GRANDMASTER

GRANDMASTER

A Story of Struggle, Triumph and Taekwondo

Won Chik Park
with Melinda Folse Kaitcer

Grandmaster: A Story of Struggle, Triumph and Taekwondo.
Copyright © 2010 by Melinda Folse Kaitcer (The Kaitcer Group LLC) and Won Chik Park.
All Rights reserved. Printed in the United States of America.

ISBN (hardcover): 978-0-9826960-0-2

No part of this book may be used or reproduced in any manner whatsoever without written permission except in the case of brief quotations embodied in critical articles and review. Special discounts apply for resale, education, business, or sales promotional use. For information, please contact Melinda@melindakaitcer.com, or call 1.888.773.8187.

Photos provided courtesy of Grandmaster Won Chik Park.

Design by JO Design, Fort Worth, Texas.
Cover photo from iStockphoto.com

19 18 17 16 15 14 13 12 11 10   1 2 3 4 5

This book is dedicated to my family, my friends, and every life that has been touched by the spirit of taekwondo.

Contents

	Foreword	*i*
	Preface: a Note to Readers from Grandmaster Won Chik Park	*iii*
Chapter 1:	Escape from North Korea	1
Chapter 2:	Struggle for Survival	13
Chapter 3:	New Life, New Challenges	43
Chapter 4:	Lessons in Triumph and Humility	67
Chapter 5:	A Teacher is Born	97
Chapter 6:	Dreams Clash with Reality	117
Chapter 7:	A Glimpse of the American Dream	139
Chapter 8:	Job, Family and Dojang of His Own	153
Chapter 9:	Opportunity on the American Horizon	211
Chapter 10:	Detour to Detroit	229
Chapter 11:	Competitive Edge	239

Chapter 12:	Challenges and Choices	259
Chapter 13:	Land of Warmth and Possibility	273
Chapter 14:	Walking Tall in Fort Worth, Texas	285
Chapter 15:	Magic in the U.S. Media	295
Chapter 16:	Visionary Connections of Old and New	303
Chapter 17:	Grandmaster Won Chik Park	317
Chapter 18:	Celebrating the Master-Student Circle	329
Chapter 19:	Taekwondo's Changing Image in the World	353
Chapter 20:	A New Dream	373
Chapter 21:	Rally Cry for the Future	385
	Acknowledgements	423
	Appendix	425

Foreword

I have known Grandmaster Won Chik Park for more than forty years. He is my teacher, mentor, friend, and one of the most amazing human beings I've ever met. In 1970, the United States Army assigned me to duty at the Yong San Compound in Seoul, Korea. When we first met, Grandmaster Park was a confident 5th degree who possessed a warm smile and looked as though he had been carved from stone. Not only was he incredibly fast and powerful, he had superb technique. Grandmaster Park has guided me on an exciting journey of traditional Taekwondo.

He taught me the history and philosophy of Taekwondo, and introduced me to the Korean culture. He spoke of the values of humility, character, integrity, courage, and indomitable spirit.

I have met many great fighters and martial artists during the last forty-five years. He is, quite simply, the BEST. His physical abilities are astounding, matched only by his intellect, teaching skills, and compassion. Grandmaster Park would never say such things about himself. He is a very humble man. He has changed the lives of thousands of students through teaching and by example.

This book is about the life of a great human being – a true Grandmaster.

Roy D. Kurban

8th Degree Grandmaster
Retired Judge, Tarrant County, Texas

Preface

A special note to readers from Grandmaster Won Chik Park:

What has my life been about? When I think about my life as a journey, I always come back to its basic driving forces. In Korean culture, we have a term for quiet strength we call *"Aeyoo Naekang."* We also place very high importance on the ancient proverb, "If a man gets knocked down seven times, he must get up eight times." The Korean expression of this relentless tenacity is *"Chil Jeon Phal Gi."* The other element present throughout my life has been a spirit of thankfulness. I realize now that in everything that happened to me in my life, finding something to be thankful for helped me turn obstacles into opportunities. Hidden in some of my life's great misfortunes were the seeds of my greatest fortune.

In the opening ceremony of the 1990 United States National Junior Olympics, I recognized my master, the late Great Grandmaster Hyon Chong Park, in a traditional Korean salute of respect and tribute. When I saw the impact this ancient gesture had on my American audience, as well as on the Korean masters and Korean-American guests present, I began thinking about the power of the unique between a taekwondo master and his students.

When Melinda Kaitcer came to me back in 1994, just after she became a first dan black belt — and a year after I became one of just a handful of taekwondo Grandmasters in the United States — and said, "Kwan Jang Neem, I want to write your story." at first I just laughed. I didn't even know she was a writer.

"Why do you want to write my story?" I asked her.

"It's a great story," she said. "I think it has many important messages that could inspire people, especially those who struggle with challenges in their life and think their opportunity is limited by circumstance."

"I don't know," I told her.

She persisted.

"It's important," she said, looking at the awards and photos lining my office walls. "You have accomplished so much and touched so many lives with taekwondo. You overcame so many things, just in your childhood, that would have made most people give up. Your story will demonstrate what amazing things can happen in your life if you just keep finding the opportunity in whatever happens, and no matter what, never giving up. It is the spirit of Jidokwan — and the story of your life!"

So I said "yes" to the book, still not convinced it would be that interesting, but hoping, as she said, that telling my story could be of help to others. Years later, when she brought me the finished chapters one by one, I saw what she saw — the message of hope hidden in my journey. So I offer my story to you now with the wish that it will help you recognize your own "Aeyoo Naekang," and no matter what happens in your life, remind you, "Chil Jeon Phal Gi" and the power of saying, "thank you" to the opportunities hidden in adversity.

CHAPTER ONE:

Escape from North Korea

My feet slapped the ground as if they belonged to someone else. My sister, half dragging me to keep pace with the urgent pack, tightened her grip on my hand as she propelled us both toward the small fishing boats anchored in the shallows about a hundred yards offshore. My lungs ached from running in the December air, and as I fought to gain control of my wobbling legs, my tearless sobs came in steady, soundless heaves.

Why were we running like this? Why had my father sent us away tonight, right when the party was about to begin? I longed for the warmth of our house, remembering the intoxicating smells of the special foods being prepared, the excited anticipation of my grandfather's 70th birthday celebration. Because my father was the oldest of his siblings, Korean custom dictated that it was his privilege to host the huge *koh cui* - (old and rare) party, and all the family was gathering at our house. One minute we were greeting guests, the next we were running for the boats.

But even in my misery I was fascinated. I had seen the fishing boats in the distance, but I had never seen one up close. I had listened to the fishermen's stories and tried to imagine what it would be like to row out to sea for a day's catch. Now, it appeared, I was about to find out. After our hurried steps carried us down to the shore and across the snow covered sand, we divided ourselves between the boats and huddled in the boats' cabins to wait for the morning tide to carry us to safety.

The first rays of daylight brought concerned whispers, first in our group, then between groups. Awakened from the light sleep that had finally found me, I watched the anxious glances and gestures toward the small mountains that ran south of our village. We heard shooting in the distance, coming from that direction.

"Should we go back?" one voice asked. From where I was huddled next to my sister I couldn't see any faces; shadowy figures gathered outside our cabin in impromptu meeting.

"No," answered another. "There's nothing we could do."

About what? I wondered. Fear began to rise.

"Our best chance is the mountains," another voice said.

"But the boats are here to take us to Yeon Pyong," argued still another.

"We can't just sit there and wait," the first voice said, intensity rising. "The shooting is getting closer. What if they get here before the tide?"

Who? I wondered. I looked at Young Soon for a clue. She stared straight ahead.

"We must go to the mountains," the first voice repeated. "The mountains are south of the DMZ and they can't get us there."

"But there's nothing there," another protested. "What will we do once we get there? How will we eat? Where will we sleep? On Yeon Pyong we have family waiting for us — the mountains have nothing."

"I don't know, but we can't stay here."

With this decided, we climbed down off the boats and trudged through the snowy muck, back toward shore and the mountains that lay just beyond the beach.

More shooting sounded from the direction of our village. No one spoke. Some people cried softly. I was too scared and confused to cry, so I clutched Young Soon's hand and concentrated on keeping my freezing feet moving. We were almost back to the shoreline when the boat crews began yelling, *"Balee! Balee!"* (or "Hurry! Hurry!) The tide is coming! Hurry back here and we can make it! The water is coming in fast!"

We turned and ran, as fast as we could, racing to beat the incoming tide. As we neared the rising boats, the icy water closed first around my ankles, then rose up my legs to my knees, then to my waist, and then to my shoulders. I struggled to breathe in this unimaginable cold, relieved that at least the rising water made it easier for Young

Soon to drag me.

The numbness in my feet soon spread throughout my body. I looked at my sister's hand gripping my arm, knuckles white, and I wondered how long she could hold onto me. Then the side of the boat loomed over us, and strong hands pulled me up out of the water and deposited me onto the floor of the boat. I didn't move, except to curl up right where I fell.

My sister was next over the side. She pulled me tight next to her, trying to warm me while compressing the two of us into the smallest space possible. One by one, people were pulled into the boat just as we had been until there was no more room.

Hushed whispers and intensity passed between the eyes of the adults, then back in the direction of our village. The boats' sails caught wind, and we began to pick up speed, moving at last toward Yeon Pyong and safety from whatever or whoever was chasing us. After a short time, the boat's crew cheered, "We're across the line! We're safe!" Everyone on the boat clapped and echoed this cheer, in voices strangely out of sync with the worry still clinging to their faces. The sun rose on our left, casting an achingly beautiful light on the boat and the faces still straining to see our disappearing shoreline.

What was all this about? What happened? I knew better than to ask the questions pounding the inside of my head. As everyone began to settle down, my mind went back to Young Soon's angry words as she pulled me away from playing in what seemed like another lifetime, but was actually only a few hours ago.

It was almost sunset when she found us. I had slipped away from the party preparations to play with my best friend from the village and thought no one had seen me. It took me a minute to realize that she had come there just to get me.

Young Soon grabbed my hand and said, without looking at my friend, "Father is calling you. We must go." On the way back to our house she hissed, "Don't you know? He's communist. You must not play with him any more."

I had no understanding of what "communist" meant—except that it was something bad. Although our village lay technically in North Korea, it was right on the edge of what would soon become known to the world as the DMZ, the demilitarized zone. It was a very important distinction to my family that we were not communists. In fact, to demonstrate our family's political affiliation with the South, two of my older brothers were soldiers in the Republic of Korea (ROK) Army.

My earlier dream of riding on a boat going out to sea far from my mind now, I noted the boat's movement through the water with detachment. Traveling to the Yeon Pyong Do fishing community to meet the uncle from my father's stories was no longer an exciting adventure, but now a circumstance I couldn't comprehend. How did such a simple instruction from my father turn into this desperate run for safety?

My mind went back to my father's face as he said, pointing first to my sister and then to me, "You two, go now with the group leaving for Yeon Pyong Do. We will all stay there with our relatives until things settle down. We will join you there after your grandfather's koh cui." Although he was trying to sound matter-of-fact, I felt the concern behind his casual words.

Without any kind of reliable communication between villages, no one knew what was happening to the north of us. Word of mouth reports told us the communist armies — North Koreans and the Chinese — were moving south. How far south or how fast they were moving, no one knew. We knew the United States and the United Nations were trying to help, but meanwhile these communist forces, although minimally armed, had lots of people on the move.

"Don't worry," Father tried to assure us, "this kind of thing has happened many times before." Again I felt his apprehension. "They'll move through, cause a lot of trouble, and then go back to the North in about a month."

Why us? I wanted to ask. Why do we have to leave all the fun and all my favorite foods when everybody else was staying? Something in Father's tone stopped my questions. It was settled; he was sending us to Yeon Pyong. Now.

"Your Uncle, Ki Hoon Song will take care of you until we come, and then we will decide what to do," Father said. Uncle Ki Hoon, actually my father's older cousin, was an exciting character from my father's childhood stories, but I had never met him. He and my father were very close when they were young, but even they had not seen each other in years. *Why him?* I wondered as we said our goodbyes and prepared to leave.

We moved silently through the water, still straining as if to hear and understand what was going on in the distance behind us. Continued shooting and several explosions, and other sounds we couldn't identify, became muffled by wind and distance. We drifted and rowed all day and all through the night, huddled together for warmth in the numbing cold. Just as the sun was again starting to rise, we landed on Yeon Pyong Do. A large group of people I assumed were our relatives stood waiting for us. Then, as we struggled out of the boats and tried to revive our cramped, frozen feet and legs, it seemed that everyone started crying at once.

No one knew what was happening on the mainland, but we all knew the situation we left behind us was serious. We told of the sounds we heard. The unspoken fear and dread hung heavy in the air as we made our way to my uncle's house. Our relatives said there would be another boat later that day. It seems that boats from the mainland villages had started to arrive twice a day— and they were making room as best as they could.

Our uncle kept going back to the shoreline each time a boat arrived, asking every group if they had seen Father and the group he was bringing. Young Soon and I sat together in silence, too worried to speak.

◊◊

The Korean War separated and destroyed many Korean families such as mine. My name is Won Chik Park. I was born May 15, 1940, seventh of nine children — four boys and five girls, in Hae Joo City,

Hwang Hae Do, a state in North Korea that was very close to what would soon and forever be known as the DMZ. Even as a very young child, I realized the importance of all that was going on around me during that time. This is my story — and the beginning of a lifelong illustration of the ancient proverb I came to know as a fundamental tenet of Taekwondo's Jidokwan philosophy, *"Chil Jeon Phal Gi,"* or, "If a man falls down seven times, he must get up eight times." It was from this ancient wisdom that I drew the courage I needed many times in my life to never give up, no matter how hopeless things seemed.

It was December of 1950 when fishing boats carried my sister, Young Soon, and me away from all I had ever known — and the life I thought I would have. I was 10 years old, and the Korean War had officially begun. In my young mind, however, it was hard to make any distinction between the steady undercurrent of political strife that was a way of life in Korea and this new thing called the Korean War.

My home country, small and innocuous as it may seem, has always been one of the world's political hotspots. It wasn't so much South Korea itself that everyone wanted, but rather, the access to the sea it offered its neighboring landlocked superpowers. For China and Russia, control of South Korea meant access to opportunity for trade, technology and progress, not only with nearby Japan, but ultimately, with the rest of the world. For Japan, controlling South Korea was key to blocking this Chinese and Russian access and protecting its trade monopoly. That was why my country had been forcibly occupied by Japan since 1910.

Some of my earliest memories were of the small Japanese police officers strutting through our village, their fearsome Samurai swords nearly dragging the ground. They were there "to keep order," and they terrorized anyone who crossed their path.

My parents were owners of a local restaurant, and my family, along with all the employees of the restaurant, lived in the back of it. Our living space was one big room with a well in the center, surrounded by four small rooms. As a young child, I slept in the room with my parents. The house sat right on the edge of a packed dirt street; a small fence surrounded the yard, which was mostly dirt with a few tufts of coarse grass.

As my father's only son still at home, I was his constant companion. Almost every day we went to my grandfather's fruit farm just outside the village to help Grandfather tend his crops and gather fruit to bring back to the restaurant and to our home to eat. My father was a quiet and serious, but kind man. I practiced imitating his gestures and mannerisms so that when I grew up I could be just like him.

Next door to my parents' restaurant and our home was the police station. In the back of the police station was a yard surrounded by a tall reed fence. This was where the Japanese officers held their prisoners.

Because the Japanese police were there to patrol and arrest any Korean whom they believed did something — anything — against them, arrests were almost constant. When they brought their prisoners to the station next door, it was to interrogate them, which most often meant beatings and torture. We heard these beatings at all hours of the day and night.

I remember covering my ears with my hands to try to block out the sounds of the Japanese yelling and the prisoners screaming in pain. Sometimes my mother closed the doors to try to block some of these horrible sounds, but in the summertime it also blocked the breeze that was our only air conditioning. I dreaded the sight of new prisoners.

"What is that sound?" I once asked my parents.

Anger and fear flashed in their eyes before they answered, "Someone's hurt."

The Japanese police sometimes rode loud motorcycles, and this tremendous noise always heralded their arrivals and departures from the station. Then on August 15, 1945, after the United States dropped the bomb on Hiroshima and Japan surrendered to the Allied forces, Korea was free from Japanese tyranny and the motcrcycles roared away for the last time.

I remember the hushed, urgent whispers in my village on the day the Japanese police left. Instead of releasing all their prisoners as ordered, they had killed them and thrown their bodies into the well at the center of their main room. I watched through our back window as my parents and many others from the village ran into the station as soon as Japanese police were out of sight. When they came back out, they were all crying, overcome with grief at this final indignation. It was a horrible, horrible time in my country's history.

◊◊

Relief over the absence of the Japanese, however, opened the door to a new concern. The end of World War II also divided Korea. The North, now under the jurisdiction of a new Communist government, became The North Korean Democratic People's Republic of Korea (DPRK); the South, under the supervision of the United States, became The Republic of Korea (ROK). After Russia and China established the Communist government in North Korea, their attention once again turned to South Korea and control of the access to world trade. Soon the fear of the Japanese who tortured us transferred to the nameless, faceless threat of the Communists that would now try to gain control of our fledgling republic.

My village cheered when the US military came in the South, rumbling down our main street in trucks and huge tanks. The talk in my village was that the Russians were likewise rolling their tanks and troops into the North.

That time was also the beginning of the confused whispers about communists, and more important, endless speculation about who was and who wasn't. My parents told me which friends I could no longer play with; these included my very best friend. Neither of us understood what "being communist" had to do with kids playing together. We didn't know what "communist" meant, but we could tell it was something very, very bad.

◊◊

My mother owned the only sewing machine in our village. The machine was large, heavy and operated by foot pedal. I remember standing, still and silent beside her, mesmerized by her hands, swift and sure, moving over the fabric, turning, sewing, stopping, pulling it out, clipping the thread. Her small feet moved in a constant, steady rocking motion, independent of her hands. This was the rhythm that lulled me to sleep most evenings.

One day soon after the US military passed through our village, a giant truck pulled up. Men in uniforms jumped out to unload large bolts of a drab cloth I would soon know as the fabric of military uniforms. With several other women, my mother dragged her heavy sewing machine to the center of our village where they formed an assembly line. Some measured, some cut, and each took a turn at the machine; they worked nonstop until all the fabric was gone. The Korean War had begun.

On Sunday, June 25, 1950, when North Korean forces crossed the 38th parallel into the Republic of Korea and attacked the South Korean capital city of Seoul, the United Nations Security Council called for "immediate cessation of hostilities." This official UN resolution was ignored, so two days later United States President Harry S. Truman ordered American forces to provide cover and support to the South Korean troops. On July 8th, the UN Security Council then issued another resolution — the establishment of a unified command in Korea — and asked the United States to appoint a commander of these forces. Within a week after US Army General Douglas MacArthur accepted this command, ROK President Syngman Rhee placed all ROK security forces under McArthur's command, consolidating the anti-Communist forces under the United Nations Command.

As a 10-year-old I was of course unaware of the political machinery, but I felt its effects whirling into motion all around me. Sudden and mysterious flurries of activity, urgency mixed with uncertainty, and a new dread that felt very different from the fear of the Japanese became the new norm.

A strange invisible line now divided our country, making it the only divided country in the world. This meant little to most of us until word came that the North Koreans were tunneling through the mountains that served as the visual geographic dividing line between the North and the South. These were the mountains just outside my village; the war was getting closer every day.

The people in our village who did have guns began to practice shooting in the open areas outside our village. My friends and I ventured out into these areas when no one was watching to collect shell casings. Oblivious to the macabre implications of living so close to the war zone, we made up a wonderful game involving these strange and fascinating new toys. Squatting a few yards away from a circle we drew in the dirt with a stick, we'd take turns trying to flick the shells into the circle. We spent hours perfecting our technique; this was the game we were playing when my father sent Young Soon to find me on the eve of my grandfather's party. It is also the last memory I have of life as I knew it in my village.

My sister, Young Soon Park (indicated by box), with our cousins, circa 1952.

My second oldest brother, Ung Chik Park, in his military uniform, circa 1951.

CHAPTER TWO:

Struggle for Survival

Every day after Young Soon and I arrived on Yeon Pyong Do island, we climbed to the island's highest point to scan the 200 kilometers of sea that now separated us from the mainland. We hoped against hope to see the boat carrying our parents and the rest of our family. Many boats did come; almost every day brought others trying to escape the path of war.

Each time we saw new boats arriving, we ran to the shore, where we'd go from boat to boat, asking anyone we saw if they had seen our parents. When they would shake their heads to say, "No, I'm sorry," we'd start to cry again. Our tears flowed constantly those first days, and then weeks. Each "no" compounded our sadness and fear until it became almost unbearable.

Then one day the answer we had been both seeking and dreading came at last. One group arrived who had passed through what was left of our village. As they described the carnage they saw there, we realized what must have happened just hours after Young Soon and I left. The truth was harsh but clear. We would never see our parents again.

This group had seen the place where the North Koreans executed my family. With faces twisted with the grief of having to be the ones to give us this news, they delivered the words that destroyed all our hopes.

"Are you sure everyone was killed?" We kept asking. "Was it the family having the party?"

Each nod to our questions felt like a physical blow. They saw where the invading communist troops had lined up everyone in the village and shot them. There was a party, they nodded. All were dead. My mind created a picture of this scene that I would never be able to erase. What were their last thoughts when they knew their life was over?

I remembered the shots we heard behind us as we ran that night. In my nightmares I would hear them again and again, and the truth transformed my unspeakable fear into harsh reality. One of those shots killed my mother. Another took my father. One by one, those shots announced the end of my family, my friends, and any hope that my life would ever be the same again.

Of the large extended family that had once filled my parents' home, only Young Soon and I remained. If our two older brothers in the military, Ung Chik and Yung Chik, were still alive, we had no way of knowing. In the course of fulfilling their mandatory military service, the responsibility of all young Korean men, they were swept away from us in this war that destroyed countless other families like mine.

◊◊

As word spread that Yeon Pyong Do was a safe refuge, my uncle's house grew more crowded as more relatives fled the North and the terrors of the communist invasion. The house was small, but as more people arrived, we made room. Soon, people were everywhere; at night we slept packed together like the skewered fish I had seen drying on the beach.

The winter's cold, crowded conditions and close quarters also made my uncle's house a breeding ground for germs and illness that rippled through the group in varying forms and intensities. When I started to cough, I tried to ignore it; I was determined not to get sick. I grew sicker, but continued my charade as if willpower alone could ward off the inevitable.

Just before dawn on a fitful night when the tightness in my chest and the constant coughing of others made it impossible to sleep, I looked over at Young Soon to see if she was awake. She was staring into space. Even from a few feet away I could see the tears in her eyes. She caught me looking at her and swiped the back of her hand across her eyes. I pointed to the door. She nodded. We picked our way through the sleeping but restless carpet of people to the back door.

Once outside, I sucked in the sweet predawn air, over and over again, then exhaled as deeply as I could, trying to force the smell of that house out of my nostrils. With so many people in such close quarters and no way to get clean, the oppressive stench seemed to cling to me like a filmy cloud. Young Soon and I took a lot of walks, looking for firewood and relief from the smell in the fresh, cold, salty air.

These walks were also opportunity for just the two of us to think and talk about what happened — and what we would do next. Where should we go? Were we supposed to stay here on the island? No one was talking about the future; it was all we could do to get through the present. What would our parents have wanted us to do?

Uncle Ki Hoon was very kind and good, and we both liked him very much, but it was easy to see that he already had more family here than he could take care of. With the conditions in his house growing worse each day, how long could we live there?

Part of our ritual as we searched for firewood was to climb to that same perch at the highest point of the island and look back toward our village in remembrance of our parents. This spot became our special place of mourning, the place where we felt closest to our parents, where we last experienced thoughts that they might be alive and on their way to meet us as planned. This point on the island gave focus to our grief, much like a crash site where families visit to lay flowers and share remembrances. Some days we talked. Some days we just sat silent, crying together.

"What will happen to us?" I'd ask Young Soon, as we stared out at the surrounding sea.

"I don't know," she'd reply. "But I'll take care of you."

"I'll take care of you, too," I'd promise in return.

◊◊

My teeth chattered out of control as chills and fever overtook me. Despite my best evasive efforts, the sickness caught me. Young Soon was there, wiping my face with a cool wet cloth. She piled any unoccupied blankets or coverings she could find on top of me, but I could not feel their warmth. My awareness was fleeting, drifting in and out without warning. Once I thought my mother was there, but when I opened my eyes she was gone. Then I was picking fruit with my father, back in Grandfather's orchard. I could almost smell the sweetness of the ripe fruit, but when I bent over to pick up a peach from the ground, I saw my family all lying dead in a shallow trench, faces staring, bullet holes in each of their heads.

My uncle owned the only store on the island, and he was the island's only source of medicine. Educated on the mainland, he returned to Yeon Pyong to raise his family and start his business to help provide for the people of Yeon Pyong. Every day he brought medicine from his store to see if it would help me.

My first knowledge of my uncle's medical expertise came just after we arrived on the island. Some time between the icy water and the long night huddled in that tiny boat, my feet had frozen. The sensation in them was unbearable, alternating between excruciating ache and tremendous itch. I tried to be brave, but my misery was not lost on my uncle. He came to me one day with a large bag of beans.

"Sleep with your feet in these beans," he told me. "It will help."

He said there was something in the raw beans that would draw out the poison from the frostbite, so every night I slept that way. It did seem to help some, but mostly it helped to know he cared and was trying to help.

Then the illness they called pneumonia made the constant pain and itching in my feet a mere annoyance. Struggling for every breath and too weak to lift my head, I didn't know whether it was night or day. Every time I did open my eyes I saw Young Soon's face. She was taking care of me, just as she had promised. I heard the whispers of voices I didn't know, wondering if I would die. I knew I would not; I couldn't leave Young Soon all alone.

Once I awoke to an unfamiliar hiss accompanied by a strange, sweet, clean smell. Something was being sprayed all around the area where we slept. Then I went back to sleep, returning to a psychedelic blend of days and nights, faces and sounds, dreams and reality.

Then one day I awoke and felt hungry. I was able to sip some broth and eat a little of the rice Young Soon offered me, and this seemed to make Young Soon very happy. She smiled and sang to me as she smoothed my hair. I knew for sure that I was getting better when I again became aware of the achy, itchy throb in my feet. When I asked Young Soon for my bag of beans, she nearly danced with glee.

When I was strong enough to get up and around a bit, my uncle invited me to go with him to check on something at his store. This reminded me of all the times when I went with my father, following him like a shadow, mimicking his mannerisms and expressions. It was a bittersweet outing; the ache of missing my father interwoven with the comfort of my uncle's attention.

Uncle Ki Hoon Song, however, was a different sort of man from my father — or any other man I had ever known. In a culture that was predominately Buddhist, he was Christian. In a community of thatched roofs, his was the only one made of metal. Rather than traditional Korean clothing, he wore Japanese and Western-influenced clothing; he had a remarkable collection of jackets.

When I was well enough, Uncle Ki Hoon began taking me to church with him every Sunday. Sitting with him in church, I remember studying him when I thought he wasn't looking. Sometimes he caught me and I flushed with embarrassment. I always wanted to touch his shiny, narrow black shoes.

The thing I treasured most about my uncle, however, was the knowledge he had about my parents. Within the expanse of his memory lay my family's entire history. I never grew tired of hearing my uncle's stories about growing up with my father, Yong Jim Park. Closer in many ways than most brothers, they were constant childhood companions. On our daily walks he told me stories about my father when he was my age, of how my mother and father met, and what they were both like before they became my parents. I absorbed every detail, committing these stories to my own memory that I could recall for the rest of my life whenever I needed to remember and feel close to my parents.

"Was my mother beautiful when she was a young girl?" I'd ask.

"Oh, yes," he'd say, replaying the memory of her in his mind. "She was tall and beautiful and loved to dance."

These small details of my parents' earlier lives provided strange comfort to me, somehow bringing them back to life in my mind, if even for just a few moments.

"Who do I look like?" I'd ask, already knowing the answer, but wanting to hear it again.

"Your mother's sister," he'd say, smiling. "You have the shape of her face and the sweetness of her smile." He'd pause, peering at me as if intent on discovering something new. "And I think you have her *'aeyoo naekang'*"

"*Aeyoo naekang?*" I had never heard this term before, but even the way he said it sounded special.

"Yes. *Aeyoo naekang* means having a quiet, gentle appearance and strong inner spirit," he said.

Aeyoo Naekang. I said the term over and over to myself, thanking my mother's sister for this gift.

"Was my father strong?" I asked Uncle Ki Hoon one day as we unloaded supplies for the store together.

Uncle Ki Hoon smiled. "Yes, Won Chik, he was," he said. He stopped stacking bags of rice for a moment, remembering. "But you know what was funny? Even though he was smaller than other boys his age he could always lift more than any of us — and he could move faster than anyone I ever knew." Uncle returned to his stacking. "The other thing I remember about your father's strength is that no matter how long or hard he worked, he never seemed to get tired."

My uncle hoisted a big box onto his shoulder and then handed a smaller, lighter one to me. I tried to put it on my shoulder. It fell off and we both laughed. It was genuine laughter, and it felt good. It was the first time I had laughed in months.

◊◊

Struggle for Survival

Young Soon and I stood at the water's edge, scanning the shimmering horizon for the first sign of the day's fishing boats returning with their catch. We were at the beach first today, far ahead of our competition. Soon a crowd of children would be there, scampering to meet the boats, pushing and shoving to be the first ones on board to help the fishermen glean the choki from their nets. For Young Soon and me, this was a way to contribute to our uncle's household and help to feed the many people gathered there. We tried to be on the beach first whenever we could.

Choki, an unusual fish that swims in the Yellow Sea surrounding Yeon Pyong Island, provided much of the island's livelihood. Used to prepare a great Korean delicacy, choki brought the best price by far in the mainland market. Because the choki were very small and delicate fish, they had to be pulled from the nets first. Island children vied for opportunity to help, because the grateful fishermen then allowed them to keep whatever crabs were also in the net.

Just as we spotted the day's first boats, we heard the clamor behind us of others catching up. Our feet were already churning through the sand to the water's edge, ready to hop the first boat that got close enough. I grinned at Young Soon; she smiled back. I was glad she was with me.

In normal circumstances, Young Soon would never be allowed to be here. She was of age to be helping the women at the house, but because of our situation and my illness, the other women had looked the other way, allowing her to remain a child and be my caretaker at the same time. She was serious about this responsibility, never letting me out of her sight. In other circumstances, this would have been annoying to a boy my age, but I didn't mind. She was doing her best to be both mother and sister to me.

The first boat landed and we splashed through the water to help drag it ashore. We climbed aboard and pulled open the heavy nets to begin our work. The other boats were coming in fast, so the other children left this one to us.

It was a delicate situation. The fishermen were glad for the help, but they didn't like it when too many children boarded their boat. Sometimes if they felt too mobbed, they sent everyone away. So a strange etiquette had evolved, with respectful distance and silent understanding of how many of us could approach each boat.

As I worked, I breathed in the smells of salt water and fish. It was a good smell, and I was so grateful to breathe without coughing. I was still a little weak, but feeling stronger every day. The sun and sea air felt good on my skin. A small shell in the net captured my attention — it was a color I had never seen in a shell before. I picked it up to examine its exquisite design, and then I felt Young Soon's eyes on me. I shoved the shell in my pocket. As I returned to work, a baby octopus wriggled under a pile of seaweed to hide. One glance at Young Soon told me she was still watching me, so I resisted the urge to play with the octopus and returned to the choki harvest at hand.

When the fisherman was satisfied that all the choki had been cleared from the nets, he gestured at the squirming pile of crabs we had tossed in the front of the boat. Taking care to avoid their menacing, snapping claws, I gingerly gathered them into our pail, trying not to look at these ugly creatures. Crabs made good food for my uncle's table and I liked their taste, but their creepy appearance was unsettling to me. We thanked the fishermen, picked up the pail, and began the walk back to our uncle's house.

On less fortunate days when we were not first to the shoreline and had no crabs to take home, we stayed and watched the fishermen thread the choki onto long skewers, salt them and set them on straw mats to dry in the sun. They turned these skewers every few hours until the salted and sun-dried fish were ready for market. About once a week the fishermen stacked these loaded skewers back onto the boats and hauled them to the mainland to sell.

"What do you think they taste like?" I asked Young Soon one day as we watched the laden boats depart.

"I don't know," she had said, shielding her eyes with one hand to watch the last bit of boat fade into the horizon. "Salty fish, I guess. I've heard they're very expensive in the market ."

Our mother had been a wonderful cook — and our family's restaurant was the favorite in our village. She served many special dishes there, but never choki.

Several times when we were too late to get a boat, some of the other children contributed their extra crabs to our bucket. This kind gesture from children our own age touched our hearts. It seemed that everywhere we went on the island, strangers reached out to us. So many people there had lost homes and families. The people who had not endured this tragedy took care of the rest of us. While I appreciated their compassionate help, seeing the sorrow in their eyes when they looked at us only escalated my own grief. I didn't want to feel sorry for myself. Most of all, I didn't want there to be a reason to feel sorry for myself. But there it was, reflected in everyone's eyes as they showered us with kindness I knew I could never repay.

I looked at Young Soon as she walked silently beside me on one of these days of charity. The crabs clanked and clawed inside the pail.

"Someday we will sit in a beautiful restaurant and I will buy you choki," I told her. She didn't look up. "We will eat an entire meal of nothing but choki."

Young Soon just smiled and kept walking. I knew she didn't believe me, but I was glad the thought made her smile. I felt a surge of indignation. *You just wait and see,* I huffed inwardly. *I will show you.* Just like Uncle Ki Hoon, I was determined to find my own way to follow whatever dream sparked the fire I already felt smoldering in my belly. Someday I would eat nothing but choki for dinner.

◊◊

"Do you think Ung Chik and Yung Chik are still alive?" I asked Young Soon one day as we gathered firewood. The question that would not stop rolling through my mind, but asking it aloud could open the door to an answer I didn't want to hear.

Young Soon was quiet for so long that I wondered if she knew something she hadn't told me — or if she shared my superstitious fear of the question itself. Finally she spoke. "I don't know. And I don't know if we'll ever know," she said. "How would they even know where to find us?"

Another thing that had been worrying me lately was the question of what would happen to Young Soon. Like me she was plucked from the normal order of things. But unlike me, it was at a time that she would normally be preparing for womanhood. With her sixteenth birthday nearing, she should be preparing for marriage, not picking crabs with the children or caring for her younger brother. I wondered how she felt about this raw hand life had dealt her. Losing her parents at her age meant her chances for traditional courtship and marriage rituals were also gone. What would happen to her? If she was concerned about any of this, she didn't let me see it.

While there were plenty of days when I still felt like a small child, lost and alone, orphaned and clinging to my sister's skirts for protection, there were now days when I felt that I should be doing more to take care of her. Like Young Soon and so many others I was trapped between traditional generational responsibilities with no idea of who I was supposed to be or what I was supposed to do. For now, everything we once knew as normal seemed frozen in time, but one day this frozen existence would thaw. What would we do?

If some day, by some miracle we discover our brothers are alive, would we go to where they are? Or would we stay here and make our home on the island with the family that took us in? I was torn. The island and its people were starting to feel comfortable. Not home, exactly, but a good place to be with many people connected in some way to us. More than anything, however, I wanted to see my brothers again. Yung Chik left for the service before I was old enough to know him, but Ung Chik was just 17 and I missed him every day since he left for his required military service.

"As long as we hear nothing, they are still alive," Young Soon said, setting her small chin as if that settled it. It was hard to read her expression, but I knew the emotions were bubbling just under her surface calm. "If we find out where they are, we will go to them." She answered my unasked question with certainty.

I took the load of firewood from her arms, trying not to wobble under its weight. It was maybe a little too heavy for me to carry with ease, but carrying the wood was something we both realized I needed to do.

"You're growing very strong," she said, a smile playing at the corners of her mouth. "You will be a very strong man some day."

Suddenly the load seemed lighter, the hill less steep, and the distance to my uncle's house a little shorter. "Thank you," I said.

By the time winter on Yeon Pyong Island ebbed into spring, the crowd at my uncle's house settled into a new sense of community. Young Soon and I were stronger, more settled and less fearful than we were when we first arrived, and a new restlessness was growing within both of us. We needed answers and a revised plan for our lives, some idea of what we were supposed to do now. We realized that with no parents or true guardians, there was no one to make those decisions and tell us what to do now. Relatives could make suggestions and take care of us, but we had no clear direction.

Our uncle, no longer a stranger, had become a source of comfort and camaraderie — a connection we both enjoyed. I helped him at the store, doing odd jobs, loading and unloading merchandise, and whatever else he needed help with. Because he had only daughters, having this kind of help was a new experience for him. The irony of our situation was not lost on either of us — just as I was given a surrogate father, he was given a surrogate son. I admired his independence, his quiet strength, his knowledge of who he was and what was important, regardless of the noise and uncertainty around him. He was a steadying influence in unsteady times.

"I hope we stay here forever," I told him one day as we unloaded sacks of grain and stacked them in his storage area. "I really like it here. When I am older I can help you even more."

"I hope so too," he said, stopping to look at me as if for the first time. He looked at the size of bag I was carrying. "You're already a lot of help."

I loved the days when supplies arrived, an entire day with my uncle, away from the stench of the overcrowded house, and physical work that felt good to my growing muscles. Life at our Uncle's house provided us with a roof over our head, plenty to eat and a dry place to sleep, but I could not imagine living this way forever. I missed my home. I missed my friends. I missed my bed, my house, and my life. These thoughts I kept at bay during the day, but each night as I drifted off to sleep they returned in an unstoppable river of tears. I missed my parents and I had no idea what was going to become of me.

◊◊

Young Soon shook me awake. It was barely dawn and the urgency in her manner alarmed me. I sat straight up, wild eyed. What happened? I shook my sleep-fogged head, then scrambled to get up, get dressed and follow her as she directed without words. She stood at the door, waiting, looking out into the distance. I could feel her impatience.

"What is it?" I asked, hurrying to keep up once we were finally on the packed dirt road to the shoreline where we had landed nearly a year before.

"Ok Sun is here with Sung Hoon," she said, peering through the dawn mist. "The others came in and told me."

I had never met them, but I remembered that Ok Sun was Yung Chik's wife, and Sung Hoon was his son. How did they find us? Did they know we were here? Maybe they had news of my oldest brother's whereabouts. "Where's Yung Chik?" I asked, the words escaping me before I could stop them. "Is he with them?"

"No." Her tone said everything. Tears stung at the backs of my eyes and my throat joined in with its all-too-familiar tightness. When we got to the beach, one look at Ok Sun's face confirmed my worst fear. My oldest brother was dead.

Sung Hoon, my brother's son, just three years younger than me, looked as lost and scared as I had when my feet first touched this same shore. Our eyes met and instant understanding passed between us — the bond of bottomless misery.

We grieved together over the next few days. My brother's death ripped the scab off of our own deep wound. We made room at Uncle's house for Ok Sun and Sung Hoon. Young Soon and Ok Sun spent time together and I tried my best to interest Sung Hoon in exploring the island, meeting the boats, anything to help take his mind off his pain. Focusing on helping him through this pain was welcome distraction from my own.

"Your father was my oldest brother," I told him one day as we walked the shoreline a few weeks after they arrived.

He looked at me with a tear-streaked face. It was the first time he had made eye contact with me since they arrived.

Encouraged by this small breakthrough, I went on, remembering the comfort of my uncle's stories. "Your father was the fastest runner in our whole village."

Sung Hoon moved closer, saying nothing, but hanging on my words.

"All the other boys, even the older and stronger ones, challenged him, but he always won."

Sung Hoon, still silent, kept walking beside me, head down. "Do I look like my father did when he was young?" he asked. These were the first words I ever heard him speak. He searched my face for the answer he wanted to hear.

I studied his face, searching my mind for an answer that would help him. The truth was my memory of Yung Chik was minimal. What did he look like? I closed my eyes, trying to summon any detail of Yung Chik's face through my hazy memory. Then, my mind's eye saw him sitting across from me at the table, eating with gusto. Looking up and smiling at something someone said. Throwing his head back in laughter.

I opened my eyes. "Smile," I said to Sung Hoon.

"I can't." Sung Hoon said.

"Can you laugh?"

"Nothing's funny."

"Did your father ever make you laugh?"

Struggle for Survival

"Yes." Sung Hoon started to cry again. Not quite the reaction I was hoping for. He looked at me through his tears. "Sometimes he would chase me and make funny sounds. I always laughed then."

"What sounds?" I asked. "Can you make them for me?"

Sung Hoon cried harder. I could see that this was just making matters worse. My uncle was much better at this than I was. Still, something made me persist. "Can you close your eyes and imagine that he is chasing you now and making those funny sounds?"

"No."

"Was it a little bit like this?" I stretched my arms out and pumped my feet up and down fast in place, uttering a sort of screeching growl that all at once felt familiar to me. I remembered Yung Chik doing this very thing with his friends.

Sung Hoon looked startled. He said nothing. I moved toward him, feet still pumping. No reaction. Then I flapped my arms in a giant semi-circle just as I had seen Yung Chik do. Sung Hoon took off running and I took off after him, arms, feet and a strange, screeching growl gaining momentum with each step. I caught up with him in a flat grassy area behind my uncle's house. I tackled him and we both fell to the ground. He was laughing and crying at the same time. So was I.

"Yes, now I'm sure," I told him when I was able to speak. "You do have your father's smile."

◊◊

Young Soon's hands trembled as she opened the letter from Ung Chik, my second oldest brother. I watched as she read it, first to herself, and then again, out loud, to me and to the rest of the small crowd gathered around us. My mind whirled. If he wrote a letter, he must be alive. How did he know we were here?

In the days and weeks of grieving over Yung Chik, I think we also gave up on Ung Chik. Somehow it seemed easier to assume that he was dead, too, than to try to keep hoping he was still alive. Now, to our surprise, not only was he alive — or at least had been recently enough to write this letter — somehow he had found us. His letter said his military unit was now in Kun San City. He wanted us to come there to be near him.

The thought made my heart race. Then it filled me with dread of leaving my uncle's house. "How did he find us?" I asked Young Soon when we were alone.

"It seems like he knew about the plan to come to Yeon Pyong if things got worse near our village," she said. She was mending a rip in one of my shirts. She kept sewing without looking up; this made it hard to read her true reaction to this news — and this request. "He knew our family would be here." She paused. "I'm sure he doesn't know about the rest of the family. We will have to tell him."

New dread plummeted to the bottom of my stomach. "So we're going to Kun San?"

"He's our older brother," she said after a pause. She handed me the shirt. "He told us to come there, so we'll go."

I stood there for a moment, letting it all sink in. Ung Chik lived in the barracks of a military base. We would not be allowed to stay there with him. "Where will we live?" I asked, following her as she walked.

"I don't know," she said. "I think there are places where people are staying who have nowhere else to go."

"When?" I was somehow able to force that one word out.

"Tomorrow," she said. "Uncle is arranging for a boat to take us to the mainland." She paused, looking at me for the first time. "We should get our things together."

The decision was made. I was both angry and relieved not to have to make this decision. While I couldn't wait to see my brother, and I couldn't bear the thought of not going to see him, I didn't want to leave our uncle. None of my thoughts mattered. We were going to Kun San. Tomorrow.

◊◊

Struggle for Survival

Young Soon and I, along with Ok Sun and Sung Hoon, watched the island disappear into the distance, each of us too full of thoughts, emotions, and unanswerable questions to speak. As we neared the shore of the mainland, I saw Ung Chik first. Standing on the pier, looking very official in his military uniform, he looked much older than I remembered. I tried to recognize something familiar in his face as he helped Young Soon out of the boat. After so many months of assuming I would never see him again, it seemed incredible that he was here waiting for us.

It was hard to tell him the news of what happened to our parents and Yung Chik, but the war had wearied him and he was not as surprised as I thought he would be. He said he had heard our village was destroyed, but had hoped we all escaped as planned. I couldn't imagine how much death and pain Ung Chik had seen. We all cried together and held onto each other for the short time he had to be with us and get us settled in one of the schools where refugees were staying. Ung Chik explained that in Kun San, just like in most of the South's cities, a large population of refugees from the North found temporary housing in the girls' middle school and high school auditoriums.

"I wish you could come stay on the base with me," he said as we walked, "but a lot of our military families are staying at school auditoriums until things settle down."

I had no idea what any of this meant, so I kept quiet. My experience of school was very limited, so of course I had no idea what an auditorium was. And how would we know when things settled down? What did that even mean? How could things ever settle down for us, alone in a strange city with no parents, no home and no family besides each other? Once things "settled down" how would we live then? At least on the island we had a home and food; I wondered if we made a mistake by coming here.

These thoughts pounded in time with my footsteps as we drew nearer to a large square building. People were milling around, and quiet conversations were taking place in small groups. The smells of food cooking over small fires around the building's perimeter mingled with human stench reminded me of the smell of my uncle's house, the smell of too many people in too close quarters.

"How long do you think we'll be here?" I asked Young Soon as we entered our designated space. She shook her head, telling me to be quiet.

One of the people who seemed to be in charge gestured to a spot near the back corner. I was happy to find small a window in this area, and I unrolled my sleeping mat there, grateful for its natural light. I found a small cloth and wiped the window a little cleaner; I needed somewhere to look besides across this packed roomful of strangers. At least we had some connection to the people in Uncle Ki Hoon's crowded house. Here I felt thrown into a strange but familiar zoo — as both resident and visitor.

"Now what?" I asked Young Soon as she unrolled her mat next to mine.

"I don't know," she said for the hundredth time that day, in a voice that carried weariness and exhaustion beyond her years.

Not too far down the same row of mats, Ok Sun was also settling in. Sung Hoon's face was a muddy roadway of tears. He never seemed to stop crying, and it was wearing through my patience. Ok Sun had not spoken all day, and it was hard to imagine what she was thinking. On those few occasions when she did speak, her voice was so soft it was difficult to understand what she was saying. We tried to be kind to her, to engage and involve her, but her impenetrable shell of despondent hopelessness made this difficult.

It became clear from our first day in that auditorium packed with war refugees that our only work was survival — and trying to find food would be a full-time job. This was new to us, because even though the conditions on the island were crowded and disease infested, there was always plenty to eat.

Now a new gnawing sensation in my stomach kept me awake at night, and my feet still itched and burned, but there was no big bag of beans to put them in. During these sleepless nights I missed my uncle and how he took care of us. He always knew what to do. Why did we have to leave?

"What can we do to get more to eat?" I asked Young Soon.

She shrugged. "There are supposed to be people who bring food here," she said. "We have to wait." The certainty in her voice did not match the worry in her eyes.

"There has to be another way," I told her.

The next morning, when my gnawing stomach awakened me earlier than usual, urgent movement outside the small window near my bed drew my attention. Far different from the aimless wandering I usually observed outside my portal, people seemed to be in a hurry to get to some common destination. Where were they going?

I got dressed and outside as fast as I could, running to catch up with the last group of hurrying people. I trailed them through several streets to discover that the destination was the bus station. I had heard talk of busses and stations before, but I had never actually seen either one of these things.

The activity in and around this building reminded me of the hive of bees I used to watch for hours back on my grandfather's farm. Then I noticed something peculiar. Children about my age, carrying a small armload of newspapers, ran up to people getting on or off of the busses. As they ran, they waved one of the papers in the air, shouting the headlines, the price, and the urgency of purchasing a paper.

To my amazement, it worked. One by one, these children sold their armload, ran off, and then came back with more. I stopped one of them, a friendly looking boy who seemed to be about my age but a little bit taller than me.

"What are you doing?" I asked.

"Selling newspapers," he said, not breaking his stride. I hurried along beside him, wanting to know more and not wanting to slow him down. "How do you get to do that?" I asked. "Do you get to keep the money?"

He looked at me as if I were being ridiculous. "Yes. But we don't keep all the money — just a little of it. It's how we buy food."

Like the crabs in the choki nets, I thought.

"See that man over there?" the boy gestured at an old man standing at the far corner of the station. "Go ask him. If he likes you he will give you papers to sell. And if you sell them, you get to keep some of the money."

"Thank you," I said, bowing as my uncle always did in business situations. Then I turned and ran as fast as my legs would take me to the old man in the corner.

"Sir," I began, stopping to bow again to demonstrate my business manners. "May I sell some papers for you? My family is very hungry and I need to help earn money for food."

He looked at me for a long time without any response. Then he handed me a stack of papers. "Sell these and bring me back the money." His tone was gruff, but his eyes were kind. I could tell he liked me. "When you bring me the money for these I will give you more," he said. "At the end of the day I will give you part of the money to keep."

"Thank you, sir!" I said, bowing. I was so excited I could barely speak. We would have food to eat. Today.

"And if you don't bring the money back to me," he said in the sternest tone I had ever heard, "don't ever come here again."

This warning puzzled me. Who in their right mind would ruin their chance at steady money by taking just one day's booty? "Yes sir," I said, bowing again. My father had taught me to always say, "Yes, sir" to my elders.

Then I took off for the buses. It was harder than it looked to run with that heavy load of newspapers. And not everyone wanted a newspaper. After a few attempts, my natural speed and persistence —and my experience at beating the other children to the choki boats — and paid off; I soon sold my first stack of papers. Each triumphant return to the old man was rewarded with another stack of papers to sell as soon as I handed him the money. Then there were no more papers.

"May I have more papers to sell?" I asked, puzzled.

The man gestured to the emptying station around us. The station was clearing out and the busses were gone. "The busses are gone until evening," he said, handing me my morning's wages. "Come back then."

"Thank you, sir," I said, bowing again. "I will see you later!

"Good," he said, not even looking up as he counted his money.

I turned the money over and over in my hand all the way back to the auditorium. Marveling at my good fortune, I tried to imagine the surprise on Young Soon's face when she saw it. Then I imagined how my aching belly would feel when at last it was filled with food. I couldn't begin to count the times in just the past few days I wished for just one of those ugly crabs to crack open.

Young Soon had her back to me as I approached. She turned when she heard me approach. Saying nothing, I held out my small handful of money. She took a step back, covering her mouth. "What did you do?" she asked, eyes wide. She looked around to see if anyone was listening, then whispered, "Did you steal that money from someone?"

I laughed. Sometimes she could be so silly. "Of course not," I said. "I sold newspapers at the bus station. And I am going back tonight and tomorrow and every morning and every night. I will sell newspapers so we will have enough food."

Young Soon, Ok Sun and Sung Hoon gathered closer to hear the details of how I discovered the morning rush hour, and with it, a way to help feed our family. Young Soon turned to Ok Sun and said, "First thing tomorrow we can go to the market for food!"

Ok Sun said nothing, but smiled and placed her hand on Sung Hoon's shoulder. Young Soon looked at the boy with empathy in her eyes I had never seen before. "Now we will not be so hungry."

I felt a rush of pride. I had helped. At last I was doing my part to take care of our family. Things just might not be hopeless after all.

The next morning after the buses were gone, the old man called me aside. He handed me a huge stack of papers. I looked around at the empty station, then back at him, confused. He handed me a scrap of paper. "Deliver newspapers to the houses on this list," he said. He held up a stack of coins. "I will pay you this much extra to deliver these and then sell any leftover door-to-door in the neighborhoods around here to the people who don't take the bus or subscribe. When you come back, I'll give you more to sell to the bus passengers."

I learned from the angry stares and outraged whispers of the other children selling papers that this was the plum assignment they all wanted. I ignored them, focusing instead on doing a good job in this new opportunity.

Newspapers were a crucial commodity of that time, the only source of any information about the war. Unlike in my village where news traveled only by word of mouth, Kun San was a bigger city, with a newspaper to provide information, good or bad, that at least gave people some idea about what was going on around them.

There weren't many houses on my designated route — maybe 50 or 60 in all to deliver each day. Once subscribers were taken care of, I went from house to house on those streets, knocking on the doors, bowing politely and trying to sell the rest of the papers in my stack. Then each day I chose a different route back to the station to offer a newspaper to anyone who didn't take the bus.

Once back at the station, I positioned myself near the ticket window to be first to approach people after they purchased their ticket for the bus. When ticket sales slowed, I stood near where the incoming busses unloaded so I could make my move toward each opening bus door. If I timed it just right, I could always get there first. Then, finding the correct mix of aggression and humility, I worked the crowd and each day sold stack after stack of papers.

For the next six months, we lived in the auditorium, subsisting on the barley and rice that came from the UN, plus any food we were able to buy with my newspaper money. We saw Ung Chik from time to time in short visits, but his days were filled with military duties just as ours were filled with getting food and staying alive.

Then Ung Chik came to us one afternoon. The distress on his face frightened me. "My unit is being moved again," he said. "We're leaving tomorrow, and I don't know when I will see you again."

Now what will happen to us? I wanted to ask, but I kept silent, watching and waiting for more. Do we have to stay here in this horrible auditorium? Can't we go back to Yeon Pyong? In these times, a lot could change in six months. I felt panic and dread for the first time since the day I started selling newspapers.

Young Soon was silent, Ok Sun turned and walked away, and Sung Hoon started crying. Again. I sighed. There were no words for the despair I was feeling.

"Once I know where we'll stop for a while again, I'll send for you," Ung Chik said. "I'm very sorry." Torn between obligation to his family and his more official military duty, Ung Chik's choices, like mine, were made for him. Because we had followed him here, these choices were also made for us. We hugged and cried together, aware once again that this might be the last time we would see each other.

◊◊

When Fall came with no word from Ung Chik, we had a new problem. For the past year the war had suspended all schools throughout Korea, but now word came that Kun San was planning to reopen its upper schools on time. This, of course, would return the school auditorium we were living in to its intended use.

Once again Young Soon and I packed our things. Ok Sun and Sung Hoon, packed their belongings in expressionless silence. Waiting for word about where we would go next, we only hoped the four of us could stay together.

As groups began to depart, a man came to where we were standing. He spoke without looking at any of us. "Your family will go to the elementary school just outside Kun San," he said. "Follow the group leaving now."

Moving to the outskirts of Kun San meant that I would be too far from the bus station to sell newspapers.

"Is there any place closer we could be?" I asked, trying to quell my rising panic. If I couldn't get to the bus station, how would we have money for food?

"I'm sorry," he said. "All who are staying here must go to the lower school."

I looked at Young Soon. She looked away. I could already feel the gnawing hunger returning. Then a strange calm settled over me.

Struggle for Survival

I didn't know about the newspaper job when we came here. I would find something else.

"It will be all right," I told the others with confidence in my voice I tried to coax into my heart. "I will find another way to help us get food."

In addition to the elementary school, the area of Kun San we were going to was home to an industrial district where clothing was made. I explored this area each day, looking for work. The rations from the UN were dwindling, giving my urgency with a new desperation. Beyond not wanting to be hungry, I now realized that if we didn't find a way to get food we would die.

I walked through an open door at the end of a long row of low-slung buildings. It was a factory of some sort, with an oddly familiar odor permeating the air inside. A man was working in the front room.

"May I help you?" he asked, looking up to acknowledge me.

"What do you make here?" I asked, looking around the room for a clue.

"Clothes for school children," he said.

In Korea, school is considered preparation for military life. So just like in the military, every child in school wears a uniform — the same color and style of school shirt is required for every school child in the country. This factory first sewed and then dyed these shirts for all of South Korea's schoolchildren. He explained that because school was about to re-open, the factory faced a very busy production schedule.

"Are there any jobs here?" I asked. "My family is hungry and I need to earn money to help buy food." I paused, noting the knowing look on his face. I looked at the ground, then back at him. "We were staying in a school near the bus station in Kun San, and there I was selling newspapers at the bus station." I tried to read his expression, then continued, "I am a very hard worker and will do any job you have. I just have to help my family."

"Come with me," he said.

◊◊

I stood on a rickety scaffold over a huge vat of scalding water and watched the cakes of dye dissolve. Adult workers around me stirred the vat with long poles to mix the dye into the water, and then they dropped the uniform shirts into the dye one at a time. They stirred this mass of cloth, poles bending under the weight, to distribute the dye evenly. After the prescribed amount of time, the clothes were to be removed from the vats, wrung out by hand and spread on large racks to dry.

The man told me that wringing the dye water from the scalding shirts and then spreading them out to dry would be my job. One of the workers pulled a shirt out of the vat and placed it on a mat beside the drying rack. "You must twist the wet shirts hard with your hands to get all the water out," he said. "Then lay it out flat on the rack to dry," he said, pointing to the large, empty racks. The worker went back to his stirring.

I nodded and reached for the steaming shirt, trying not to wince as I wrapped my small fingers around the scalding cloth and forced myself to tighten my grip. Ignoring the pain, I twisted the cloth as I had seen the women in my village do on laundry day. The pain was intense, worse than anything I had ever experienced, including the frostbite on my feet and the labored breathing of pneumonia. The pain was not worse, however, than watching my family starve to death like so many were around us, so I twisted the water from the shirts, one by one, stifling my pain, trying not to cry out loud as I wrung the cloth. If anyone noticed, they didn't say anything.

It got easier once the calluses formed over the blisters on my hands, and it was that job that saved us. The meager handfuls of barley UN workers gave each family diminished until the rations became a watery barley soup. Then the grain stopped coming at all. When Young Soon looked at my scalded, dye-stained hands, I could never tell whether her sadness was because of what I was having to endure to earn money, or because she wondered if it would make any difference.

South Korea was literally starving. The hunger was widespread and oppressive — like what the world would later see in Africa. I wondered how much longer we would be alive to worry about Ung Chik.

We sat together at night and looked up at the sky, reminding each other that we were still alive, and that if Ung Chik was still alive, too, he was looking up at the same stars we were. Somehow that comforted us.

Unlike before, we now realized that not knowing was much better than knowing. If we knew he was alive, we'd worry about tomorrow. If we knew he was dead, he was gone forever. Not knowing became a strange place of peace, an unexpected rest for our worn-out emotions.

◊◊

Once again, survival found a new rhythm. Both Young Soon and Ok Sun got jobs sewing uniforms in the factory where I worked. With three people working and Sung Hoon doing whatever he could to help out, we were getting by. The sheer exhaustion of our daily struggle for survival blessed us with the lack of strength to wonder what would happen next.

Then one morning as I entered the factory for work, a young man hurried up to me. "Won Chik Park?" he said.

I looked at him, trying to imagine how he could know my name. Did I know this man?

"I just heard you and your sister are here." he said. "My name is Yong Woo Lee, and I am your cousin — your mother's sister's son. We, too, came here from a small village in the North."

"I'm glad to see you." I said, bowing to him.

He laughed, bowing in return. "I'm glad I found you. When we heard that two young refugees from the North who had been staying with relatives on Yeon Pyong were here, we knew it had to be our family." He grew quiet. "We also heard what happened to your parents and the rest of the family. I also know that your older brother in the military brought you here, and then he had to leave."

"Yes," I said, glad to make this new connection with family. "Ung Chik found us on Yeon Pyong and sent for us — but then his unit got moved. We lived in the high school until school started up again." I paused, looking down at my dye-stained hands. "It's been harder here, but now we all have jobs at the school uniform factory, so at least we have enough to eat."

"Today after work you will all come to live at my house and we will help you," he said. It was not a question or offer. "There is another young boy with you?"

"Yes, he is my oldest brother's son," I said. "Yung Chik was also killed in the war, and his wife, Ok Sun, and his son, Sung Hoon, are with us. We are all that is left of my family except for Ung Chik."

"We will take care of you all," he said. The matter seemed settled, and I didn't argue or question. "You and your sister, sister-in-law and nephew can stay with us for as long as you need to." He paused, tears filling his eyes. "I am so glad we found you!"

I blinked back tears of my own. "I'm glad too. My mother would be so happy to know of your kindness to us. Thank you very much for helping us."

I barely remember the scalding water or the weight of the dripping shirts that day. I couldn't wait to tell Young Soon the news that at last we would have a place to go that wasn't a big crawling stinking mass of people we didn't know. It was a home. A family. Our family. Even though we didn't know them, either, it was the connection we had all been missing. My heart was feather light as I waited outside the factory at the end of the day for Young Soon and Ok Sun. For the first time in a long time, I felt hope.

◊◊

One afternoon after work, Ung Chik was waiting outside the factory doors.

When I recognized him, I grabbed and hugged him with a fierceness that surprised me.

At last he took a step back and looked me up and down. "You've grown up so much," he said.

I tried to conceal my pride. "I am doing the best I can to take care of our family," I told him. I looked at my hands, scarred and dyed from months of hard labor. "I have a good job and now that we found our cousins, we have a nice place to live and plenty to eat. It was really bad for a while, but everything is much better now."

Relief flooded his face. "I am so glad to know you're all right," he said. "The stories coming from this area were so bad I was afraid of what might have happened to you all. You have done a very good job taking care of them."

"Thank you," I said. My brother's words were unexpected balm to all the pain, uncertainty and suffering I had endured for the past year and a half. Even though I was very young to feel such responsibility, it was a role I now embraced. To be recognized in that way by him made me even more determined to continue.

"Let's go surprise Young Soon," I said.

When Young Soon saw Ung Chik, she clapped her hands and danced with him in a circle. I had not seen such animation from her in a very long time. The pent up anguish of our struggle mixed with the relief of seeing him alive was a tidal wave of emotion even Young Soon couldn't contain.

"You're here!" she kept saying. "I can't believe you're really here!"

To my surprise, even Ok Sun and Sung Hoon joined in the jubilation, and soon we were all laughing, hugging each other and dancing in circles until we could not catch our breath.

"How long can you stay?" we all asked Ung Chik at once.

"Not long," he said. "We were coming through here and my commanding officer gave me a few hours to try to find you."

"Can you stay for dinner and meet our cousins?" I asked.

Over dinner Ung Chik told us how he found us. When his commanding officer gave him the afternoon and evening off to spend with us, he first went to the first auditorium where he was told the refugees had been moved to the elementary school; when we weren't at the elementary school, someone told him we were working at a factory and living with relatives. He had checked every factory in the district until he saw me coming out to empty a bucket. He didn't want to disrupt my work, so he waited there until the end of the workday.

Right after dinner, it was time for Ung Chik to return to his unit. He didn't know when he'd be back, but it seemed to give him great relief to know where we were and that we were safe. That was the last we heard from Ung Chik for seven more months.

Ung Chik Park in his wedding photo, 1954.

CHAPTER THREE:
New Life, New Challenges

Once again, it was a letter from Ung Chik that changed everything in my life. The letter informed us of his upcoming wedding in Inchon, a harbor town on the midwest coast of Korea, and we were all invited.

"Can we go?" I asked Young Soon, watching her face for reaction. No clue there. I had never seen a wedding, but if my brother was in it, I wanted to be there.

"No," she said, shaking her head. I noted the set to her chin, a sure sign the issue was settled.

Nevertheless, I pushed it. "Why not?"

"It's too far and we have jobs," she said. "We must stay here and work." Pragmatic Young Soon saw no reason to risk any of what we had worked so hard to attain for a wedding.

"How far is Inchon?" I persisted. I was not so ready to dismiss the idea.

"Six or seven hours." She looked at me hard, as if willing me to let it go. "By train."

Wow. When I was selling newspapers at the Kun San bus station, I could almost imagine traveling by bus, but I had never even seen a train. I had heard them in the distance, and I had walked across their tracks, but traveling by train was something beyond the reach of even my active imagination. My disappointment was raw.

"Isn't there any way we could go?" I asked her, risking one more try. I usually didn't question Young Soon once her mind was made up, but this was big.

She stopped what she was doing and studied me for a moment. "You can go," she said.

"By myself?"

"Yes."

I paused. She couldn't be serious. I searched her face for any sign of playfulness, a teasing smile hiding in her eyes, but found nothing of the sort. While the idea was at first unthinkable, my brain began to nibble at the edges of its possibility. "Maybe I could," I said.

"We can spare enough money for one ticket," she said. "You can go and we can stay here and work," she said, warming up to the idea. "You'll lose your job, but we'll still have ours. When you come back we will take care of you until you find another one."

I thought about this for a moment. The idea was as exciting as it was frightening. And how could I leave them here working while I went off on what I was certain would be a big adventure?

"You must go to represent our family," she said, replacing guilt with responsibility. It was settled. I would go to Inchon for Ung Chik's wedding.

I followed the directions our cousin gave me to walk to the Kun San train station. I tried to hide my excitement and nervousness as I purchased a ticket like I had watched others do at the bus station. I stood for a moment, looking and listening to the monstrous, hissing train before I climbed up the steps and chose a seat near a window.

As the train whined and growled out of its Kun San station, my stomach was a knot of nervous anticipation. In my hand I held the address of my brother's future family. Even though I had never traveled alone, and I was going to a city many times larger than any I had ever seen, I knew that somehow I would find Ung Chik. I would represent our family at his wedding and get to spend time with him and his future family. Then I would come back to Young Soon and maybe even find a new job. I felt like the luckiest person alive, a bird out of a cage. I looked down at my bag and the well worn, but clean clothes I packed for the trip. I couldn't wait to see my brother.

I had not considered how long a six or seven-hour train trip would feel. It seemed like every time the train began to pick up speed, it was time to stop again, sit on the track for varying intervals, then cough and whine back into motion. At first these stops were interesting; soon they grew annoying. Would we ever just go? I ate the food

Young Soon put in my bag and wished I had more. I put my head back and tried to sleep, but the excitement put springs in my eyelids, requiring more effort to keep them closed than to let them fly back open.

To occupy my mind, I told myself the story of all that happened to me during the past two years. It was still all so unbelievable to me. With the now-dulled ache of loss a constant in my heart, I also felt the pride of surviving all we had been through.

My mind played across the fear and the danger of our escape, the heart wrenching time on Yeon Pyong and the kindness of our uncle and family there, the awful times and near starvation in the refugee camps, the moments of victory selling newspapers and the painful factory job that kept us from starving. In my story the triumph played alongside the sorrow to create a symphony of experiences I still couldn't believe.

And now I'm on a train, all by myself, going to a wedding in a far-away city, I thought. What will come next in this unfolding story? Just as I never could have imagined any of what happened to me in the past two years, I knew I was now walking through the door to another unimaginable experience.

After what seemed like a million stops, the train entered a large station that I knew had to be Inchon. In the distance I could see the sea, just as Ung Chik described in his letter. Excitement fluttered as my thoughts turned to finding Ung Chik. I dug the wrinkled paper from my bag and looked at the address again. The first thing I need to do when I get off this train, I thought, is to ask someone for directions.

An older man who reminded me of the newspaper seller in the Kun San bus station stood looking at the train as I climbed down the steps to the platform. I asked him where I could find the address on the paper. He shrugged and turned away. Next, I approached a woman who reminded me of Young Soon. She pretended not to notice me and hurried past. I walked down the steps of the station and out into the street. The city was large, stretching as far as I could see. People were everywhere, but everyone seemed too absorbed in their own activities to notice a young, confused boy.

I walked down the main street that led from the station toward more residential areas and looked for any sign, any street that was marked. Frustrated, I stood in the middle of an intersection, trying to get someone's attention. An older man stopped, looked at my paper and then pointed toward a street in the opposite direction. "Turn right at that corner, then left, then another right," he said. And then he was gone.

I repeated his instructions over and over as I followed them. This placed me in the middle of a residential neighborhood whose houses and streets also were not marked. I was even more confused than before, and with far less foot traffic, there was no one else to ask.

This was too much. The excitement and anticipation of making the trip collided with disappointment, fear, and the realization that I might never find my brother in this unfriendly, unmarked city. I sat down beside the road and started to cry. In violent shudders, the tears erupted. These were tears from far beyond this day's events. I had been so brave for so long; these tears came from the very depths of my sorrow.

Behind me, a door opened. A woman older than my mother, but not quite the age of a grandmother, put her hand on my shoulder. Her kindness made me cry even harder.

"What's wrong?" she asked.

"I came here on the train, all the way from Kun San for my brother's wedding," I managed to say between sobs. "And now I can't find him. All I have is this address. I don't know the family's name, and none of the houses and streets are marked."

Putting my plight into words added velocity to my wailing. Here where no one knew me and I knew no one, in the company of this kind woman, I was too distraught to be embarrassed. She took my arm and guided me into her house.

"Let's see that paper," she said, offering me a drink of water.

"Thank you," I said, wiping my face with my sleeve and trying to compose myself. I took the water and drank it. She refilled my glass. It was cool, and the day's trip plus the tears had made me thirstier than I realized.

"Just a moment," she said as she left the room.

I looked around me. It was a nice house. Very small, but with all the good smells of a home. I wondered if my brother's future relatives lived in a house like this. I heard voices in the back of the house and then the woman returned with the good news that the house I was looking for may be on the next street.

"They are preparing for a wedding there," she said. "I think it might be the house you are looking for." She walked with me back to the road and pointed me in the direction of the house, which she described in great detail. "If that's not it, come back here and we'll help you," she called after me.

With new energy, my feet hurried to the doorstep I recognized at once from the woman's description. As I approached the house the front door opened and a man walked out.

"I'm looking for Ung Chik Park," I told him.

He peered at me. "Who are you?"

I bowed. "I'm Ung Chik Park's brother, Won Chik," I said. "He sent me a letter inviting me to come to his wedding." I looked at the tattered scrap of paper in my hand. "He gave me this address, and I have been looking for it all day," I said. "A very nice lady on the next street told me she thought this might be the right house."

"Yes, this is the right house," he said, still looking at me with an expression I couldn't read. He did not return the bow. "Please come in. I am the father of your future sister-in-law."

I stood at the doorway and looked around the room filled with people who were all looking back at me. As my gaze traveled from face to face, I grew more self-conscious. Nobody spoke.

I turned back to the man who had invited me in. "Is Ung Chik here?"

"No, he went out for a while," he said. "He will be back later. Is he expecting you?"

"No," I said. I looked around at the roomful of people. "Our sister, Young Soon, sister-in-law, and nephew are also in Kun San," I explained. "Ung Chik sent a letter to invite all of us, but we all work at the school uniform factory there, and we decided that only I would come to represent our family. They stayed there to work. He doesn't know I'm coming — I wanted to surprise him."

The words stammered and tumbled out of my mouth long past their usefulness. Realizing we should have responded to the letter, and with the lack of response from the room, I willed myself to shut up. I looked down at my clothes and the bag I was holding that contained others just like them. I realized how poor I looked to this roomful of well-dressed future relatives. My face grew hot with embarrassment, and I looked down at my feet. I wanted to leave, forget the wedding, and go back to Kun San. But more than that, I wanted to see my brother.

Then a woman entered the room. She stopped, looked at me, and said, "Who is this boy?"

Gathering what was left of my pride, I bowed. "I'm Won Chik Park, Ung Chik's younger brother, here for the wedding," I said. Noticing her kind eyes, I hoped she could somehow remove me from my awkward encounter with the others.

She did. "Come with me," she said.

She led me to the small kitchen in the back of the house and seated me at the table. The aroma in this kitchen was intoxicating, and when she placed a loaded plateful of food in front of me, I realized how hungry I was. I tried to eat slowly, to savor this wonderful food, but before I knew it the plate was empty.

She laughed at my dismay and brought me another. "You're here just in time," she told me as I ate. "The wedding is tomorrow."

Young Soon had explained to me that Korean weddings are huge family affairs, and everyone comes — and stays — for the days and often weeks leading up to and following the wedding. According to Korean custom, the wedding ceremony itself is held in the bride's family's home, and the entire family stayed there for days, eating, drinking and celebrating together.

If Young Soon's information was correct and the food I had just enjoyed was any indication, I would be eating very well for the next few days. I couldn't believe my good fortune. Suddenly the upsetting

New Life, New Challenges

events of the day, including the strange reception I had received in the other room, all but disappeared. I looked down at my clothes, hoping Ung Chik wouldn't be embarrassed by my appearance.

The woman followed my glance and seemed to understand my uneasiness. "Don't worry about anything," she said. "We will help you get ready for the wedding. You are an honored guest and a very special part of this celebration. Ung Chik will be so glad that you are here — and we are also very glad to meet you!"

"Thank you," I said, smiling at her. She was a good dream come true.

It was past dark when my brother returned. The look on his face when he walked through the door to find me sitting there told me I had done the right thing by coming. Now it was his turn to hug me and dance around, much as Young Soon had done when he surprised us in Kun San. He held my face in his hands and then hugged me again. I looked around the room to discover that many of those former stone faces were now crying along with us.

◊◊

The day of my brother's wedding was a magical blur. I awoke just after dawn to the wonderful aromas of many foods cooking, and I tried to go back to sleep, assuming it was a delicious dream and closing my eyes tighter in an effort to return to it. Then a sound from the kitchen startled my eyes open and I remembered where I was. I sat straight up, smiling.

I dressed quickly and followed my nose to the kitchen. Greeting me with a smile, the woman who had been so kind to me the night before, who I now understood to be Sun Jun, one of my brother's future sisters-in-law, seated me again at the table and placed another plate of food in front of me. Remembering all the days of barley, I marveled at this feast steaming before me.

"Thank you," I said, smiling at her.

She smiled back and gestured to the plate. "Go ahead," she said, laughing. "Eat all you want. There is plenty."

"Thank you," I said again, digging into my food.

"When you are finished eating, some of our relatives will take you to get clothes for the wedding," she said.

I looked down at my worn clothes and felt the heat of embarrassment again creeping up my neck.

She seemed to read my thoughts. "Don't worry," she said gently. "We'll help you. You haven't had a mother to take care of your clothes for a long time. It would be our honor to make sure you have the clothes your mother would want you to wear for the wedding, if she were here."

If my mother were here. This thought brought the familiar tug of sorrow. This wedding was the first normal family event she would miss, the first time her absence would be as palpable to others as it was every day to me.

"I'm so sorry about all that has happened to you and your family," Sun Jun said. "They should all be here today with us. But we'll remember and honor them as we welcome your brother — and you and you sister — as part of our family now."

I appreciated her kind words, but being part of someone else's family just wasn't the same. Nothing would ever be the same again, and I was only just beginning to realize in how many ways this was true.

Later that day, outfitted in new clothes and shoes, with several more sets of clothing to spare, I returned to the house. Ung Chik was there, and the place was a bustling hive of last minute wedding preparations.

"Look at you!" he said as I walked in the door. "What a well-dressed young man you are," he teased. "You must be here for a wedding!"

I looked down at my new clothes, then back at my brother. I still couldn't believe any of this was really happening. Catching my reflection in a mirror, I confirmed that with the wave of some invisible magic wand, and the efforts of several future relatives, the street urchin had disappeared and in his place was a handsome young man I struggled to recognize.

As the ceremony began, I stood silent, trying to absorb every detail. If I had been to a wedding before, I didn't remember it. Every unfamiliar detail was beautiful to me. The clothes, the rituals, and the significance of each word and action all swirled like magic.

Sun Jun had explained that according to custom, the courtyard of the house was prepared with a folding screen set to the north. Just as she described, the *Choilyh* table was in the center, set with two candlesticks, one red and one blue. Two vases also stood on the table, one with a branch of pine and one with bamboo. There were also other items including bowls, food, washbasins, towels and two smaller wine tables, all carefully placed, organized and separated according to Korean custom.

Ung Chik and Soon Jun Kang, my future sister-in-law, stood facing each other in front of the Choilyh table. In an elaborate display I didn't understand, but with beauty that took my breath away, my brother and Soon Jun did a series of bows to each other, a ritual of some kind involving wine, and exchanged some of the food items in several different ways.

I watched each precise, orchestrated movement in complete awe. While much of the beautiful symbolism was lost on me, the greater significance this ceremony held for me was confirmation that there was still order, tradition, and future hope in a world that many of my people believed was gone forever. Comparing this beautiful scene unfolding before me to the dirt and desperation of the world I had been living in, I felt a great fluttering of hope. This wedding also meant that our family tree would now continue, rather than being mown down as so many were in the violent ugliness of war.

After the ceremony, the nonstop flow of food, music, dancing, and laughter began and, as Sun Jun and Young Soon promised, lasted for days. I ate and ate and reveled in what had gone missing from my life. I wished for time to slow down, and as I watched Ung Chik prepare to leave with his new wife for something called a honeymoon, I was filled with despair that this miracle was ending. I didn't want to think about returning to my life in Kun San.

"Thank you very much for inviting me," I told my brother as he packed.

"I'm glad you came," he said. He stopped packing and looked at me. "Do you want to stay here until I get back?" he asked. "Sun Jun said you are welcome to stay here for a while longer if you like. She enjoys watching you eat!"

I looked down, embarrassed. "It was such good food," I said. "She is very kind and I do like it here, but I should get back to Young Soon."

"She'll be OK," Ung Chik said. He looked at me with a tenderness I had not seen from him before. "Will you please stay until I get back so we can spend more time together before you go back to Kun San?"

This idea sounded reasonable to me. I missed Young Soon, and I couldn't wait to tell her about the wedding, but she and my Kun San life could wait a little while longer. Grateful for the reprieve, I settled into this blissful purgatory of good food and kindness.

By the time Ung Chik returned from his honeymoon, I had explored the streets of Inchon, played with some local kids, and discovered a world I never knew existed. Sun Jun and the rest of the family had seen to my care in a way that warmed my heart and made me want to stay there forever. Still, the tug of obligation and sadness when I thought of Young Soon made me realize it was time to return to Kun San. I had been gone for only a few weeks, but it seemed like years.

◊◊

"I've been thinking about your future," Ung Chik said as we walked to the nearby soccer field on the day after he returned.

I loved to play this game called soccer with the kids who gathered there every day to play, and I wanted to show my brother all I had learned. The great thing about soccer was that with just one ball, everyone who showed up could play. It was a fun game and it didn't take me long to catch on. All that running and kicking and laughing felt good.

"What about my future?" I asked as I scanned the horizon.

"I think you should come to live with me and Soon Jun in Pusan," he said.

New Life, New Challenges

I stopped walking. Was he serious? "What about Young Soon?" I protested. After all we had been through together, and the way she had taken care of me, how could I just leave her?

"Young Soon is with our relatives, she has a job, and someday soon, she will meet someone and marry," Ung Chik said, watching my face. "But you need to go to school. You need a home and a family to take care of you."

This was something I hadn't considered. We, like so many others, had been frozen in time by the war and the day-to-day struggle to survive. Although this trip had shown me that life was going on for others, I hadn't considered what could be next for me beyond working at the factory.

"What about your family — your own children?" I said, remembering the wedding vows and their promise to have a family.

Ung Chik laughed. "We don't have children yet; that takes a while. And even when we do, it makes no difference. You are my family, and I want to take care of you. You need to stay here with us so you can start school in the fall."

By his tone I could tell that this was another of those matters already settled, and once again I was relieved that the decision wasn't mine. Despite the tug of sadness over leaving Young Soon, I was happy to live in Pusan with Ung Chik and Soon Jun and to go to school instead of working in the clothing factory. I was nearly 13 years old, and I could almost hear the doors closing on the most terrible two years of my life.

◊◊

When the time came to register for school, I was a bundle of nervous excitement. Ung Chik went with me to register and pay the tuition. Public school in Korea was not free; they all charged tuition. Although Ung Chik tried to seem unconcerned, I heard the quiet whispers about money trouble. His military paycheck was barely enough to cover our basic living expenses, and my tuition would put a new financial strain on them.

"Can I get a job to help?" I asked him on the way back from registering for school. I already knew how to work hard, and to get to go to school would be well worth it.

"No," he said. "Your job is to go to school and get an education."

"But it's expensive," I protested. "I don't feel right taking your money to go to school."

"I want to take care of you," he said. "Please let me do this. Our parents would want me to."

"Thank you," I said, because it seemed very important to Ung Chik to do this for me. I wondered how I could help without insulting him.

The war had left the whole country lagging behind in so many ways; among the most significant was the three-year delay in every child's education. I was placed in middle school because of my age, but this meant I had to skip three grades. Despite the school's assurance that they would help me catch up, I wondered if I was smart enough to pass.

◊◊

One afternoon near the end of the first term, my teacher asked me to stay after school. "I need to talk to you," was all he said.

I prepared myself for the worst. I worked hard and did my best, but with so much catching up to do, maybe I wasn't doing as well as I thought. During those first six months of school I arrived early every day, studied late into every night, asked incessant questions of my teachers and maintained single-minded dedication to understanding every lesson. True to their word, the teachers all made extra efforts to help everyone catch up to his grade level. It was a different kind of work than I had ever done, but as my mind began to take to it my confidence rose, as did the marks on my papers.

"Won Chik, I have your grades here," my teacher began.

"Yes?" was all I could manage to say. I realized I was holding my breath.

"They are very good."

I breathed my relief.

"At this school we offer scholarships to the top three students in every grade," he said.

"What does that mean?" I asked. I had no idea what a scholarship was.

"If your grades are in the top three out of the 70 students in your class," he explained, "your tuition is free."

"Oh," I said, excited at the thought. "How much do I need to improve to get into the top three?"

He laughed. "You already have," he said. "We are pleased to award you a scholarship to recognize your hard work. As long as you keep your grades in the top three, your tuition will remain free."

I will never forget the look on my brother's face when I told him this news. He hugged me tight. "I am so proud of you," he said. "I always knew you were smart!"

I was too choked up to speak — it was one of the proudest moments of my life. My brother's words and the feeling behind them gave me the determination that kept that scholarship for the next six years. It was the perfect way to honor my brother's kindness and generosity in taking me in and giving me a chance at a life that I never would have otherwise had.

◊◊

The transition to living at my brother's house was much easier than I thought it would be. To my surprise, Young Soon agreed to this plan, and I communicated regularly with her in letters. I was sorry that she had to stay in Kun San, but she seemed happy there and had a good job. Remembering Ung Chik's prediction, I wondered when she would find someone to marry so she could have a home and a family, too.

One evening after dinner we opened Young Soon's latest letter. Reporting that Ok Sun and Sung Hoon were gone when she woke up one morning, this letter set off an almost forgotten alarm in my heart.

"Gone?" I addressed the letter as if it were Young Soon. "What happened to them?"

Young Soon's letter went on to say that she thought Ok Sun may have left to marry a man from another village.

I was puzzled. "Why didn't she tell anyone?" I asked. "Why wouldn't she say goodbye?" Weddings, after all, were something to be celebrated, as I just witnessed. Why wouldn't she want us all to be part of that?

Ung Chik shrugged. "I don't know," he said. "It's different when a woman has been married before, even if her husband died. And she has a child. Maybe she was embarrassed to tell them because she was afraid we'd think she was being disloyal to Yung Chik. Or maybe she just didn't want to feel bad about leaving them, so she left when no one was looking."

"Does Young Soon feel all alone?" I asked.

Ung Chik looked at me. Then he looked at Soon Jun. "I think it is time for Young Soon to come here and be with us," he said.

I looked at Soon Jun. Her face was expressionless. Soon Jun was always kind to me, and if she minded my being there, I never knew. I wondered if adding yet another person to their household would place new emotional as well as financial strain on their new marriage. Although these were worries that were not mine to address, they plagued the adult side of my youth. Nevertheless, I couldn't wait to see Young Soon.

◊◊

It was almost sunset as I walked toward the soccer field after dinner, but the August heat still radiated through my shoes. Every evening, once my chores and studies were done, I went to the soccer fields to play until dark with kids of all ages who gathered there. My low center of gravity, strength, and quick reflexes made me a natural for soccer, often allowing me to outmaneuver even older and more skilled players. The same sense of timing that had been key to being first to the fishing boats and first to the buses now, more often than not, made me first to the soccer ball.

Passing an elementary school with a very popular soccer field for my age group, I paused to watch a group of six or seven boys already embroiled in a game. The first thing I noticed was that they were playing with a real soccer ball. I smiled as I remembered the makeshift soccer balls I had seen. In this time of scarcity, almost anything that rolled could serve as a soccer ball. But a real soccer ball was a treasure few could afford and we all longed for. *Someday, I will have my own soccer ball,* I thought. Then I could practice and play soccer whenever I want to, wherever I want to. It was not lost on me that the kid who owned the ball controlled the game.

As if summoned by my thoughts, the ball from the game I was watching glanced off one boy's knee and came flying my direction. It landed right in front of me, landing right in my path like a gift from above. Before I could stop myself, I moved forward into it and gave it a mighty, satisfying kick.

Kicking a real ball was even better than I had imagined it could be. I watched it soar, delighting in its amazing arc. My delight turned to horror as the ball kept going, then disappeared out of sight, coming down behind a tall wooden fence. The sound of shattering glass told me the ball had found a window. I heard a door open, then angry yelling; my mistake had not gone unnoticed. In my shock and concern about the enraged homeowner, I didn't even notice the angry mob of boys now surrounding me.

My eyes widened at the murderous expressions on their faces. The shockwave of their collective anger hit me first, followed by fists, feet and elbows. As they continued to pound me I closed my eyes and wished for the earth to somehow swallow me.

It didn't. I'm not sure how much longer they would have beaten me if the homeowner hadn't appeared around the fence. When they saw him approaching, they scattered like cockroaches.

"I will keep this ball as payment for my window," he shouted after them. Then I felt his eyes turn to me.

I couldn't bring myself to return his angry gaze, so I just sat there, crying, looking down at the dirt. My face was already beginning to swell, and I fought the urge to wipe away the blood I felt trickling down my cheek and chin. "I'm very sorry," I said, still not looking up.

He said nothing, waiting, I suppose, for me to say more.

I didn't know what else to say, so I just sat there, silent.

Then he turned and walked away, taking the ball with him.

I dragged myself to my feet and began the long walk back home. I walked around and around the neighborhood, hoping to think of some explanation, something to tell Ung Chik about what happened that wouldn't make me an embarrassment to him. I didn't know what was worse —my mistake of kicking the ball, my weakness of getting beaten up, my guilt in breaking the window, or how badly I had had handled my encounter with the angry homeowner.

I washed myself off the best I could, tried to smooth the dirt and blood out of my shirt, and then tiptoed into the house. I waited as late as I could, hoping the darkness would provide the extra cover I needed. It was about 9:30, and with any luck my brother and sister-in-law would already be asleep. It was not my lucky day.

"Who's there?" Ung Chik called as I entered the house.

His voice startled me and I bumped into something in my path. "It's just me," I said, trying to sound casual.

I heard movement as Ung Chik entered the room. I tried to keep my back to him so he couldn't see my bloody, throbbing, misshapen face.

"Come over here."

I turned away even more so he couldn't see my face. "It's late — I'm tired," I said, faking a yawn. I knew my voice sounded different.

"Something wrong," he persisted.

I turned and stepped into the light.

He gasped and took a step back. "What happened?"

I told him the whole story, apologizing to him over and over. More than anything else, I didn't want my brother to be angry with me.

He was angry, all right, but not at me. "Who are these boys?" he demanded.

"I don't know," I said. "I never saw them before."

"Where they older?"

"No," I said, "I don't think so. I think they were about my age." I was miserable. "It's not their fault. I took their ball," I said, fighting back the tears of shame. "I just wanted to see what it felt like to kick it really hard." I looked at Ung Chik for the first time. "I made a terrible mistake," I said. "They had a right to be angry."

"Yes," he said, "but they did not have the right to do this to you." He got some cool water and helped me wash the cuts and abrasions that covered my face, arms and back. The water stung and the rag hurt, but nothing was hurt as much as my pride.

"What did you do to try to protect yourself?" Ung Chik asked.

"Nothing," I said. It was true. I had just let them pummel me. At first, perhaps, because I thought I deserved it. But at some point I had realized that I had no idea how to stop them. Or whether they would stop before killing me.

"I need to help you learn how to protect yourself," Ung Chik said, as if somehow reading my recollection. "You are a strong, smart young man. You must learn how to protect yourself."

◊◊

"I'm going to learn boxing," I told my best friend, Wan Kyu, one day a few weeks later as we walked to school for the first day that year. He knew the story of the soccer ball. The bruises were still barely visible, and it didn't take long for word to get around. The embarrassment was a shadow that followed me everywhere.

"How will you learn boxing?" Wan Kyu was intrigued. Gang Jun Ho, a Korean boxer who had just won a bronze medal in boxing at the Helsinki Olympics, was the new idol of all the boys my age. His medal had put boxing in the national limelight and made Gang Jun Ho an instant national hero. He also happened to be one of Ung Chik's very best friends from the ROK Army.

I was star struck every time Gang Jun Ho came to visit. Laughing at this, he would always punch me in the arm and say, "Little Won Chik, when you are sixteen, I will teach you how to box."

"Really? Will you?" I'd say, breathless at the possibility.

The he'd laugh. "I will make you a champion," he'd say. I could hardly wait. It was never clear to me why I had to be sixteen to learn how to box; I decided that the next time Gang Jun Ho came to visit I would somehow persuade him to let me start my training early.

"When is Gang Jun Ho coming to visit?" I began to ask Ung Chik every single day.

"Soon," he'd say. "Why are you always asking me that?"

"He's going to teach me boxing," I'd say.

Ung Chik would just shrug. He had bigger things to worry about. Even though my moment of supreme humiliation had faded for him, it was still very fresh in my own mind.

◊◊

Wan Kyu was waiting for me outside the school at the end of the day. We always walked home together, but today I could see something different in his face — excitement and a new sense of purpose.

"Come with me," he said. "I want to show you something."

"Where?" I asked, following him. It was not like Wan Kyu to be mysterious, but today he had a secret. What could it could be?

We were both still angry about what happened on "the day of the soccer ball," as we called it. For some reason Wan Kyu seemed as angry as I was, even though he only heard about it after the fact. I think it frightened him, maybe making him realize he was just as vulnerable as I was.

"Remember what happened on the day of the soccer ball?" he said.

How could I forget? We talked about it every day. "Of course," I said. "But soon I am going to learn boxing. That will never happen to me again."

"I know something better," he said. "And you don't have to wait for Gang Jun Ho to learn this. Come see."

New Life, New Challenges

Now it was my turn to be intrigued. Better than learning boxing from Gang Jun Ho? Not possible.

Wan Kyu stopped in front of an old building with a sign that said, "Grand Opening."

"What is this?" I asked.

"It's a taekwondo dojang. It is just opening."

I frowned. I had never heard of such a thing. "What is taekwondo — and what makes it better than boxing?" I asked.

"With boxing you just hit and hit and hit," he said. "With this," he gestured toward the building. "Just one strike is all it takes. The fight is finished." He gestured with his hands, flat out.

"One strike is better than boxing?" I asked, skeptical. "How could that be? Boxing is strong, tough." I made a fist and hit my other palm, hard. "One strike is enough in boxing, too."

"This is nothing like boxing," he said. "It is . . ." he paused, making a big circle with his arms, eyes wide, "Wow . . . so much more."

I frowned. I didn't understand. "Wow?"

Wan Kyu tried again. "With taekwondo, every finger, every kick, even your elbow — everything on your body is a weapon," he said. He held up his index finger, right under my nose. "With this one finger, you can kill someone."

I laughed at his seriousness. "That's OK, " I said, waving him off. "You go ahead. I'm going to learn boxing."

"We're here," he persisted, following me down the street. "Will you please just come in and watch with me today? You don't have to do it if you don't want to, but I want to see it." He paused. "Will you come with me? Please? Just today?"

"OK," I said. Wan Kyu had never asked anything of me before. I had no idea why this was so important to him, but I could see the urgency in his eyes, hear it in his voice. I realized that he was scared that what had happened to me would happen to him. And above all, he was my friend, and he said "please."

We inched our way into the old building and climbed the stairs to the third floor. The only light came through a few small windows along one side of the room and a single bulb in the center of the low ceiling. The wood floors were worn smooth from years of varied use. The school had only been open for a few weeks, but it already smelled of stale sweat.

As our eyes adjusted to the light, we realized there were six or seven students standing in the middle of the room. A man standing before them let out a tremendous yell. We jumped back, ready to bolt. This caught the attention of the man, who then began walking toward us. Behind him his students, all wearing the white belts of beginners, stood frozen in place in a funny half-crouched position, feet parallel. What had we walked into?

The man got closer. He peered at us as if sizing us up. "Do you want to learn taekwondo?" he asked, looking first at me, then at Wan Kyu.

If we said, "No," we knew we'd have to leave, and by then both of us were curious about what that small, straight line of side-by-side students was learning. The yell was impressive, too. We wanted to know more. We looked at each other, then back at the man. "Yes, sir," we said in unison.

"Class has already started today, so today you can watch," he said. "Go sit over there and be quiet." He turned back toward his students, but still spoke to us. "If you talk, you leave."

"Yes, sir!" We didn't know much about this place, but we knew that of all times to be respectful, this was without a doubt one of them.

We sat there for the next hour and a half without talking or moving. Even though our legs went to sleep, we were too enthralled and too intimidated to move. After the class was over and the students started to leave, we chanced a few short whispers to each other.

"Did you see how they kept doing that same thing over and over?" Wan Kyu whispered.

"Did you see how long they had to stand there that way?" I answered, matching his tone exactly. "How boring!"

"They were all sweating at the end, just from doing that one simple movement, over and over," he said. "It must be very hard to do."

"It doesn't look that hard," I said. But I, too, had noticed the discipline this taekwondo required, and in spite of myself, I was fascinated.

"The master seems very strong," Wan Kyu said. "I bet he can kill someone with one finger."

We were so caught up in our musing that we didn't even notice that the master was standing right behind us. We jumped up when we saw him, wondering how much of our conversation he had heard.

He was quiet for a moment. Then he said, looking at both of us, "Do you want to join?"

Neither one of us had to think about it. Each of us, for our own private reasons, said, "Yes, sir!"

On the way home we kept going over and over what we saw in class, and Wan Kyu told me more about what he had heard about this ancient fighting art. All the old masters had hidden it for many years from the Japanese. It had been illegal, punishable by death, to practice taekwondo during Korea's Japanese occupation, but somehow the masters had kept it alive in private.

Now dojangs were opening all over my country and this beautiful ancient art was making a big comeback. I was beside myself with excitement. Then, as we drew nearer to Ung Chik's house, reality came crashing down on my euphoria.

"I can't do it," I said.

"Why not?" Wan Kyu was confused.

"I don't have any money," I said.

"Can't your brother pay?" Wan Kyu had no concept of the poverty I had seen and lived. His family was better off than most, and he couldn't imagine doing without.

"No," I said, "and I would never ask him to." Money was getting even tighter, and I was acutely aware of being another mouth to feed. I didn't want to be any more of a burden on Ung Chik and Soon Jun than I already was.

"I have some money," Wan Kyu said. "My parents can pay for me and I can pay for you."

"I can't let you do that," I said.

"Why not?"

"Because I don't know if I can ever pay you back."

"It's OK," he said. "You don't have to. I want you to come to class with me, so I will pay your way for the first month. We'll figure something else out after that."

"OK," I said, "but just for one month." Maybe if I liked it I could find a job and earn the money to pay for my training. Or maybe I wouldn't like it and then I could go back to my boxing plan. Either way, I couldn't wait to learn more about this amazing, mysterious and powerful thing called taekwondo.

Grand Opening of a dojang in Pusan, circa 1954. After the war, taekwondo masters all over Korea were opening dojangs to begin the revival of this almost forgotten ancient Korean martial art.

Left to right is my master, Great Grandmaster Hyon Chong Park (left) and his friends. Far right is Great Grandmaster Chong Woo Lee, and standing next to him, dressed in the monk's robe, is our mental master, Dong Ho Bub Sa.

CHAPTER FOUR:
Lessons in Triumph and Humility

We started with *choon bi sohgi,* ready position. Again and again we practiced, feet parallel and shoulder-width apart, making a fist just the way the master demonstrated, raising our hands, palms forward, making a good fist by first closing our fingers, then wrapping our thumbs tightly around our closed fingers.

Inhaling slowly just as he did, we pulled our fists back to our belts, palms up. Then, pausing for an instant, we straightened our arms quickly, twisting our palms toward each other as we did until they were parallel in front of us, stretched downward in front of the knot on our belt.

"There should always be one fist's distance between your fists in choon bi sohgi," the master said, walking slowly to each one of us and placing his fist between our hands to check the distance. He'd also straighten arms, turn fists slightly, move thumbs almost imperceptivity and adjust the distance between our feet by nudging a foot with his toe until he was satisfied that each one of us had the choon bi sohgi just right.

"Now, again!" he'd say, and the process would start over.

For the first few classes, choon bi sohgi was all we did. Then, at last we moved on to the basic stances, *ahp sohgi,* front stance, *dwi sohgi,* back stance, and *juchoom sohgi,* horseback riding stance. We learned each technique the same way, with the master breaking down each one into its smallest parts, which we practiced again and again until he was satisfied. Then we'd put the parts together and practice the whole movement again and again until the details melded into fluid perfection every time. We practiced each stance until our legs ached, each block until our arms and shoulders throbbed.

Learning juchoom sohgi was the most difficult. To do this stance properly, the master explained, required training your body to stand in a half squat with feet parallel, back straight. This in itself was not difficult. What was difficult about juchoom sohgi is that he'd leave us in this almost-sitting position while he went from person to person, correcting details.

When our legs would start to shake, he'd say, "Shaking is good— it means you are building strength." Then he'd seem to walk even slower between us, telling us stories, sometimes adding, "Tell your legs to be still."

I went to the dojang every day after school during that first month. Although we were learning just one small technique at a time, moving tediously from stances to punching and then basic blocks, I practiced each one with single-minded intensity, over and over, visualizing the master's demonstration as I practiced. In class, out of class, walking down the street, while I was doing my household chores, my individual practice was constant. I was obsessed.

I knew that the master, whose last name was Park, just like mine, often watched me practice. He nodded from time to time when I did a movement especially well; this made me work even harder. Wan Kyu liked the classes, but not as much as I did. He was always impatient, bored with our slow progress, wanting to do something more exciting than the blocks and stances we practiced over and over each day.

"I want to learn kicks," he said one day as we walked home. He executed what he thought was a good kick, then lost his balance and fell to the ground.

I laughed. "Maybe we're not ready for kicking," I said.

"I want to learn elbow striking, punching, and how to break things," he said.

Normally I was the more impatient of the two of us, but for some reason I was in no hurry. I sensed the importance of building a strong foundation step by step. I was happy to practice each thing the master taught us over and over until he thought we were ready to learn something new. It was a strange journey of discovery for me, and for some reason, I didn't want to rush it.

Before I knew it, my free month was over. Heartsick, but determined not to ask Ung Chik to pay, I stopped going to the dojang, but continued practicing by myself at home. Wan Kyu promised to come by each day and show me what they had practiced and anything new he learned. It wasn't ideal, but it was better than nothing.

"Master Park asked about you today," Wan Kyu said toward the end of that first miserable week of no taekwondo class.

"What did you tell him?"

"I told him that you didn't have any parents and you were living with your brother who was military and couldn't afford to pay."

"Why did you tell him that?" I asked. I was angry with Wan Kyu, but angrier at the situation.

Wan Kyu took a step back, surprised by the sharpness of my tone. "Don't be mad at me," he said. "I just told him the truth. What was I supposed to say?"

He had a point. "I'm sorry," I said, feeling bad for taking it out on him. He was telling the truth. And what else could he have said? "What did he say?"

"He said to tell you to come talk to him tomorrow before class," Wan Kyu said, still looking nervous.

◊◊

"My military unit has been transferred to another city," Ung Chik said when he got home that day.

I felt the old familiar panic rising. "Do we have to move?" I asked, trying not to let him see my eyes. I had found a home here in Pusan. School. Friends. Taekwondo. I fought back the tears.

"No," he said, looking away to spare me embarrassment. "Our home is here and Soon Jun's family is here," he said. "We have decided that I will go with my unit and you will stay here and help Soon Jun take care of the house."

I breathed out relief. I would miss Ung Chik, but remembering what it was like to live near him but never to see him because he was on active duty, this decision came as a huge relief. "Don't worry," I said. "I will take care of everything while you are gone."

"Thank you, Won Chik," he said. "I will feel better knowing you are here to help Soon Jun and watch over our home. You are a good brother and a very strong, smart young man." He stepped back and looked me up and down. "You're growing up fast," he said. "Soon it will be your time for military service." He paused. "I think you will be an officer."

My heart pounded with pride as I looked down in humility. These were big words to live up to. I hoped he was right.

◊◊

I arrived at the dojang early, but Master Park was not there. I began practicing my high block, the *ahrae makee*. Paying special attention to breathing, just like Master Park showed us, I mimicked my mind's picture of him executing the block. I inhaled as I positioned my arms, inside wrist to inside wrist, tucked at my side, just above my belt. A slight pause. Then with a strong exhale I twisted my body as I raised my top forearm across my face to a spot just above my eyebrows and parallel to the ground, fist facing out, just high enough to block an overhead blow from an imaginary attacker. Master Park showed us the type of attack the ahrae makee would block. With a ferocious yell, called the *kihap,* he swung an imaginary weapon overhand from above, straight down toward the tops of our heads.

Over and over I practiced. Inhale. Wait. Exhale and block at the same precise moment, imagining blocking this dangerous attack. There were now eight of us in our class, the charter class of Master Park's new school, and we learned the basic movements one at a time, first the stances, then punching, now the blocks. One at a time, repeated more times than any of us could count, every day.

Seeing the practical purpose for this block whetted our appetites even more for learning the more advanced techniques of kicking, fighting and self-defense. None of us had the nerve to ask Master Park about when we would start learning these things, but sensing our eagerness, he explained that to be a strong fighter, the basic techniques we had learned so far must be practiced until they are automatic, like breathing.

"Feet must know how to find only the right stance," he said. "Shoulders and arms must remember on their own how to set themselves up for exactly the right block. When your mind moves on to other things," he told us, "your body must remember this foundation on its own to support your other techniques. Making the foundation strong makes the building strong."

It was nice to be back in the dojang, but I couldn't imagine why Master Park asked me to come. Wan Kyu told him I didn't have any money. That part wouldn't change until I got a job. If I got a job, the only time to work would be during class time. There seemed to be no solution. Maybe I was here to face that truth and tell Master Park I would not be returning to class.

"I'm glad you came," the master's voice behind me startled me from my practice.

I stopped, turned and bowed. "Yes sir," I said. *"Anyong ham shamika,"* I said. This traditional Korean greeting also opened every class.

Master Park bowed and returned my greeting. "Good practice," he added.

"Thank you, sir."

"You are younger and smaller than the rest of the class," he said.

I nodded. "Yes, sir."

"You started out behind everyone, but now you've caught up — and passed — most of the other students. Soon you will lead this class."

I didn't know what to say. The dread in my stomach kept me from enjoying this high compliment. I had to tell him the truth. Now, before he started counting on me.

Master Park took a step closer. "What's wrong?" he asked.

"I cannot come back," I said. There. I said it out loud.

"Why not?"

"I cannot afford to pay for my training," I said. "My parents were killed in the war and now I live with my brother. He is in the military and we are barely getting by as it is. I couldn't ask him to pay, and if I get a job I would have to work during class time." I looked at my feet. "I'm sorry, sir. I have no choice. " More than anything I did not want to cry, and I was afraid that if I looked at Master Park's face I would not be able to stop the tears from embarrassing me further.

"I see," he said. He paused, thoughtful. "You're going to school," he said. "Who's paying for that?"

"I am on scholarship because of my good grades."

"OK, then," he said, "your hard work and good practice has earned a scholarship here, too. To keep it, you will also help me at the school."

I was too stunned to speak. This was a solution I never imagined.

"Come every day thirty minutes early," he said, turning to walk away. The matter was settled. "Not to clean," he added over his shoulder. It was the job of all the lower ranking students to clean the dojang together; they mopped the floor by hand at the end of class every day. Master Park stopped and turned back toward me. "You will bring water every day for cleaning," he said. "After the students clean, you will stay ten or fifteen minutes to make sure everything is prepared for the next day."

I looked at the spotless dojang floor. I had never considered that someone had to bring the water before we cleaned the floors and then someone came behind us to make sure the school was ready for the next day's training. "Thank you, sir," I said, bowing, my eyes now brimming with grateful tears I had no wish to stop.

He returned the bow and disappeared into the shadows. We never spoke of my scholarship again.

◊◊

The thirty minutes before class at the dojang soon became my favorite part of each day. I entered carrying a large wooden bucket of water in each hand, trying not to slosh as I walked. I stowed the buckets in an out-of-the-way corner for later use, put on my uniform and began to practice in the perfect stillness of the quiet dojang. Moving from technique to technique, I reenacted from memory what we practiced the day before.

My solitary practice before class each day became an important personal ritual. Then after class, when the cleaning was finished and everyone was gone, the quiet dojang became a place of reverent meditation. The smell of the dojang was distinctive. Powerful. Privileged. It was the smell of belonging to something important — this rare combination of physical and mental accomplishment that nothing else could touch. As I took my final walk around the training floor, I breathed in this musty blend of old and new sweat, the sacred smell of hard work and our collective spirit. As I breathed in this unique aroma, I let each day's training soak even more deeply into my being.

At the end of class each day we hung our sweat-soaked *doboks* on the straight line of hooks bolted high on the walls surrounding the training floor. As I walked, I always let my eyes travel from hook to hook, uniform to uniform, thinking about each of my classmates. The yellow, then grey sweat stains and even black dots of mildew on the doboks were badges of honor, the surest sign of consistent hard work and progress that new students in their perfect white doboks first envied, then strived for, then celebrated. Washing a dobok was only for testing day, Master Park explained, when, with the the stains of hard work still visible, a clean, pressed uniform showed our pride, spirit, and readiness to begin our next level of our training.

During this time I also I tried to imagine testing. The now-silent room filled with people, Master Park and two other masters would be seated in the front behind a draped table. I pictured myself standing in the center of the room, lined up with my classmates, our clean uniforms pressed stiff with starch.

The traditional Korean gup system of ranking dictated a 7th gup test to mark our progress from beginner to advanced beginner, confirming our readiness to begin more serious training. It wasn't until we passed our 6th gup test, however, that our belt would change color, from white to green. After 6th gup, each test was for a new color of belt, progressing from green to blue, blue to red, and then, at last, red to first dan black belt. First dan black belt, Master Park told us, was like a college degree. It prepared us for the real learning. I couldn't even imagine what that meant, but our first testing day was coming soon. As far as I was concerned, it couldn't come soon enough.

◊◊

"Won Chik Park!" It was testing day at last, and Master Park called me first.

"Yes sir!" I said, with all the bravado I could muster. Upon hearing my name, the knot of butterflies in my stomach became a swarm. It was a curious sensation to be so terrified and so excited at the same time. *Why me? Why me? Why me?* My thoughts kept time with my footsteps to the center of the room. *I'm the youngest and the smallest. Let one of the older guys go first!*

As members of our master's first class of nine students, all of whom were testing for the very first time, we were in a special position of privilege. For as long as we continued to train and progress, we would always be our dojang's highest-ranking students; anyone who joined after would be our juniors.

I knew I was ready. I trained hard for more than three months, practicing the basic stances, blocks and punches over and over until they were embedded in my memory. Was the strong foundation Master Park described enough to overcome this nervousness I never could have imagined?

The crowd surrounding us was silent, watching and waiting. As I took my place I stole a glance around the room. Even my wildest imaginings had not prepared me for the size of this crowd. They were already waiting when I arrived, even earlier than usual, for the test.

Master Park prepared us for this the day before. "A taekwondo test," he said, "is for more than just the person who is testing. It's a community event. Everyone is invited, and for the most part, everyone comes." He added that because it was also our dojang's very first promotion test, it would be a community celebration. Everyone present at this test was part of the rebirth of a part of our culture that had long been dormant, nearly extinguished, and was now rising throughout our country like the phoenix from its proverbial ashes. He said he wanted us to understand the honor of being part of this rebirth.

Two other masters, Master Park's friends, were here to help officiate the test. They were seated, one on each side of him. Master Park stood to welcome his guests and visitors, and he then introduced each of us— his first students and his dojang's charter class — with pride. We each bowed when we were introduced.

Then the test began. Once my body began to move, its ingrained memory of each movement forced out the wobbliness of nerves. With each technique I felt stronger and more focused. Soon the crowd disappeared from my awareness and I executed each technique with precision born of hours of repetitious perfectionism.

At last, the test was over. I looked around the room, seeing again the spectators, feeling the returning rush of nervous excitement, my insides again turning to jelly. I longed to sit down but somehow remained standing, a rock-steady exterior masking my inner quaking.

Once we were dismissed, and Master Park gave his thanks and concluding remarks to the crowd, he invited us all to the celebration. On this cue, volunteers carried in long tables of food and a community celebration began. With our personal ordeal behind us my classmates and I were all too glad to join this excited gathering as its honored members. The question on all our minds, however, we could not ask. Did we pass the test?

We stood in a corner and whispered, "How will we know? What happens now?" The masters' expressionless faces yielded no clues. And, because we were the first class, there was no one to ask. We didn't have any idea what to expect.

Master Park approached the group. We stopped our whispering, turned to face him, and bowed in unison. He returned the bow. "I will post results of the test on this wall," he said, pointing.

Our eyes all tracked in unison to the place on the wall he had chosen.

"If your name is on the list, you passed."

"Yes sir!" we said together. He didn't say when he would post this result, and none of us dared ask. It was Saturday. The next class would be Monday afternoon. The wait loomed like a thundercloud.

"Why won't he tell us?" Wan Kyu asked as we walked home after the test. "He already knows who was good enough and who wasn't."

I shrugged. "I'm sure there is a reason," I said. With Master Park, there was always a reason for what he said and did, but sometimes it took a while to discover it.

"Do you think we passed?" Wan Kyu continued, unable to let it go.

"I don't know," I said. I thought we all did everything pretty well, but since we had never had a test before and we were all so nervous, we had no way of knowing how good we really had to be to pass. "We'll just have to wait and see."

Wan Kyu sighed and kicked the dirt. "I don't know if I can wait. I have to know now," he said.

"Maybe patience is part of the test," I said. I had no idea how right I was.

On the Monday following our test, class began as usual. No mention of the test. The wall was blank, and I tried not to stare at the spot where we had so hoped the results would be posted. We came back to class on Tuesday. It was class as usual — and still, a blank wall. No one mentioned it, even to each other. By Wednesday, I forced it from my mind and willed myself to just focus on each technique as if it was new. We continued to practice the basics, nothing more, as if we were still preparing for the test. Did we all fail? We couldn't help but wonder.

After class on Wednesday, Master Park said, "Results of your test will be posted next Monday."

We all passed.

◊◊

As we entered the next phase of our training, Master Park explained how each aspect of training would build upon our foundation of basics. Practicing hyung, or forms, would build our concentration, balance and strength; sparring would develop our focus, timing and execution; meditation would teach us how to consciously quiet our minds and control our breathing; special training would improve our stamina, conditioning and mental toughness, and consistent practice with something he called the *dalyun ki* would toughen striking surfaces for breaking.

The dalyun ki was a wood post-like contraption set deep into the ground and wedged between rocks for stability. Target areas for striking with punches, kicks and hand and elbow attacks were wrapped with thick rope. Master Park explained that repeated striking the dalyun ki with a variety of kicks, punches and strikes would toughen up our hands, knuckles, elbows and feet by building calluses and strengthening our bones and joints. This, he said, would protect us from pain and injury during sparring and breaking. We would not learn breaking technique until we reached the green belt level, but by starting our dalyun ki training now, we'd be ready when the time came.

We attacked the dalyun ki daily, before and after class. As the power and focus of my punches and strikes improved this practice, I also pounded out years of hurt, anger, frustration and fear. Before class, after class, and even on a makeshift dalyun ki I built in one corner of Ung Chik's yard, each blow to the center of the dalyun ki target area fed the new power I felt growing in my forearms and shoulders, as well as in my focus and my concentration.

I was punching the dalyun ki one evening after class when the lights went out in one of Pusan's frequent power outages. I kept punching, picturing the target in my mind. In the darkness I discovered a new kind of focus. My fists found their mark time after time, keeping in cadence with my breathing, just the way Master Park demonstrated. My stance was low, my feet and legs, conditioned by hours of practice, could now hold the right depth indefinitely. The clear, meditative state brought about by the connection between breath and movement made time irrelevant. When the lights came back on, I realized I had no idea how long I was there punching the dalyun ki. I looked down at my knuckles only to see a bloody mess that took weeks to heal; however, this experience marked a new threshold of understanding, along with massive knuckles that were the envy of my friends.

◊◊

I sat in *mukyum,* meditation, observing the ritual that began each day's training. Behind me, I heard the soft footfalls of Dong Ho Bub Sa, the monk who visited our class about twice a week. He was a longtime friend of our master, a smoky presence, who was there, Master Park said, to help us with our *jung shin soo yang,* the training of our minds. Beside me, Wan Kyu fidgeted, I knew what would come next.

Whack.

The bamboo stick wielded by the monk came down hard between his shoulder blades. No one dared look toward the source of this noise. The monk's very presence was a reminder to keep our minds clear and focused on the nothingness of meditation. Physical movement was indicator of mental movement, so complete stillness during meditation was paramount — and very difficult for our fidgety adolescent bodies. We never knew exactly when the monk came or went until someone felt the sting of his stick. For about thirty minutes at the beginning of each training session we practiced emptying our minds, concentrating only on our breathing, and willed our bodies to be as still as our minds.

"Why does he *do* that?" Wan Kyu asked as we walked home after class. The stick's sting had left its mark on his mind as well as his back.

"To help us concentrate." I said, wishing I had a better answer. Because of my own experience with meditation, my understanding was deeper than what I could put into words.

"But why does he have to *hit* us?" Wan Kyu persisted. "How does that help?"

"I don't know," I said. "Maybe to make sure we don't forget."

Even though my back never felt the sting of the monk's stick, I didn't forget. These lessons in concentration taught me how to command stillness in my own mind — and how to hold onto that stillness for as long as I needed to.

◊◊

We stood on the high mountainous spot Master Park chose for another important aspect of our training, the *kihap*. He explained that more than just yelling as we execute a technique, the kihap is key to gathering, focusing and expending our maximum power. Developing a good kihap requires special practice, he said, because it requires precise control of our breathing.

"What many people do not understand," he added, "is that the kihap is not something we do to convince others of our power — it brings your power into your own focus."

One by one we sent our first tentative kihaps into the face of the surrounding mountains. These self-conscious attempts drew immediate reprimand.

"What is this weakness I hear?" Master Park asked no one of us in particular. He paced back and forth in front of our single line. "The kihap shows your ability to gather up all the power and spirit inside you. Is that *really* all the power you have inside of you?

With that he turned his back to us and faced the mountains. He drew in a deep breath, paused, and then arched his entire body and let go of a ferocious yell that seemed to shake the mountains. This more than illustrated his point. I stole a glance at Wan Kyu. His mouth was open, expressing the awe we all felt.

Master Park turned back to face us, once again the small, unassuming man we recognized as our master. "Now, you practice," he commanded. Without another word, he climbed to the top of a nearby boulder, crossed his small feet into *bah ro angi,* the lotus position, and fixed his gaze on some distant point only he could see.

We paused for a moment, letting it all sink in. Then, one by one, we stood on the precise spot where our master had stood and did our best to mimic his ferocious kihap. By the time we left, our weakened, hoarse voices were in sharp contrast to the voices of our inner spirit now made stronger by that one afternoon's concentrated practice.

◊◊

It was a Saturday when I awakened to the surprising chill of my first Pusan winter. I scraped the frost off the window and wondered what impact the cold would have on my taekwondo training. I hurried through my chores and got to the dojang extra early, trying to still the chattering of my teeth as I dressed for class. My uniform was still damp from the night before, and to make matters worse several panes of missing glass allowed a steady flow of moist, frigid air to swirl around us as the school's cold floor numbed our bare feet.

Master Park began class as usual, then noticing our shivering, said, "Training in the cold will teach you to control your mind and have patience with your body." He stopped, turned and looked at each one of us as if measuring our grit. "Welcome to Special Winter Training."

"Yes sir!" we said, trying not to fidget against this opportunity. We didn't dare look at each other.

"The most important thing when it is cold outside is to keep moving to keep your muscles warm," he said. From that point on, Special Winter Training became just another class time, only longer and much colder.

At first, moving at all was easier said than done. Our kicks were low, our blocks were slow, and our feet didn't want to move at all. Then, as we did begin to get warm, everything returned to the form we were accustomed to. The energy of our kicks, blocks, and punches stoked the fire we worked hard to keep burning in the dojang for more than five hours, three times our regular class time. To our surprise and delight we discovered that in this cold we didn't tire — we felt invincible.

I even welcomed the bite of cold air blasting my face on our way home from the dojang. We defeated the cold with our concentration, with our spirit, and with the heat of our combined energy. We trained on many cold days after that, but the magic of Special Winter Training on that first cold Saturday afternoon was, as Master Park predicted, a lesson in adversity we would never forget. I glanced behind me as I left the dojang that day, just in time to catch the look of deep satisfaction and pride on my master's face as we walked away.

◊◊

As the first green of spring spread across the Pusan countryside, it was another kind of green that commanded my attention.

"We will have a belt test this Saturday," Master Park told us, granting my daily silent wish, at the end of class on Monday. "Four students are ready to test for green belt." He paused. "The rest of you will wait until next time."

Wan Kyu and I were both among the four. We tried to hide our excitement and remain humble in front of the others, but we felt their eyes upon us.

Master Park turned his gaze to the new students who had just joined. "This line will test for 8th keup," said, indicating the middle line. Then he gestured to the last line, the newest students. "This line will wait till next time."

"Yes sir!" everyone said in unison.

The green belt test was a vast difference from the first test. This time the spectators did not concern me; once the test started, they just faded into the walls of the dojang.

Again, I was called first, but this time, I didn't mind. I stood up, saying, "Yes, Sir!" as I moved to the mark in the center of the room with confidence. Standing before the masters' table, the familiar swarm of butterflies filled my stomach. Then as I began my test, my deep, rhythmic breathing sent them away as fast as they appeared.

With each new requirement of the test, my body showed the fruits of my practice, executing kicks, blocks, and punches with precision, power and timing. My mind was clear and present, but somehow disconnected from the physical effort. When it was over, I knew the result posted the next week on the wall would confirm that I was a green belt. Now my serious training can begin, I thought to myself as I walked home from the dojang after my test.

◊◊

From the first moment that new green belt was tied around my waist, I felt different. I was still by far the smallest in the class, but now I was always called upon to demonstrate, to count, and often, to call the commands that constituted the formal opening and closing of the class.

A few weeks later my master called me into his office as I was about to leave the dojang for the day.

"Yes, Sir!" I answered in usual form.

"I need to speak with you." His tone was different – one I hadn't heard before. I searched my mind for something I had done wrong or neglected to do.

"Yes, Sir?" I asked.

"I saw you wearing your dobok outside of the dojang yesterday," he said.

"Yes, Sir." Since I was last to leave, the influx of new students left no place for me to hang my dobok. I also enjoyed the feeling of wearing my dobok out on the streets, as if to let others know the source of my newfound power.

"You are a green belt now."

"Yes, Sir!" I answered, hoping to return this conversation to the tone of our usual exchanges.

"Green belts should NEVER show their dobok or their belt outside of the dojang," he said. His tone was harsh — one I knew better than to question.

Master Park looked at the setting sun. "It will be night soon," he said. "All over Korea, people are still very hungry and poor and angry because of the war. Crime is everywhere. On the side streets, people wait for someone to rob or beat up. They will say, 'Come here, I want to ask you something' and then pull you into the alley and rob you. If a woman has a purse, they will take it. Even if you don't have any money, they will beat you up anyway. The streets are not safe for anyone."

I nodded. *Isn't this the kind of thing we trained for?* I wanted to argue. I thought about my strong blocks, kicks and punches, relishing the idea of using them in a real street fight.

As if reading my mind, he said, "You are a good taekwondo student and you have learned a lot." He paused, pinning me into place with the piercing intensity in his eyes. "If it were not for taekwondo, you might even be one of those people on the street who robs and beats others for clothes, money or just in anger over their situation. Taekwondo has saved you, but you still have a lot to learn."

"Yes, Sir." He had never spoken to me this way — or this much. I knew he was right, but a part of me still imagined how I could fend off attackers.

"Even though you train here, you must not talk about it," Master Park continued. "No bragging or showing off to your friends." He gathered the collar of my uniform in his fist. "And when you leave here, put your uniform inside a bag."

"I do not have a bag, sir," I said.

"Then fold it and put it inside your shirt," he said, exasperation nibbling at his patience. "You must not ever let people on the street see your uniform."

"Why not, sir?" My curiosity had gotten the best of me. "Shouldn't I be proud of my taekwondo training?"

He seemed a little taken aback with this bold question, but he paused, thoughtful, trying to find the explanation that would penetrate my ego and incite my obedience.

"If they know you train in taekwondo, they will attack you in a different way," he explained. "For example, they might use weapons that you don't yet know how to defend against. If they don't know you are training, you will have a much better chance of using what you do know to defend yourself."

I nodded, understanding the concept, but my heart still questioned.

Seeing this, my master added, "When you are a black belt, you are prepared physically and mentally to take on any attacker with confidence." He patted my arm. "Then you can show your uniform. I will show you the special way we fold it, with your black belt tied across the bottom to display it with pride." He strutted around me in a circle, carrying an imaginary uniform draped over his arm. He stopped in front of me and repeated, "In early training, we never show our uniform. When we are black belts, then we show it with great pride."

It was just one week later, one Sunday evening as Wan Kyu and I walked to church, when we saw five older boys standing on the corner ahead. Even though I heeded my master's instruction and stopped showing my uniform outside the dojang, I was unable to resist the temptation to put my taekwondo to the street test.

"Hey," one of the boys called out to us. "Come over here."

My ears perked up. It was exactly what my master said they would say. How did he know?

"Don't go," Wan Kyu whispered, keeping his eyes on the boys. "There are five of them."

"So what?" I said, eyes locked on to the one who called out to us. The boys were now heading our way.

"Let's go, Won Chik." Wan Kyu begged.

"No," I said, speeding up a little to meet the boy halfway, "I'm going to see what they want. You just stay where you are. I'll handle this."

Wan Kyu stopped walking. "Won Chik, please come back," he said. "What they want is trouble."

"Don't worry," I said, pushing up my sleeves to show the muscle in my forearms, taking care to make sure my large knuckles were clearly visible. If I couldn't show the uniform or talk about my training, I'd let my appearance do the talking. "If what they want is trouble, they found it."

Those boys beat me to a pulp.

As I lay bleeding and coughing in the street, Wan Kyu rushed to my side. "Won Chik, are you OK?" he asked. "This looks bad," he said, dabbing at the cuts on my face and bleeding mouth with his sleeve.

The cuts and abrasions were superficial, the bruises would heal, but the wound to my ego was the most painful of all. I dreaded the reproach on Master Park's face when he saw me.

He took one long look — up, then down, then up and down again. Then he asked, "What happened?"

"Five older boys jumped me."

"Did you try to defend yourself?"

"Yes, but they were too fast and there were too many of them."

"I see," he said.

A few days later Master Park again called me into his office. "A little bit of knowledge can create more trouble than no knowledge," he said, examining the gash over my eyebrow. "When you are a black belt, you will be able to take care of yourself in these situations." He patted my shoulder and smiled. "I'm sorry this happened to you, but maybe now you understand what I was trying to explain about false confidence."

◊◊

As a greenbelt, we began to learn jump kicks, which as red belts would lead to flying kicks. Jump kicks were of special interest to me, because by then I realized that most people were always going to be bigger than me, and to spar well against them I would need to offset my lack of stature with good jumping and flying kicks.

To strengthen my legs and improve my jumping ability, I fashioned crude ankle weights from a pair of discarded soccer shin guards I found by removing the vertical bamboo stays and filling them with sand. I tied these weights around my ankles and wore them to school every day. Remembering Master Park's instruction not to tell people about my training, I always wore long pants to cover these weights, even when the days grew warm enough for shorts. When I heard people whispering, speculating on why I walked so funny and wondering what was wrong with my legs, I just smiled to myself, enjoying my secret. Then, when I went to the dojang after school, I removed the weights after our warm-up exercises and was amazed at how much higher I could jump. As my legs grew stronger and got used to the weights, I looked for ways to make the weights heavier. When I found a large pair of discarded military boots I began wearing those as well when I practiced my basic kicks. Big, thick and heavy, these old boots were far too large to wear to school, but they made the perfect training tool.

Another aspect of green belt training that spoke especially to me was increasing our power. Because I was small I knew I needed both reach and power to hold my own against bigger boys like the ones who beat me up. Master Park demonstrated how to stop a heavy bag swinging toward you with a kick, then a punch. With his own deceptive power, he made this look easy. The first time I tried this drill, the bag, oblivious to my best side kick, knocked me flat on the ground. Laying there gasping for air with Master Park and my classmates standing over me, I feared the worst. Gradually I was able to walk it off, relieved that I could walk at all. On Master Park's command, I sat out the rest of the class. I kept trying every day with better and better results, and by summer when someone would swing the bag at me from the opposite direction I was able to meet that bag with a kick that stopped it. For weeks I laughed whenever I thought about how good it felt to get the best of that bag.

Just as the extreme cold of winter training taught us to focus through the discomfort of chattering teeth, the summer before my black belt test brought a new version of Master Park's "Special Training." Special Summer Training was different, he explained, and not something we were required to do. Whereas our Special Winter Training was created as a way to help us deal with the natural chill of our dojang in winter, Special Summer Training was a special privilege awarded only to top students to further enrich their training. Not all masters offered this opportunity to their, students, he added. "Maybe you're lucky, maybe not," he said, smiling at his own joke, "but if I choose you for my special training, you will improve greatly."

Loaded down with military tents borrowed from one of our master's friends, as well as food, water and provisions for a two-week stay, the 30 of us chosen for Special Summer Training arrived at the beach with just enough sunlight left to set up camp. We cooked a meal together over an open fire, then sat and listened to Master Park's stories about taekwondo and his life in a world we couldn't even imagine. One by one, as the urge for sleep overtook us, we crawled into our tents and slept, wondering what Master Park's "Special Summer Training" would be like.

Ocean sounds woke me moments before sunrise, bringing to mind dream-like thoughts of our time on Yeon Pyong Island. I lay still for a moment, listening, and I wondered if Uncle Ki Hoon and the others on Yeon Pyong ever thought about me. Stirring sounds outside my tent told me my classmates were awake and beginning to move around. Time to get started. Master Park's Special Summer Training had begun.

We stood in a straight line on the beach, facing the ocean. Master Park was facing us, ankle deep in water that swirled around his feet. "Welcome to Special Summer Training," he said.

We bowed. *"Anyong ham shamika!"*

"We are training here during the hottest time in Korea to learn more about how to mentally and physically overcome difficult conditions." He paused, looking from face to face, then continued. "We have trained in the coldest days of winter with no heat and you learned how to beat the cold by warming up your body from the inside. You discovered that when you work hard enough, cold disappears."

He turned and began to walk the length of our line. "Heat is more difficult," he said. "You cannot escape it by cooling your body from the inside. Training in hot temperatures requires mental strength. To deal well with heat, you must take good care of your body with proper food and water, and then you have to condition your mind to ignore the heat."

He gestured toward the shoreline that stretched as far as we could see. "We will start with running," he said. "We will run here, next to the water, where the sand is soft and wet."

We looked where he was pointing, noticing how the sand and water filled in his footsteps as he walked. Following our eyes, he turned and pointed to his disappearing tracks. "As the wet sand sinks, your feet and legs will have to work hard."

He pointed to an outcropping of rock in the distance. "After you run to that rock and back, we'll rest and eat breakfast," he said. "Then we will practice our jumping, kicking, and one-step sparring in the water. The resistance of the sand and water will make your legs stronger and your kicks more powerful and faster. Then we will have lunch and rest before afternoon sparring — first in the water, and then on the sand. This will be our daily training routine for the next 10 days."

There are no words to describe this kind of physical challenge. Despite all the extra training I did on my own, there were times when I wondered if my legs would carry me another step, if I could command my leg to kick one more time, or if my lungs would continue to bring in enough air to keep me upright.

We all struggled, some more than others. A few fell, a few got sick, a few passed out. We helped each other, revived the fallen, then after letting them rest a little bit, encouraged them on. I don't remember any complaining or any threats of quitting — we knew we were special enough to be chosen, and the bond of our shared commitment, concentration and focus buoyed all of us through this challenging ordeal.

For the next ten sun-scorched days, the heat oppressed us in visible waves, radiating up from the glaring sand. The salt, sand, and water chafed our sunburned skin like sandpaper as this new intensity created new soreness in our already well-trained muscles. True to his word, Master Park kept us supplied with plenty of good food and water, and each night the cool night breeze off the ocean swathed us in restorative sleep.

The morning run, so dreaded for the first several days, became the welcome friend that coaxed our stiff, sore muscles back to function each morning. Each day brought a new level of accomplishment and new surprises of what we could do. We learned that we were stronger than we thought, and our bodies responded to the intensity of this training as we could never have imagined. What began as pure physical torture ended as a gift of self-realization that would be with each of us for the rest of our lives.

As word spread, a growing crowd of spectators came each day to watch us train, and this impromptu opportunity to demonstrate spurred us through the fatigue of those last few days. Having such a rapt audience changed our focus from our own survival to giving them a beautiful exhibition of taekwondo's ultimate expression of power, grace and beauty.

As we stood in three lines of ten at the water's edge to do our final poomse, I was overcome with gratitude. The sand had made us strong, the heat had made us tough, and the audience had taught us to overcome challenge by changing our focus to serving others. Rather than a life shaped by tragedy, taekwondo's many lessons had already given me at age 15 an identity and self-awareness that many people never achieve. Regardless of what the future held, I knew I had finally found my way.

◊◊

"Why do we always have to do this exercise? Who do you think you are?" Kang, my ever-sneering taekwondo classmate heckled my leadership whenever our master was out of earshot. Three years older and much bigger than me, Kang made no secret of his disdain for me. He glared at me when I led the class, glowered when I was asked to demonstrate, and grumbled regularly when he didn't like the exercises I selected.

I ignored him and continued to lead the exercises. It was just another day at the dojang, and by now I was used to trouble from the older students who did not practice as much as I did, who did not understand why I was getting better so much faster than they were.

"He thinks he is a master but he's just a stupid kid," Kang's muttering continued.

"Cha ryot!" unbeknownst to any of us, Master Park had entered the room behind us. We all turned and snapped to attention.

Master Park entered the room, walked straight over to Kang and jabbed a finger in the center of his chest. "You have something to say?"

"No sir."

"I heard what you said," Master Park said. "Do you want to say it again — to me?"

"No sir."

"One hundred pushups! *Shee-jak!*"

On this command to begin immediately, Kang dropped to the floor and began doing pushups.

Master Park looked at the class, then at me, then back to the class. "He may be smaller and younger, but he is high ranking," he said. Then he pointed that same finger at me *"Kae sok!"* he said, then, as I followed his order to continue, he walked back into his office and closed the door.

◊◊

One day just a few months after Special Summer Training, and after a year and a half of training several hours a day, six days a week, Master Park gestured to the front row as we all stood at attention at the end of class. "Front row, you are ready to begin training for your black belt test. If you do well in this training, you can test for black belt at the next testing time."

"Yes Sir!" we said in unison, trying to conceal our glee.

Later on, when no one was looking, we jumped up and down and slapped each other on the back. We knew we had worked hard. We had looked for this moment since the beginning of our training. Though we knew we were ready, the prospect of the test was both exhilarating and daunting.

We practiced each section of the test under Master Park's watchful eye. Each technique, each movement, each poomse, repeated over and over again until he was satisfied that every detail was perfect. At last, it was the day before the test when we all finished each section of the test without a single correction. We were ready, inside and out.

Master Park walked in front of our line with one last set of instructions on the day before the test. "All eyes will be on you tomorrow," he said. "Remember, you represent the best of our dojang. You are asking to wear a black belt. You will prove your physical readiness with your testing skills —Your technique and your strength. But more than that, you must demonstrate your highest character, your respect, and your commitment to taekwondo. Once you are awarded a taekwondo black belt, you are a taekwondo black belt for life. You must be ready to carry everything you are and have accomplished in this moment into everything you do for the rest of your life, both inside and outside the dojang. You are standing at a very honorable doorway, asking to step inside." He paused for almost a full minute, allowing us to process his words. "Is there anyone here who is not ready?"

"We are ready, sir!" we answered in unison.

"Good," he said. Then he nodded. "I will see you tomorrow."

◊◊

I arrived early on testing day with my friend, Young Moo Choi, who was also testing. We walked in silence, each mired in our own thoughts. As we rounded the corner onto the street of our dojang, we stopped and stared. A huge crowd was already gathered, standing under a large sign that had appeared over the door to announce our dojang's first black belt test.

I looked at Young Moo. He was chewing his nails.

"Are you nervous?" I asked, glancing at his gnawed nails.

"No," he said, not looking up. "I forgot to cut my fingernails."

"Well I hope you remembered to cut your toenails." I said.

He looked quickly at his feet, and then at me. We both burst into nervous laughter. It felt good to laugh. The knot of tension that had been growing in my stomach since dawn began to loosen.

We stood for a moment, watching the crowd. "All these people don't matter," I said, talking as much to myself as I was to Young Moo. "We've worked hard to learn what we know, and even if we're nervous, we won't forget. We're ready. Let's show them what we can do just like we showed the crowd on the beach. If we do our best, they will be impressed."

"I know," he said. He shaded his eyes with his hand as we approached the building. "But there are so many of them. Do you think there are more here than there were at the beach?"

"No," I said, holding the door open for him as we entered. "It only seems like more because of the smaller space." I actually had no idea whether this was true, but my certainty was calming to both of us.

◊◊

After the initial flurry of nerves, our minds quieted and our many hours of concentrated training were reflected in each well-rehearsed section of the black belt test. I was aware of the crowd — and of my classmates executing their techniques around me — but my focus was pure.

I faced Young Moo as we lined up for one-step sparring. One-step sparring takes the basic movements of taekwondo and sets them into their intended practical applications. In these specific choreographed sequences of attack and defense, each partner takes a turn at being both attacker and defender. Young Moo and I practiced our one-step sparring for hours on our own, in addition to class time, working out several special touches to make our one-step techniques look as realistic as possible.

We bowed to the judges — Master Park and two high-ranking masters from Seoul — and then we bowed to each other. Young Moo attacked first, which he did with convincing ferociousness. Someone in the crowd gasped, and I tried not to smile as I stepped around his attack, grabbed and twisted his arm, feigned an elbow break, and then, with an ear-splitting *kihap,* executed a jump snap kick that stopped just short of the tip of his nose. The crowd was silent. Then exuberant clapping erupted. I helped Young Moo straighten up, then brushed off his dobok for a little comic relief.

I stole a glance at Master Park. He was not amused at our showmanship. We returned to our positions and executed the rest of our one-steps, each with its own small touch of additional drama. Our performance was flawless, without hesitation or error, a true reflection of our extra motivation and commitment.

Kyrogi, or free fighting, came last. Kyrogi, the ultimate measure of both technique and application, is where it all comes together. Whereas strong basic technique often prevails at lower levels of kyrogi, the black belt level requires an additional element of instinct and intuition that, although innate to some, must be honed by practice.

In my heart, I have always known that I was born a fighter. Perhaps it was this innate knowledge that led me into that fateful greenbelt street fighting experience. While my taekwondo training had built upon my strengths and minimized my weaknesses, my fighting instincts were with me all along. Even when I was getting the beating of my life, I never ran away, because my instincts told me to stay close. Now that my training had equipped me to be effective in close quarters, taking advantage of my small stature and adding quickness and power, I understood that it was a matter of patience, waiting for my opening to get inside. My relentless practice then cultivated the judgment to recognize those openings, as well as the ability to execute the correct technique with speed and power. My black belt test kyrogi was my long awaited opportunity to show that I could at last put it all together.

In round-robin fashion, we would each fight three different people. When my first match was called, I smiled. It would be the perfect test, in the truest sense of the word. I stood up. Across the room, Kang stood up. We met in the center of the room, and I was careful not to look at his face so as not to be distracted by the murderous expression I knew I'd find there. This was an added test of focus and concentration that I knew I must pass above all.

"Cha ryot!" The referee, a friend of our master's, said in a sharp and official tone.

We snapped to attention, hands at our sides.

"Kyung nae!" The referee's arms were bent at the elbow in a stiff pair of matched right angles, fingertips up. We bowed to each other. I met Kang's eyes with a detachment oblivious to his intensity.

I smiled to myself as I realized that it was Kang himself who had provided me with the best possible preparation for the battle to come. Although I mostly ignored Kang's continuous jibes, insults, and how he tried to get others to turn against me, on those days when Kang's jealous competition got a rise out of me, our in-class sparring bouts took on the grit of true battle. I learned from the resulting bruises and injuries how to acknowledge pain, but not to give in to it; those experiences were perfect practice for this perfect test.

"Sah bum nim, kyung nae!" We turned and bowed to our Master.

Like everyone else in our class, Kang was taller and bigger than me, and his legs were long to the point of gangliness. Those long legs were dangerous, and everyone was scared of their reach and power. But if you are quick enough to get inside their range, long legs are useless.

"Kyorugi sohgi!" The referee put a stiff outstretched arm between us as he issued the command that snapped us into sparring position, each signifying our readiness with an earsplitting kihap.

Just as I had learned in class, no matter where Kang moved or what he did, I continued to move in. He needed distance to deliver a fully extended kick, and I made sure he didn't get it. When Kang tried to punch me away, I blocked and countered, matching him blow for blow, moving in behind each counterpunch.

I heard the crowd laughing and clapping. Even they could see the frustration my dogged closing in was creating in Kang. Finally the bell sounded and it was over. I smiled as I bowed to Kang and shook his hand. He said nothing, but the starch was completely gone from his demeanor. Even though we never spoke of it, after that day his animosity toward me was gone. There was nothing else that needed to be said.

"Why didn't you ever back up?" Young Moo asked me as soon as we began the walk back to our respective homes.

I shrugged. "I'm small. I have to stay close."

He grinned. "Impressive."

I returned his grin. "And besides," I said, "if I had backed up even one step, Kang would have kicked my head off."

There was no greater influence on my life and my teaching than the wisdom of my master, Great Grandmaster Hyon Chong Park.

1957 With my taekwondo classmates (that's me in the back row, center) at my master's Special Summer Training at Su Young Beach in Pusan.

CHAPTER FIVE:
A Teacher is Born

The next time Ung Chik's unit was transferred out of Pusan things were different. This time Soon Jun had to go with him, he said, and I could not go. The agony on his face as he told me brought a knot to my throat. I blinked the tears back, lest he thought they were for myself.

"It's OK," I rushed to say, trying to make him feel better. He had done more for me than most brothers in his position would have done. He and Soon Jun had given me a home and a stable life. Without them I would not be in school or taekwondo or have any of the friends or opportunities that were just beginning to show themselves to me.

"I have spoken with Young Soon," he said. "She and Taeil Hwang, have invited you to live with them so you can finish high school here in Pusan."

About a year after Young Soon joined us in Pusan, someone had introduced her to Taeil Hwang. After a period of formal courtship, they were married in a ceremony very similar to Ung Chik's. I was so glad that she at last had someone to take care of her.

"She says they will be very happy for you to live with them."

The tumult of emotions brought on by this news made me dizzy. In an instant, my life in Ung Chik's home was over and he was going away again. I couldn't even imagine how much I was going to miss my *hyong neem*, older brother, and his presence in my life. Now I would begin another new life with my *noo neem*, older sister, and my *mae hyong neem*, brother in law.

What kind of man is Taeil Hwang, I wondered. *Will he like me? Will he mind sharing his home with me?* A big part of Korean culture is for family to always take care of each other, and we have specific titles and structure to reflect this tradition, but sometimes the load of that responsibility is easier to bear than others. I wondered how this new arrangement would go.

◊◊

As I had already seen so many times in my life, another important bond of commitment in Korean culture is how friends take care of friends as if they're family. Once I started to school, began taekwon-do training and lived in my brother's home, the friends I made — and their families — all became my extended family. Even though we had plenty to eat at Ung Chik's house, my friends and their families were always giving me food and clothing.

"Everyone likes you," Wan Kyu said one day. "Especially the mothers." He laughed. "All the mothers want to take care of you and for their sons to be more like you."

I smiled. "Because of my good friends, I also have many mothers," I said. Even though it was no substitute for having my own mother to take care of me, and in truth it sometimes made me miss her even more, my friends' mothers formed a safety net for me — a sense of security in an uncertain world. They listened to me, encouraged me, and made sure I always had a place to go and a good home-cooked meal.

◊◊

Life at Young Soon's house was quite different from Ung Chik's. They owned a small store in Pusan and struggled to make ends meet. Although they never said anything about it, I knew that my being there was an extra burden on them financially, and I tried to help out all I could. I was still on full scholarship for school, and I tried very hard to cover my other expenses so I didn't cost them any extra money.

To help out even more, I began tutoring two boys at their homes after dinner. Payment was dinner with their family. My days consisted of going to school, training at the dojang, and then on to the home of this family that hired me to tutor their sons in all subjects to improve their skills and understanding. It made for long days, and there were many times I just wanted to go home and go to sleep, but the lure of a good hot meal always won out.

"You're never here," Young Soon observed one night after waiting up late for me to come home. I could see that there was something on her mind.

"I have a lot to do," I said. "Is everything OK?"

"Yes," she said. "Everything's fine. I just miss you." She paused, weighing her words. "I hope you are not getting into any trouble when you are out so late."

"No," I laughed. "I don't have time to get into trouble. Besides, what trouble would I get into?"

"I don't know." She looked at me as if trying to see into my head. "You never talk and you are always watching us. You seem very worried and anxious when you are here. Are you uncomfortable here?"

"No," I said. "I just don't want to be a burden to you."

"You're not a burden. Why do you think you're a burden?"

"I am not your child, but you have always had to take care of me," I said. I paused before deciding to say my real thoughts aloud. "I am almost grown up now. Maybe it is time for me to take care of myself."

"We are your family," Young Soon said. "Family takes care of each other. I love you and I love having you here. It is also very important that you have a good home so you can finish school. After that, you will go away for your military service and be on your own. You can take care of yourself then."

Young Soon went to bed, but I sat there for a while longer, pondering my unexpected words. I didn't want to disappoint Young Soon, but I knew it was time to find a place of my own.

◊◊

My middle school math teacher, Keun Soo Lee, had long ago made me his "honorary younger brother," and after Ung Chik left Pusan, I was glad to have another *hyong neem,* older brother, available whenever I needed one. Keun Soo's older brother was commander of a ship in the ROK navy — and he was stationed at the nearby Gin Hae naval base on the edge of a small military harbor outside Pusan. "I'll take you there some time," he said one day when I stopped by for a visit.

"When?" I asked. My talk with Young Soon made me start me thinking about my upcoming military service. Four years of Military service was still required of all young Korean men, and I was beginning to consider the different branches and which one I might like best. A visit to Keun Soo's brother on the naval base would be a great start on my exploration.

"How about Saturday?" Came the quick answer. I knew he was worried about my future because of all the questions he had been asking me lately. This was the first interest I had shown in anything besides taekwondo, so he jumped at the chance to help me.

◊◊

We arrived at the base during early morning maneuvers. We stood at the front gate and a straight line of soldiers marched in front of us. I studied them, intent on every detail of their uniforms, their faces, their boots and the positioning of their hands as they marched. Their precision was beautiful.

"Wow," I whispered to Keun Soo, mesmerized by the rhythm of their steps.

On command, the line of soldiers made a sharp, 90-degree turn. The base stretched out before us and in the distance I saw the ships lined up in the harbor, mirroring the line of soldiers marching before us. Trying to take everything in at once, I could hardly catch my breath. This was a future worth dreaming of.

Later that evening, when Keun Soo's older brother, Un Soo, the base commander, joined us for dinner, Keun Soo introduced me to him as "our new younger brother." Too shy to say very much to this great military leader, I was proud to be included in this new "family."

"I think Won Chik is officer material," Keun Soo told his brother.

Un Soo looked me over. "We need good officers," he said. "The exam for officer's school is difficult, but if you can pass it, you will have the opportunity to become a great leader."

I nodded. My grades were good. I was always helping other people study, and I was learning how to lead others at the dojang. I saw my path laid out clearly before me. I couldn't wait to take that test.

"What else do you have to do to apply to officer's school?" I asked.

"You have to have recommendations of two military officers," he said. I will be glad to write one for you but you need to find one more officer in a different branch of the military.

That wouldn't be hard. Ung Chik's best childhood friend was now an officer, and my good friend Kwang Jo's brother's friend was a general. "I have one more year of high school," I told them. I will use that time to get ready."

◊◊

We stood in the *joon bee,* ready position, waiting for Master Park to speak.

"You here on the front line" he said, his sweeping open hand identifying five of us, "will test for second dan black belt in Seoul next month."

After more than a year of hard training, this was big news. To test in Seoul was the highest of honors. Only the best black belts at each level tested there. For a master to take students to Seoul for advanced testing meant that we were the students he was most proud of. Beyond being a test for the students, the Seoul testing was also a competition between masters to compare their teaching ability and display the strength of their dojang.

"We will practice each section of the test for the next three weeks," he said. "If I think you are ready for Seoul, I will take you to the test there. If you are not," he shrugged, "you will test for 2nd dan here at our next regular promotion test."

We practiced every section of the test every day until our muscles failed. At the end of this three-week intensive, the likes of which none of us had ever seen, only two of the original five on that front line were selected to go to Seoul for the test. Man Sup Lee and I would go to Seoul for our second dan test, representing our dojang, our master, and ourselves.

The test in Seoul would require a train ticket, an overnight stay in a hotel, and of course, the testing fee itself. Even saving every cent I earned since I first knew of the test, I had not been able earn enough in time. I didn't want to let Master Park down, but how could I go? I couldn't ask Young Soon and her husband for money. Miserable beyond words, I waited for Master Park after class.

"What's wrong with you?" he said, "Why is your head down?"

"I'm sorry, but I cannot go to Seoul for the test," I said. As strong as I was physically, it took everything I had to utter those words. But they had to be said. I had pretended it would all somehow work out, but the time had come to face reality.

"The others have already donated the money to pay the rest of your way," Master Park said. "You pay what you have and we will take care of the rest."

I was overwhelmed. "Why?" I asked. I couldn't believe that in these hard times my taekwondo classmates had donated their own money to help pay my testing expenses.

"It is very important to our dojang that we be well represented at this test," Master Park said. "It will be a show of our strength, and you and Man Sup will honor us with your good performance on the test."

No words could describe my gratitude. "Thank you, sir," I said.

"Say thank you to all of us with a perfect test," he said.

◊◊

My mind whirled as we entered Seoul by train. This city of about three million people was three times the size of Pusan, and my senses strained to absorb all the new sights, sounds and smells at once. The test was held in the gymnasium of the Korean National University in Seoul, where Kwye Byung Yoon, our *Kwan Jang Neem,* our master's master, was a professor, and at that time, president of Jidokwan.

A Teacher is Born

We arrived at the small motel near the university, and I followed the others into the single room we would all share. We wouldn't see the gym until morning, and somehow we had to calm ourselves enough to get a good night's sleep. After dinner in a nearby restaurant and some stretching and deep breathing, I managed to fall asleep, going over and over the test in my mind.

"It's time!" Man Sup shook me awake. I sat up, shaking my head. I didn't think I had slept for very long, but my grogginess told me otherwise. After a quick breakfast, we stretched and did a light warm up before walking over to the gym to look around and make our final preparations for the test.

"Are you nervous?" Man Sup asked.

"Yes," I said. "I'm ready to get started. Waiting is much harder than testing."

"That's true," he agreed.

We stood together in the center of the gym, and I let my eyes travel the immense perimeter of this place, noticing all the different dojangs represented. I looked at Man Sup, who was making the same mental calculations.

"How many do you think are here?" he asked, his eyes still traveling from group to group.

"More than I want to count," I said. "Let's not think about it. We're here, we're ready, and it is the same test we have been going over and over in our own dojang."

"I know, but there are so many people," he said.

"We will all be doing the same thing," I said. Then, seeing the only person here we knew, I said, "Look, Man Sup, there's our Kwan Jang Neem!"

Our Kwan Jang Neem was a special person to all of us. He had come to Pusan to help with our Special Summer Training, for many of our promotion tests, and often, to visit Master Park. To see a familiar face — especially one I liked and respected so much — put me at ease.

"I wish Master Park had come with us," Man Sup said. "Why did he stay in Pusan?"

"I don't know," I said, looking around the room again, this time with a new attitude of calm assurance. "Maybe he just wanted us to do this on our own."

It seemed strange that our master would miss something so important. I hoped that the money for my expenses had not come from his pocket. "Say thank you with a perfect test," he had said. With all the determination my seventeen years could muster, I vowed to do just that.

◊◊

When it came time for the 2nd dan test, 30 or 40 people lined up in front of the four masters judging the test. We were called up one at a time, answering, "Yes, Sir!" as we took our place in line. We stood in four straight lines in our starched white uniforms; nervous anticipation crackling through the air in a palpable current.

When at last the physical maneuvers of the test began, my mind shifted into that floating sense of detached focus that happens when preparation is so complete, so much a part of you that everything flows perfectly together without thought or effort. Almost as soon it began, the preliminary sections of the test were complete. Free fighting was next.

I stood with my toes on the tape and waited for the familiar signals to begin. What seemed like just moments later, the sparring section of the test was over as well — and just as clean, perfect and solid as the other sections had been.

Finished with our required two rounds of sparring, Man Sup and I sat in the back, congratulating each other on a job well done. Master Park had done an extremely good job of preparing us for this test, and he would be very proud of our scores. We sat cross-legged, relaxed and happy, to watch the final moments of the test.

Then the door to the gymnasium opened and a student in his dobok rushed into the room. He would have been big and tall by any measure, but was gigantic in this room full of Koreans. His appearance caused a stir in the sea of students sitting around us. Man Sup and I looked at each other and shrugged, then our gaze followed the big boy as he went straight to the front of the room, right up to the judge's table.

He bowed to them. They nodded in return, irritated, but politely curious. In a low, urgent and earnest voice, he spoke to them. We could not hear his exact words, but we could tell that he had some compelling reason for being so late, and he was trying to convince them to let him take the test.

They told him to sit down.

When the free fighting was finished, Kwan Jang Neem called the big boy back to the front of the room. Alone, he did his poomse. With the help of various students called up when he needed a partner, he completed each section of the test. His technique was good, but not perfect. However, what he lacked in precision he more than made up for in power. We all watched silently, glad our test was over.

Then the big boy needed to spar.

Our Kwan Jang Neem, the second highest official there, began scanning the room. Even though I made sure not look up for fear of making eye contact, I felt his eyes lock on me.

"Won Chik Park!"

Oh no, I thought. I looked around. All eyes were suddenly on me. *Why me?* I looked at the boy standing in the center of the room. *He's so big! There are so many others here to choose from — why would he pick me out of all these people? I'm the smallest. I may be the youngest. Anyone here would be a better choice for this than me!*

While I was busy complaining inside, he called again, "Won Chik Park!"

"Yes sir!" I said, scrambling to my feet. I took my position opposite this giant. For the first time I looked at his face. Then I looked at his belt. I realized he was testing for the same ranking as me.

The referee took his position and, *"Sheejak!"* With this familiar command, the round began.

The big boy jumped right in, as if thinking he could make fast work of this short little guy and, with an impressive showing, secure enough points to earn a passing score. Because the masters assessed a point penalty for his being so late, he had a lot of points to make up and this was his last chance to do it. In taekwondo testing, each technique and section is valued at a specific number of maximum points. Each master officiating a test awards points as he sees fit for each technique and section, and these scores are averaged, then averages tallied, to arrive at a candidate's total score. In this way if someone is weak in one section he can make up the lost points in another for an overall passing score.

He had very long legs, and his first attack was a roundhouse kick to my face. I moved quickly to the side, out of its reach, and while his leg was still extended, closed in to land a solid sidekick to his ribs. The success of this exchange told me that although he was big and powerful, he was also a little bit slow. And, like so many others I fought who where bigger than me, he needed distance to execute his technique well. So I kept moving in and attacking, keeping the distance between us as short as possible.

This annoyed the big boy. To teach me a lesson, he tried a quick, short front snap kick with his front leg. Reading this, I shifted my weight to the side but didn't move my feet. His balance wavered a bit as he tried to make a last-minute adjustment to follow my movement. That slight wobble was all I needed. I closed in and landed another side kick to the same spot on his ribs. Because he was already a little off balance, the power I was able to pack into this kick knocked him to the ground with a resounding thud. Everyone laughed.

I glanced up for a second. I imagined how it must have looked from the sidelines to see this little guy moving in on this huge guy — and then knocking him down. It probably was a funny thing to watch, but I wasn't laughing. I knew that when this big boy got up, he was going to be mad.

He clambered to his feet and glared at me across the referee's hand at me. I took a deep breath and cleared my mind. *Just keep closing,* I told myself. *If you give him distance now, he will kill you.*

A Teacher is Born

On the referee's cue, we continued. Keeping my mind locked on defense I stayed in close, thwarting his kicking attack. Frustrated by this, he started punching — hard. Grateful for my speed and quick reflexes, I was able to stay out of the path of those punches until at last, after what seemed like hours but was really only two minutes, the bell rang and it was over.

The big boy fought several times more, and he did manage to make up quite a few points on those less fortunate than I was. I was thankful to have had the first round with him — to get it over with first before I saw what he did to the others.

I met him in the hallway after the test was over. We were alone there, and I was a little nervous, not knowing what his reaction to me would be with no referee to control the situation.

"I'm not mad," he said, sensing my apprehension. "You did a good job!" He laughed. "You're such a little guy, but you got me!"

Relief rushed through me. "I'm sorry," I said. "I hope our round didn't hurt your score."

"Nothing to be sorry about," he said. "You did a good job. When you get knocked to the ground by someone so much smaller than you, at first it makes you angry, but later, you have to say, "Wow. " He bowed to me. "You're very good."

◊◊

My taekwondo classmates who didn't test for 2nd dan in Seoul tested two weeks later at our dojang. Even though Man Sup and I were awarded our new black belts one week after we got back from the test in Seoul, Master Park held a special awarding ceremony to recognize all has new 2nd dans equally. Or so I thought.

We stood in three straight lines. The first two lines were all of the new second dans, the third line, our newest 1st dan black belts. Master Park stood facing us in the front of the room and began to speak.

"Today, as we honor your great accomplishments with pride, we also must recognize that this is the time for each of you to set a new goal. You have worked very hard to get to this place. Now you must continue to work hard to reach your next place of honor."

Master Park began walking as he talked. "Earning your black belt — and each new level of black belt — brings both honor and responsibility. You must accept both with humility and devote yourself to fulfilling this commitment whenever you are asked, whether in teaching others, helping those less fortunate, or setting an example of courage, strength and honor in your life, no matter what happens to you."

He came to a stop in front of me. As he continued to talk about our responsibilities as black belts, he began taking off his own belt. We stood, three rows of statues, eyes fixed on him, minds racing. What is he doing? Why is he taking off his belt? What does this mean? What is about to happen?

"Won Chik Park, please step forward."

I stepped forward, puzzled.

Then, extending the belt toward me, Master Park said, "I present this belt to Won Chik Park. I give my belt to him to honor his accomplishment and his future in taekwondo."

He looked at me straight in the eyes, and then bowed. I accepted the belt and bowed in return, too stunned to speak. Long ago, when I had first begun working at the dojang in exchange for my training, Master Park had said that with hard work and continued commitment to taekwondo I could one day take over his school. Assuming that he was just trying to give encouragement to a young man in danger of being lost, I had dismissed these words. Until now. Now I understood the connection between this heartfelt presentation and those earlier words, as well as the confidence and trust he was now placing in me.

"Won Chik Park is my student, but he has also become my teacher," Master Park said. "Watching him grow from a scared, shy boy to this strong, powerful and humble 2nd dan black belt who just became the talk of the Seoul promotion test is a lesson I will never forget. Taekwondo gives human beings a powerful opportunity to transform ourselves and others with its spirit, honor and strength. To share this opportunity with others is our gift and our responsibility as black belts. Won Chik Park is a true example of how honor, commitment and responsibility can overcome tremendous personal obstacles. Today I recognize the example Won Chik sets and salute him with the presentation of my own black belt."

I felt the mixture of surprise, congratulations and questioning jealousy coming at me from all directions. "Why him?" I could almost hear some of them thinking. "Good for him!" would likely come from the others. The room was silent. Master Park remained silent.

Tears rolled down my cheeks. It was an odd sensation, extremes of pride and humility, awe and responsibility. I knew that my response to this presentation was very important, and the surprise of it helped me to respond with quiet humility. I bowed to my master. "Thank you, sir," was all I said. My mind, however, was spinning, trying to gain understanding of this moment.

In the days and weeks that followed I considered my future in light of this new responsibility my master just laid at my feet. His words kept echoing though my awareness, "Taekwondo gives human beings a powerful opportunity to transform ourselves... to share this opportunity with others is our gift and our responsibility." Even though my sights were still set on being a military officer — and a general if I could —I now knew that my ultimate future, after my military service was over, was to become a taekwondo master. The old black belt my master placed in my hands had forged in an instant the commitment of a lifetime.

Beyond marking my entry into a career and a future I could not yet imagine, the simple but profound gesture of master to student showed me the true nature of this special relationship — a circle of responsibility and commitment I would now carry on to others, just as Master Park did for me. He nurtured the potential he saw in me that I could not yet see in myself.

◊◊

The sense of focus, accomplishment, and leadership I honed in the dojang soon began to ripple into the other parts of my life. The high school teachers began to rely on me as someone they could call on anytime they needed help — either in work they couldn't finish or to tutor or provide leadership to other students. Parents of the students I helped often invited me to dinner, grateful for the help I gave their children. The principal of my high school, who also happened to be a friend of Master Park's, appointed me class leader, an honor bestowed each year to one of each class's three scholarship students. It was a golden time — all begun, strengthened and continued by my commitment to taekwondo.

One of the teachers who had known me since middle school — and knew of my taekwondo training — suggested that I teach a taekwondo class at the high school as a special activity. Even though I was still a student there, my rank as 2nd dan qualified me to teach taekwondo to anyone.

At first the principal was hesitant. "Do we really want to teach fighting at school?" he asked.

Master Park came to the school for a special meeting to discuss it. "Taekwondo is not about fighting," he explained to the principal. "Taekwondo is good for young people. Teaching it in school will improve their concentration, focus and discipline. If anything, it will give them tools for avoiding fighting — and a way to defend themselves if attacked." We also discussed the role of taekwondo in Korean heritage, nearly lost during Japanese occupation but now on its way back to its rightful place in our culture.

When it was my turn to speak, I described my training and how it made me strong when my life had been so full of challenges. "Taekwondo has taught me not to give up, to meet challenges with courage — and no matter how many times you get knocked down, to always get back up and begin again."

We told him that offering this class as a special activity in high school was an opportunity for me to show others by example what I had learned and introduce them to the correct philosophies and uses of taekwondo. After asking a few more questions, the principal gave me permission to begin a special taekwondo class during school in an unoccupied second floor classroom. Because this classroom was not in use, it could be a dedicated training space for my taekwondo class.

I tried to conceal my excitement and remain calm as Master Park, the principal, and I went up to view the classroom and discuss how to set it up as a training room. For the next few days I worked to clear it out and move the contents to a storage area. Then I cleaned it just as I cleaned our dojang. Master Park stopped by several times while I was working and gave his approval. Together we hung a Korean flag in the front of the room. Classes would begin the following Monday.

◊◊

Many, if not most of the high school students had never even seen taekwondo, so my first few classes were just demonstrations. As curious onlookers gathered to watch, I practiced. I started with the basic movements they would learn first, progressed through each technique at each level, and then ended with my second dan poomse.

By the end of the week I had 15 or 20 students signed up and I began to teach them, just as I had been taught, just as I had helped teach others at the dojang. From these experiences I knew how to answer their questions, how to break the techniques into small, precise steps and to require them to master each step, one at a time, before allowing them to move on.

A new student came to our high school, and several in my taekwondo class told me that he, too, was a second dan black belt in taekwondo. I had not yet met him, but he was reported to have made some negative comments about how I was conducting my class.

I ignored this talk at first. I was used to jealousy and ego-driven remarks. Then I happened upon a small group of my students talking excitedly about something. When they saw me, they stopped talking.

"What's going on?" I asked. I had an idea it was something to do with this new student, and my curiosity got the best of me.

"The new boy, the other taekwondo 2nd dan, is telling people he can beat you up."

"I see," I said, nonchalant.

"What are you going to do?"

"I'll take care of it." I wasn't sure how I would do this, but it seemed like the right thing to say. "Tell him to come see me. I'd like for him to join our class."

The next day, a new face appeared at my door. I knew by his swagger that this was Sang Soo Choi, the new student I was warned about.

"Would you like to join our class?" I asked. I kept my tone pleasant, ignoring his sullen demeanor.

"Yes."

"Good," I said. "Let me just get your information and I will add you to the class roll."

We sat down. "Where are you from?"

He told me.

"And you are you a black belt?"

"Yes."

"OK," I said.

He looked at me then, challenge in his eyes. *How should I handle this?* my mind queried. With my students looking to me as an example — and our promise to the principal — this situation was woven of serious responsibility. Rather than having my master to answer to, here my students would be measuring my actions against my words.

In class for the first few days, Sang Soo participated in the drills and practices. I ignored the building tension between us until sparring class when it became a distraction. Every student was attuned to this unspoken conflict, waiting for the coming confrontation.

Finally, I had enough. I wasn't sure exactly what I was going to do, but I knew it was time to face his challenge before he wrecked my class.

"Everyone sit down!" I called abruptly in the middle of sparring bouts. They sat, right in place.

I walked over and stood in front of Sang Soo. "Stand up!" I commanded with all the authority I could impose on this kid exactly my age who was at least a head taller — and about 30 pounds heavier — than me.

Sang Soo Choi stood up, eager for this confrontation.

Calm and strong, I reminded myself. *Aeyoo Nae-kang.*

"You will spar with me today," I said, keeping my tone even and matter-of-fact.

He smiled and bowed to me, clearly enjoying the idea of beating me up in front of my students.

I told everyone to move to the edges of the room to create a ring. I moved to the center and gestured for him to come there and face me. I bowed to him, waiting for him to follow suit. Then I snapped into *mot kyorugi sohgi,* sparring stance, with a loud kihap. He did the same.

I waited, inviting him to attack me first.

He led with a fierce roundhouse kick aimed directly for my head. Grateful for my training and extensive practice of what to do in the event of a serious attack, I moved a quick 45 degrees to the side and before he could re-chamber his missed kick I landed a short, powerful roundhouse kick to his solar plexus, right in the center of his chest. At the last instant before contact I checked this kick slightly so as not to do permanent harm. In taekwondo, *Il Kyok Pil Sal* means, "one strike must kill." I didn't want to kill this boy, but I did want to teach him a lesson he would never forget.

He doubled over, gasping for breath.

I leaned down to look him right in the face. "Do you want to continue?" I asked.

"I can't breathe," he managed to say between gasps.

I gave him a few more seconds. "Are you OK now?" I asked.

"Can I sit down?" he gasped.

Nervous laughter broke the silence from my students. I heard a loud whisper, "One kick and he gives up?"

Sang Soo heard this, too. He turned and looked at the crowd. "Not giving up, just resting." He sat down where he stood.

After about two minutes, I went to stand in front of him. "You challenged me, and I beat you," I said. "If you want to continue now, we can continue. Otherwise, either shut up and join the class or leave. Either way, if you have a problem with me, stop talking about it to the other students. Come back here and we will fight again — any time you're ready."

"Yes sir," he said, not looking up. After that day, Sang Soo Choi was a solid and productive member of my high school taekwondo class. Later on he became my assistant instructor, and as I watched him demonstrate the kindness and patience to lower ranking students that I had learned from my master — and now had passed on to him — I realized that my circle had begun.

1959 Teaching my high school class at Deok Won High School, Pusan. I'm seated, front row center; to my left (front row, second from the right) is Hong Kong Kim.

1966 Wearing ankle weights every day to school in my early training made my flying kicks powerful enough to stop the heavy bag. Here I am demonstrating this.

*1959 This was taken at the Grand Opening of my master's new school. Several of the Grandmasters and Jidokwan officials in attendance were rarely, if ever, photographed. Second row, left to right as indicated: 1. Jidokwan Vice President Young Ki Bae, 2. Great Grandmaster Hyon Chong Park (my teacher), 3. Jidokwan President Dr. Gyue Byong Yoon, 4. Great Grandmaster Il Sub Chun, 5. Grandmaster Jin Yong Chung
Third row, left to right, as indicated: 1. Grandmaster Rae Soon Park, 2. Won Chik Park, age 19, 3. Man Sup Lee*

As my time for military service grew closer, I also was beginning to excel as a taekwondo instructor, revealing two divergent paths for my life. Here I'm discussing exchanging military dreams with one of my high school classmates dressed in our school uniform.

CHAPTER SIX:
Dreams Clash with Reality

"I have decided it is time for me to move out on my own," I began. I was having dinner with Young Soon and Taeil Hwang, and the time seemed right to tell them my plans.

Young Soon started shaking her head.

I held up my hand. "Please let me explain," I said. "I have a lot of people to help me now, and I know that my being here is an extra burden on you both." I looked at Taeil Hwang. "I am very grateful for the home you have given me and for your kindness to me," I said, "but I think I can make it on my own. I only have one more year of high school before my military service."

"Why not stay until then?" they asked together, but I had already seen the relief on their faces.

"I'm almost grown up," I said. "I am a second dan black belt, I already teach in the dojang and in the high school. I have learned how to help people, and I also have many friends who help me."

I'll miss you," my sister said, eyes misting up.

"I'll still be around," I said. "I'll come and visit often. It's just time for me to be a man and live on my own."

She looked doubtful, but finally nodded. We hugged each other and that was that. I was officially on my own.

I rented a small, one-room apartment on the second floor of an old apartment house, one of the many of its kind in Pusan. The owner usually lived downstairs and there were several rental rooms upstairs, each with its own outside entrance and stairs. In my apartment there was a space for cooking, and a space for sleeping, and a space for eating and studying. The previous renter left a small table and chair, and I slept on the floor with just a blanket.

Dreams Clash with Reality

One small window served as my source of ventilation, and to my delight it also brought in the familiar smell of salty sea air. Even though I couldn't see the harbor from my window, the smell of it reminded me it was near. Dotting the gentle hill that rose inland from the harbor, apartment houses like mine revealed the poverty in this part of Pusan. It was a quiet area, populated mostly by single people who walked everywhere we went. Much the same as me, these were people who survived by helping each other. Even though I was a newcomer to this area, I felt strangely at home.

I was still settling in and getting my bearings when Hee Young arrived with food and a few essentials his mother sent. He looked around my apartment. "Nice place," he said. He had a nice home and family, but I could see a little envy that I got to have my own place now.

"It's small," I said, following his gaze, "but I don't need much room." I looked at the bundle in his arms. What do we have here?"

He shrugged. "Just some food and few things my mother thought you might need." He began unpacking. The smell of home-cooked food made my mouth water.

"Thank you," I said. "Will you stay and eat with me?"

He grinned. "Of course!"

◊◊

With fall closing in, I realized I needed to learn how to operate a *yuntan,* the traditional Korean cooking stove that doubled as a heating system. I had a vague memory of watching the women use large tongs to remove the yuntan's soot-blackened, 8-inch slate plate each night, then replacing it with a clean one. This memory took on new significance when I contemplated doing it for myself.

"I'll bring my mother tomorrow," Hee Young said as we stood before the contraption that sat about 10 inches off of the floor.

The next day after school, Hee Young's mother came with food to prepare for dinner, making with her demonstration also another home-cooked meal — this time in my home. She showed me how to use the tongs to stack and rotate the chalky slate plates that, once heated by a small fire on the grate compartment beneath them, would radiate warmth throughout my apartment. A smooth, flat lid covering the top stone served as my cooking surface, much like what Young Soon and I cooked on when we were living in the refugee camps.

Hee Young's mother gestured across the floor of my apartment, explaining that there were small passageways running underneath the floor to carry heat and smoke from the cooking fire. Flat warming stones, called kudul, lay just under the thin surface of the floor to hold and distribute the heat from the fire. The *kudul*, meaning "fired stone," was an under-floor heating system that had warmed South Korean homes since the Koguryo or Three Kingdoms period, which I remembered from my studies to be between about 37 B.C and 668 A.D.

"Wow," I said. I had never thought about what made the floors warm underneath us. It was just something I took for granted from the time I began living at Ung Chik's house.

Hee Young's mother looked at the blanket in my sleeping area. "If you build your cooking fire every day, you will be warm while you sleep," she said. A cloud of concern crossed her face. "If you are not warm when you sleep, you will get sick." She said that this system, designed to warm the body from the feet up, would help me stay healthy.

Then Hee Young's mother gestured toward a pipe in the center of the stove that provided ventilation and carried carbon monoxide exhaust outside. "These holes must always match, hole to hole," she said, "and fit tight here," she pointed to the fitting, "so the chimney will carry all the bad air outside." She looked at me hard. "You have to be very careful about this," she said. "You must change the plate and check this part every night before you sleep." She paused for effect. "Or you will die."

Hee Young and I took an involuntary step back from the thing that had been so warm and friendly just a few moments before. Maybe I was not ready to live on my own after all.

Hee Young's mother smiled, sensing my apprehension. She patted my arm. "It's OK." she now reassured. "You're a smart boy. It's not hard to do, you just have to know what to do." She looked at her own son, then back to me. "That is why I'm here."

Gathering her things to leave, Hee Young's mother told us that while this system was excellent for conducting heat in the winter, in the summer this same system allowed air circulation under the floors that kept the floors cool.

"Thank you very much for coming to show me this," I said. "I will be safe and warm this winter because of your help." I wished I felt as confident as I tried to sound. Standing alone in my apartment after they left, my eyes followed the chimney across the room to the place where it vented to the outside. "Please don't kill me," I implored the pipe.

◊◊

There were 10 people during my high school years I counted as my very best friends. Now seniors in high school, with ages varying by as much as two to three years, we began calling ourselves "The 11 Club."

Most of the 11 Club, like me, had come down from the north to escape the war; many had lost one or both of their parents to the war and were living with friends or relatives. With that common bond, we looked after one other as family, in a nurturing kind of friendship and connection that few people experience. When any one of us had a problem, all of us were there to help out. Some of The 11 Club were also in taekwondo, but everyone except me quit after his first or second dan test.

Kwang Jo, my close friend since the first year of middle school, was one of these. He trained with me in taekwondo until he got his second dan, but then he quit. "Too much work," he would say laughing. "I'm too lazy for that." At almost six feet tall, Kwang Jo towered over me. In contrast, I was always the shortest one in my age group and seeing us walking together down a street often made people laugh and wave. A shot-put champion and great natural athlete, Kwang Jo was as easygoing as I was intense, and the resulting balance was good for both of us.

Dreams Clash with Reality

Of all my friends, Kwang Jo was the most concerned about my future. Raised by his brother who was an engineer, and by Pusan standards, very well off, Kwang Jo's future plan was college, military service, and then, most likely, a lucrative career as an engineer like his brother. "Won Chik," have you decided what are you going to do next year?" he would ask me almost every day.

"We'll see," I'd always say. I was pinning my hopes on the upcoming military officer candidate school test, but to admit that would expose my vulnerability to variables beyond my control.

It was the first semester of my senior year, and my days were so full I had little time to think of the future. In addition attending my own classes and doing schoolwork that maintained my scholarship and teaching my high school taekwondo class every afternoon, I now hurried to several different homes to tutor children. This ensured a good home-cooked meal every weeknight before I went to the dojang for both evening classes. Then I trained a little bit extra on my own before closing the school and returning to my apartment to study. Most mornings, I woke with my face in my books, unsure of exactly how much study time I actually absorbed.

I have good grades, good physical conditioning and good recommendations, I'd tell myself when worry about the upcoming officer candidate test started to creep in. *I'm second in my class behind a genius and I've gone all the way through school on scholarship. How hard can this test be?*

◊◊

The idea to name our group of friends "The 11 Club," was mine, I suppose to give it a formality that felt like family. Since there were 11 of us, these literal-minded young men agreed that "The 11 Club," was a good name. As we neared graduation time, The 11 Club decided to hold a special ceremony to celebrate our friendship. We realized the time was coming when we would all go our separate ways, and though we would always be friends, after graduation it would never be the same. With life-changing events like graduation, military service, marriage, jobs and family looming our horizons, the world we knew was about to change forever.

To surprise everyone, I designed an emblem for our club, a special symbol that would always represent for each of us this unique friendship. In a solemn ceremony, we adopted this emblem and vowed our loyalty to each other for life.

After cementing our friendship in a blood oath like I had seen my older brother's friends do, we had a huge feast together of food each one brought from his mother. I stood back for a moment, deeply touched by this celebration of friendship that became family. "To the 11 Club!" I shouted, raising my glass. "To the 11 Club!" they shouted back. We laughed, drank and sang late into the night, creating a memory that these 11 friends would carry forever.

Because of the 11 Club, being alone in my meager apartment on the weekends was a rare occasion; instead of being a lonely experience, this group of friends made living alone my senior year an intensive and humbling course in the nature of true friendship. Never condescending, never pitying, but always there with support, encouragement, food and whatever help I needed, my friends and their families were a lifeline I would never forget. Late at night, however, when I was alone in my little apartment, the emptiness gave me opportunity to try to imagine what I would make of my life. With no money for college, my thoughts always went first to my military dreams. If I could pass the military officers' test, I wouldn't have to worry about money or food or a place to live for a very long time, if ever again.

The only concern I had about the upcoming military officers' test was that tuition for the Korean military academy I wanted to attend, ROK's version of America's West Point, was very expensive. Not only did I have to pass the test, but I had to pass it well enough to earn one of the few scholarships they had available for outstanding candidates. I had gone all the way through school so far on scholarships. Could I do it again?

This was a hot topic among my visiting friends, who agreed that if

Dreams Clash with Reality

I could go to this officer school on scholarship, I could be a military star. Their faith in me fueled my dreams. More than anything else I wanted to be a general. Just as Master Park advised, after the second dan test I set my new goal, and the first step toward it was acceptance into officer training school.

"My brother has a friend who is a two-star general," Kwang Jo said through a mouthful of Young Soon's kimchee and homemade noodles. Knowing how much I loved kimchee, she always made extra for me. It was rare when I was able to give something to my friends when they arrived on the weekends with food — I was happy to have something so wonderful to share.

"Can you ask him if he'd be willing to write me a recommendation for me?" I asked, hopeful. Although Keun Soo's brother also offered to write a recommendation, he had since been reassigned and we weren't sure we could find him in time. To apply to take the test I still needed one more recommendation from a military officer.

"I'll ask him tomorrow!" Kwang Jo promised.

On the words of my friend and his brother, this general wrote a recommendation for me. With everything now in order, I was accepted to take the test and, pending results, apply for Korea's elite officer training academy.

◊◊

What looked to be about 200 young men about my age lined up to begin the first part of the military officer's test, a three-day physical exam. Moving from station to station we were timed on everything from pushups to sit-ups to knee raises to all sorts of running exercises. At the end of the first day we celebrated together. "One down!" we shouted, feeling pretty good.

The second day was much like the first, only longer, with more difficult exercises and longer durations. A little less chipper at the end of day two, we spurred ourselves on with the chant, "Just one more!" On the second day, doctors at various checkpoints measured our conditions and recovery times. Because of my conditioning from years of taekwondo training, I had no problems with this part of the test, but I was glad to see day two end.

The third day was actually the easiest, with longer wait times between checkpoints. At the end of the third day of the physical exam they lined us back up, and, calling our names one by one, then called out, "Pass!" or "Did not pass!" I passed. The written test would be held in December before our high school graduation in March.

"The written test is much more difficult," said the officer who followed the results of the physical exam with instructions. "If you pass both parts of this exam, it means more to your future than college," the officer said.

Better than college? I couldn't imagine anything better than college.

"You'll have your choice between Army, Air Force and Navy — all three academies," the officer continued. I was elated. Which would I choose?

He then told us which subjects would be covered by the test. He didn't tell us exactly what to study, but since these were subjects I was already taking in school, I decided to study everything just to make sure. Just two months of hard study now stood between me and my military career.

Each night I sat with my books and tried to study. Even though I awoke most mornings with my face planted in the pages of one of these books, by test time I knew I had studied everything covered in my classes. It wasn't until about halfway through the written exam that I realized how limited my Pusan education had been. Even though I was always in the top three in my class, my relatively small town school did not prepare me for the depth and difficulty of the officer's exam.

I knew when I turned in my paper that I had not done well on the test. All the way back to my apartment, I thought about my mistakes. All the times when I was laughing with my friends when I should have been studying. Waiting until the end of the day to study when I was physically and mentally exhausted. Not digging deeper into the subjects than what I already studied in school.

Dreams Clash with Reality

Hope still flickered, though, because I scored so well on the physical exam. My resume was also strong, maintaining top of my class grades over a very long period of time. Like a taekwondo test, maybe points for those things would offset a poor written exam score.

They didn't. Just three days later the letter arrived that announced my failure. All my plans and dreams of being a general skittered away with the opening of that single page of bad news. I would have to have to enlist as a Private First Class (PFC) and serve my requisite two and a half years. My future was once again a big blank page.

I began walking, still carrying that letter, my mind rambling from thought to thought until my feet found their way to the dojang.

Master Park first looked at my face, then at the letter in my hand. "Bad news?" he asked.

"Yes," I said, too miserable to look him in the eye. I handed him the letter.

He read the letter, and then handed it back to me. He was quiet for a moment. I wondered what he could possibly say that could put this devastating turn of events into perspective.

"You missed," he said, as if reaching my goal was mere target practice. "For now you must continue training."

This was not at all what I wanted to hear. *What about the rest of my life?* My mind shouted. *What about my future?* Taekwondo is wonderful, but I had wanted to be a general. How could just going back to doing what I had always done take the place of that?

As if reading my thoughts, he stood quiet, waiting until my own mind grew quiet, too. "What you do now is up to you," he said. "A long time ago I told you that if you continue your taekwondo training and work for my school, one day it will be yours. That is still my promise, but it is your decision."

I did not go back to the dojang for two months.

At night I lay awake in my apartment, my mind a roiling sea of self-pity. *Why did this happen to me? Why is everything in my life so hard? Why didn't I study harder?* I thought about my classmates with exciting plans for their life and future. I imagined how those who passed the test were now preparing to start the new life I had imagined for myself. The future that slipped away before it began. What if I never made anything of myself? Most of these nights I cried myself to sleep, adrift in fitful dreams, awash in self-doubt. No one ever knew the misery of those low moments. Even my closest friends would have been shocked to discover that I had such fear and questioning.

"You're so strong," they'd say. "Nothing ever bothers you."

"Thank you," I would say. I was proud that taekwondo had made me strong. It had taught me how to face its challenges and never to give up. But this was a challenge I didn't want to face. What would they think of me if they saw my crying in my bed at night, knocked to the ground by this latest disappointment?

"You've already been through so much, and you have always kept going," they would say with admiration.

"God gave me this life," I'd reply. "What else could I do?"

But this was different. No matter how I thought about it, I couldn't imagine moving past this disappointment — or how it could possibly hold any opportunity I could ever be interested in.

When I returned to the dojang, Master Park said nothing about my absence, as if nothing had happened, no time had passed.

After class he said, "I'm glad to see you."

I bowed. "Thank you, sir," I said. "I just needed some time."

"I understand."

"It was a big disappointment," I said. "I am so disappointed in myself. I should have studied harder for the written test. It is my fault I failed."

"Don't worry about it," he said. "You did your best." He came over to where I was standing and put his hand on my shoulder. "I am very proud of how well you did on the physical exam," he added. "You are a taekwondo man."

"Thank you sir," I said. But I wanted more than to be just a "taekwondo man." How could I tell him that?

"It is time for you to start training for your third dan test," he said. "You must fill your mind with a new challenge."

Dreams Clash with Reality

◊◊

When Master Park received his eighth dan promotion to become a Grandmaster, I became his new chief assistant. This meant I led every class taught in the dojang, color belt through black belt, Monday through Saturday. My continuous presence at his side during every class would not only help me refine my teaching, he told me, but it was a continuous review of all I would need to know for my third dan test. At this level, my testing was starting its move away from physical challenge and more toward the base of knowledge I was building as a student and teacher of taekwondo.

Like all other tests, the third dan test had specific requirements — poomse, breaking, self-defense, and sparring. This time, however, I also would be graded on the extent of my knowledge of technique, basic movements and my deepening understanding of taekwondo philosophy. This knowledge, Grandmaster Park said, was the foundation of my teaching taekwondo to others.

My specific preparation for this part of my third dan test came in the form of daily conversations with Grandmaster Park. We sat in the middle of the dojang floor after everyone left for the day to go over each important piece of taekwondo history and philosophy. This was especially important for me to understand, he said again and again, because I was living during a pivotal time in taekwondo history.

He told me that as a martial art, taekwondo, once called "Subak, traced back to the Koguryo dynasty, which began in 37 B.C. At first it was merely of defense against animal attacks, then, because of a military, social and educational organization called Hwarangdo during the Silla Dynasty, the connection between Korean culture and this martial art was established. Its original code of honor was based on loyalty to nation, respect and obedience to parents, faithfulness to friends, courage in battle, and avoidance of unnecessary violence and killing.

During the Koryo Dynasty, Subak, already considered essential for not only military training but also for health and recreation, was first practiced as an organized sport for spectators. This happened about the same time as the rise in popularity of Kung Fu in China. Grandmaster Park stressed the importance of knowing this timetable, as it reveals taekwondo's pure Korean origin and independent development throughout Korean history.

After Japan's rise to imperial power following the Russo-Japanese War of 1904 -1905, one of its first acts was to invade, annex and occupy Korea for its natural resources, growing industrialization, and access to trade. Because the Japanese considered the study of "Subak" an attempt at revolt, it was forbidden from 1910 to 1945. Defying the threat of execution, "Subak" masters continued to practice their art in secret to preserve this important Korean legacy for future generations. Grandmaster Park was one of these masters.

When Korea was liberated from Japan in 1945, a time I recalled from my childhood, "Subak" began its re-emergence to form the roots of taekwondo. The masters decided that to honor the stylistic variations of Subak that had been taught in secret, this art would now have eight branches, or kwans: Chung Do Kwan, Moo Duk Kwan, Yun Moo Kwan, Chang Moo Kwan, Oh Do Kwan, Ji Do Kwan (Jidokwan), Han Moo Kwan, and Song Moo Kwan. We were Ji Do Kwan, Grandmaster Park said, the largest and most well-known branch of taekwondo.

In 1955 the eight kwans were united under the name of Tae Soo Do, later changed to "Taekwondo" by an influential group of masters. Soon after, South Korea's General Hong Hi Choi ordered the entire ROK army to be trained in taekwondo; taekwondo's first official students were the Korean soldiers.

This was all very interesting at first — and so important to my master, and material covered on my 3rd dan test — but as time wore on I found it more and more difficult to keep my attention from drifting.

"Pay attention, Won Chik!" Grandmaster Park said as he slammed his open palms down on the floor with a loud pop.

I jumped, startled as much by his rare intensity as I was by the sound.

"You must listen carefully so you will know and remember!" he said. "Each generation of taekwondo masters must know, share and protect taekwondo's true history and roots. If they don't, this knowledge will be lost forever."

My mind never drifted again.

Compared to my 2nd dan test, the crowd gathered for the 1960 black belt promotion test was modest. I stood in the university gym with a group of other 3rd dan candidates, and we looked around us at what looked to be about 100 people there to test; most of them seemed to be about my age. At 20, I was still among the youngest and smallest in the room, but that no longer bothered me.

The 3rd dan test was just as Grandmaster Park told me it would be; in addition to poomse, breaking and fighting, we were to have prepared three self-defense combinations. I had practiced my combinations with the same relentless determination as always, but suddenly, standing there before the test, I couldn't remember any of them. I sat down, head in my hands, trying to get control of my panic.

I remembered Grandmaster Park's advice whenever I got nervous: "Breathe, Won Chik. Deep inhale, deep exhale. Slow. Deep. Breathing." Once, to demonstrate this he had inhaled, filling his chest with air until his body looked like a balloon about ready to burst. He held this immense breath for a second, and then exhaled with force until his whole body strained to expel the last molecule of air from his lungs. "When you breathe like this, it will relax your mind," he said.

It worked. When I rose to complete my 3rd dan test, my self-defense techniques were sure and strong, as if they had never gone missing from my brain. At the end of the test, the presiding grandmaster spoke to us, complimenting our performance. He also told us that Seoul was about to become the headquarters of the Korea Taekwondo Association, to be formed the very next year. After 1960, he said, only those with an established testing record in Seoul would be allowed to test there. I was thankful that having tested there twice I would be in this elite group.

"Because you tested here today, you are forever recognized as one of our taekwondo seniors," the grandmaster in charge said. "There will always be a record here of your promotion and testing."

With my 3rd dan test behind me, I again faced the issue of what I would do with my life. Unlike the newness of first dan, the ability to teach that came with 2nd dan, the third stripe on my belt changed little in my physical training. Becoming 3rd dan, rather, marked the beginning of a new kind of journey, a path of much more subtle milestones and much bigger spaces in between them.

"Teaching is just another kind of training," Grandmaster Park said when I asked him what to do next in my own personal training. "If you are teaching, you are continuing your training."

"But how can I keep improving?" I asked Grandmaster Park. He had just been promoted to Grandmaster, the highest rank possible, and suddenly I was curious. What kind of knowledge did the four levels that lay between us hold? I realized that all the markers of dramatic physical improvement were just a phase, a stage of my training that was now complete. I felt a strange sadness over this — and a sense of confusion.

I thought again of the masters and grandmasters who had protected taekwondo from extinction during Korea's Japanese occupation, how they had risked their lives teaching this ancient art secretly to others to keep it alive and inspiring their students to mirror their dedication. Did I have this kind of courage?

Over the next several months I discovered that in addition to traditional teaching in the dojang, the growth of official competitions offered the new opportunity I was looking for. In developing students and taekwondo by helping to organize and promote competitive events, I saw a new door opening to me, and I gladly went through it.

Whenever several surrounding city branch schools would get together to have a school competition, I would make sure our dojang had a team ready to compete. The shared spirit of a group — bonded by competition was good for our school, good for the individual spirit of each competitor and good for the future of taekwondo.

◊◊

So that I could I could choose the branch of military I wanted to serve, I enlisted in the ROK army for my required two and a half years of military service. I knew that if I waited for the letter that would find me, and the rest of my age group, in the spring, the choice would be made for me. So as Private First Class Won Chik Park, I set off for Non San basic training camp, the biggest army training facility in South Korea.

I arrived at Non San by train, a very slow train that reminded me of the train to Pusan to Ung Chik's wedding. Far from being the exciting beginning of a grand adventure as that trip had been, this trip was an ongoing siege of regret and recrimination, chugging through my mind in time with the old steam engine. If I had not failed the military officers test, everything in my life would be different.

Even my departure from the train station was a sad shadow of what might have been. I tortured myself by imagining the big send off I would have had from friends and family as I boarded the train to my star military future. Instead, I went to the station alone, climbed aboard the train without looking back, and found a seat toward the back. Young Soon wanted to come; I told her no. The 11 Club had offered a Bon Voyage party; I refused. I just wanted to get on with my duty without fuss or fanfare.

I looked around me, studying the other faces on the packed train. Every young man there was from the Inchon Region. We were all headed, like so many others, to Non San for training before receiving our assignments. There was talk about going to Viet Nam, where war was already raging and the US had entered to help, just as it had with us. We all wanted to go to Viet Nam to do what we could to help the US as a national expression of gratitude for all it had done for us.

A twinge of nervous anticipation buzzed deep within me. What would army combat be like? I looked out of the dirty train windows at the countryside rolling along beside me. Military service was always a vague, shadowy, exciting thing — what would its reality be? I thought of my training at the dojang and our Special Summer and

Winter Training. How would this training be different? I remembered how Ung Chik took each move, and each new assignment, in stride, regardless of what else was going on in his personal life and in the world around him. What would my job be? I realized I had no idea what soldiers did and how it was they could learn to do these jobs in just three months of training.

◊◊

We were first directed by a man with a clipboard to long, narrow barrack. Our assigned places to sleep and store our belongings reminded me of the matchstick arrangement of the war refugee quarters in the Pusan high school gymnasium. Our beds were straw mats on the floor with a blanket folded on top of each. A wooden box sat at the head of every bed. That was where we were told to put our belongings before lining up in front of the barrack for our first inspection. One enlistee who was slow to get unpacked had to do pushups while we all watched.

The sergeant walked up and down in front of our line. Our days would start early and end early, he said as he looked us over. Our training would be hard, to prepare us for the much harder things could face in combat. There would be a wake-up call each morning, breakfast, then each day would be different, a combination of marching, conditioning, and weapons drills.

"Your weapon will be your new girlfriend," he said. This brought snickers he silenced with just one look. "You will love it, take care of it and keep it with you everywhere you go."

When the sergeant was at the other end of the line, I took a quick glance around me. Most of these young men looked scared, with no physical training outside school PE. I silently thanked taekwondo for preparing me for this experience. With my score on the officer's test, I knew the physical part of basic training would pose no problem.

The next morning, a clanging wake-up bell roused me out of a sound sleep. For a moment, I didn't know where I was. Then the scurrying around me helped me remember. We went to the mess hall for breakfast, a cup of watery soup with a handful of rice in it.

"What is this?" someone behind me asked.

"It doesn't taste very good," came another remark.

"This isn't enough," said a larger kid who had sat down next to me.

I ate my soup in silence, remembering the cups of broth with barley that were our UN rations. Looking around me, I wondered if any of these kids shared those memories. Even though it didn't taste very good and there wasn't enough of it, this watery remembrance of earlier times reminded me how far I had come in the second decade of my life.

◊◊

"PFC Park!"

It was during our final inspection one night when our sergeant singled me out. We were halfway through our basic training. What did he want with me?

"Yes, Sir!"

"Step forward, please!"

"Yes, Sir!" I stepped forward.

"Is it true that you know taekwondo?"

"Yes, Sir!"

"What is your rank?"

"Third dan black belt, Sir!"

I heard a few whispers behind me. I had not told anyone about my training. Taekwondo belonged to another part of my life that seemed out of context here. Mentioning it would have been too much like bragging.

"Will you do a demonstration for us?"

"Yes, Sir!"

I took a deep breath and began an impromptu demonstration that started with my most impressive black belt poomse as a warm up, then progressed to a series of kicking, punching and striking combinations. I ended with a humble bow and returned to my place in line.

Everyone clapped politely. Then we were dismissed.

My new friends gathered around me in the barracks afterward. "We didn't know!" They said, as if I had been hiding a secret.

No other mention was made of taekwondo for the rest of my training, but I noticed that everyone, even officers, looked at me differently after that. Taekwondo had made me stand out of this crowd, and even though it was a crowd of PFCs and not officer candidates, this unexpected mark of distinction did make me feel a little better.

After the first few weeks of training, our fumbling uncertainty with our new "girlfriends," the M1 rifle each of us was assigned, gave way to confident expertise. On the first day none of us could take it apart and put it back together in the required time; within weeks of daily practice we all finished with time to spare.

We practiced shooting while standing, kneeling, running, lying flat on our stomachs, and even while crawling on our bellies beneath a horizontal stretch of wire fence, suspended just high enough that we could get under it, but low enough to entangle us if we didn't stay completely flat as we crawled with our weapon in the ready position in front of us, using our elbows for forward traction. The fence was the last drill, done first on our stomachs, then on our backs, always keeping our cumbersome M1 girlfriends clear for shooting.

Toward the end of training, we began to talk at night of our upcoming assignments. Unlike many of the others, I didn't have a specific hope for where I would be assigned. I looked forward to moving around, seeing faraway places, going off on assignments and returning triumphant, just as Ung Chik had. After being on the other side of that picture my whole life, it was finally my turn.

"The best assignments are here in Seoul," said Hwang, my best friend in basic training.

"I want to go somewhere far away—to see someplace new," I said.

"Anywhere but the DMZ," someone across the barracks said.

"I want to go to Viet Nam," said another boy down the way.

"Not me," said another. "Too dangerous."

Then assignment day arrived. As our names were called, we were to answer, then our assignment would be announced and we would acknowledge it. As this process began, cheers and clapping accompanied each soldier as he accepted his paperwork and left for the barracks to gather his belongings. It was the last time many of us would see each other, although some would cross paths for years.

"PFC Won Chik Park!"

"Yes, Sir!" I held my breath, waiting for the exciting news of where my military adventure would begin.

"Non San Basic Training Headquarters!"

I stood in shocked silence. There must be some mistake. I looked around me. No one made eye contact. We all hated it here, but I was sure I hated it most. How could this be my assignment? What kind of assignment could it be? I'm just a private — what could I do here? My disappointment was a lead weight in my stomach as I accepted my papers and went to gather my belongings. No one clapped or cheered or said anything to me. I felt a roomful of sympathetic eyes following me to the door. I couldn't speak. I couldn't even say goodbye to my friends. I had lived through some very bad days in my life, and this one, without question, now joined them.

Circa 1960 Our school uniforms prepared us early for our required ROK military service just after high school. At this age, my only dream for the future was being a general.

A visit to the naval base in Pusan was fuel for my desire to be a military officer.

As I grew stronger, my technique continued to improve. I realized during this time how focusing on basics and relentless practice is reflected in advanced technique such as Twimyo Yop Chagi, flying side kick.

Circa 1967, Special Summer Training in the mountains surrounding Hong Chun, Kang Won Do. Front row, left to right as indicated: 1. Mental Master Dong Ho Bub Sa, 2. Young Ki Bai, 3. Chong Woo Lee, 4. Il Sub Jun
Second row, left to right, as indicated: 1. Song Wook Won, 2. Man Sup Lee, 3. Won Chik Park

Teaching American military personnel and their families opened my eyes to the richness and opportunities of life in America. In this 1969 team victory at the U.S. Military Force Taekwondo Championship, I learned how serious these students were about learning authentic techniques and competition.

CHAPTER SEVEN:
A Glimpse of the American Dream

Still despondent and confused over this strange and unfortunate assignment, I arrived at the Non San Headquarters as directed. There were 20 other soldiers gathered to await further instruction, each wearing the same expression as mine. *What will I do here — and what did I do to deserve such a terrible assignment?* I thought, over and over in an endless loop. The only consolation for not being an officer was travel and military adventure. Now that was gone, too.

In a conversation behind me someone seemed pleased with this assignment. *What can he be thinking?* I wondered. He said Non San Training Headquarters was commanded by a two-star general. *Big deal,* I thought.

We were ushered into the dining hall for dinner. While it was somewhat better than the broth and rice of basic training, it was nothing to get excited about. I refused to interact with anyone around me, especially those who seemed happy with this assignment. After dinner we were led to barracks and shown to our assigned bunks. These, too, were somewhat nicer accommodations than at basic training, but still the same basic set-up — a sleeping mat on a wood floor with a blanket and a box to hold our belongings. We were instructed to get settled and then report to the front of the barracks to introduce ourselves. This re-run seemed like a bad dream.

"I am PFC Won Chik Park," I said when it was my turn. It was the first time I spoke since arriving.

After we all introduced ourselves, the Captain said, "Thank you for introducing yourselves. However, I already know quite a bit about each of you. For example," he looked straight at me, "I know that PFC Park is a taekwondo man, isn't that right PFC Park?"

"Yes, Sir." *So what?* I thought.

"Can you do a demonstration for us?"

"Yes, Sir." *Why not?*

I repeated the demonstration I did during basic training camp, enjoying the unexpected outlet for my bottled emotions. None of the people around me were in my basic training unit, so my demonstration was new to them. As before, I finished, bowed to the Captain, bowed to the line of soldiers, then returned to my place in line. As before, everyone clapped and cheered. As before, taekwondo brought an attitude of respect from my colleagues, but this made little difference to me as we moved about our assigned daily duties to maintain and care for all Non San's training equipment and facilities. A month or two crawled by, and I wondered if I would go insane before my military service was over.

After dinner one evening, the Captain called me into his office. He shuffled through a few papers on his desk, and then looked up and said, "We have examined your records." He paused. "And we have discovered something new about you."

What now? I knew there was nothing negative in my record, but the formality of his tone was alarming.

"It appears that you not only have a third dan black belt in taekwondo, but you also have some teaching experience."

"Yes, Sir."

"It says here that you taught — and in fact created — a special program in your high school," he said. "Is that right?"

"Yes, Sir."

"You have some very high recommendations from your teachers and principal. They said your classes were very well-attended and your students learned a great deal very quickly." He sat back in his chair and looked at me. "Your master says that you are a gifted teacher."

I didn't know what to say.

"Your recommendation from your principal also says that you are a natural leader and that you went all the way through school on scholarship."

"Yes, Sir." Where was this going?

"Because of these things you have been selected to teach taekwondo here at Non San," he said.

I was too stunned to speak. Could this be true?

"Starting tomorrow, your daily duties will be assumed by someone else. You will not work any more during the day, but every evening for two hours after dinner you will be on duty to teach taekwondo."

"Yes, Sir," I said, bowing and trying to keep my face from showing my relief and excitement.

"There is one problem, though," he said.

I stood, statue still, waiting for the other shoe to drop.

"A PFC cannot teach officers — and your students here will all be officers," he said. He paused. "So you have also been promoted to corporal."

I couldn't believe my ears. "Yes, Sir!"

◊◊

Just as Master Park said, all ROK troops were ordered to be trained in taekwondo for hand-to-hand combat. General Choi's sweeping edict, as much a cultural statement as it was military strategy, marked the historic rebirth of traditional martial arts training for the Korean military, as well as a national awareness of taekwondo. For me, it was a welcome rescue from tedium and return to my taekwondo teaching.

Now that everyone — even officers who would never see combat — required taekwondo training, being a taekwondo teacher with experience made me part of an elite national commodity. The classes I began teaching at the Non San training headquarters were at first for mostly out-of-shape, desk-bound officers. Some of these had a little taekwondo experience, a few had black belts, but I was by far the highest ranking.

"Your taekwondo classes here will be like basic training school for officers," the two-star general and Non San commander explained to me. He planned to rotate groups of about 50 officers at a time through basic taekwondo training; my classes each night would consist of about 200 tired, distracted officers. I could not imagine how I would keep their attention, but since it was my only job here, I knew that I must.

"Teaching taekwondo to soldiers will not be like teaching in a regular dojang," the general said. Instead of the normal course of building skills over a two-year period, I was to compress those basics into a few weeks' practice. "No poomse or sparring," he said. "Your job is to teach these students basics, one-step sparring and self-defense techniques. They must know — and practice — *Il Kyok Pil Sal*, the one-shot strikes that will disable or kill an attacker."

The seriousness of this new responsibility was beginning to dawn on me. Their life could depend on how well they learned what I was teaching them. What I was teaching them each evening was more important — more real — than anything I had ever taught to any taekwondo students before. Even though most of these officers probably would not be sent into combat, war is uncertain. The war was escalating in Viet Nam — who knew where any of these officers might end up? I was humbled by this responsibility.

"I will do my very best, Sir," I promised the general.

About 30 minutes after dinner each evening, they'd line up for class. Fully dressed in their uniforms and heavy military boots like the ones I used to train in, they began learning taekwondo on the hard packed dirt each evening until the sun set behind them and it was too dark to see. Like every other class I had taught, we started with meditation and breathing exercises to teach them how to still their mind of chatter, then, after a few important stretching and conditioning exercises, we focused only on the basics of hand-to-hand defense and counterattack. At the end of each two-hour class they were exhausted.

"Take it easy on us!" they'd beg. Seeing their lack of conditioning, I'd comply as much as I could, but I still had a job to do. There was a fine line between accelerating their learning as the general instructed and making sure not to injure them. It was strange to me that even though these were company commanders, for those two hours each eve-

A Glimpse of the American Dream

ning I was their commander, and their respect amazed me. Even after class they were always nice to me, almost as if I were one of them.

"Corporal Park!" gasped one of these during class one day. He was a big and heavy sergeant major with too much to do. "Don't make us work so hard! We are already tired from our long day at work and extra duties. Please, take it easy!"

"You can sit down and rest whenever you need to," I told him after class. But your training is important to your safety." I explained that the general said there would be surprise inspections of our training to make sure all the officers were complying. "If an inspector comes, he must see you working hard and learning well so we will all get a good report," I said. "It is my job to train you. I understand that your body is not used to exercise, so don't push so hard that you hurt yourself, but always do the best you can."

Once, just as the hefty sergeant major was about to sit down to rest, I saw out of the corner of my eye a colonel I had not seen before, walking slowly around the perimeter of our training area.

I moved toward the sergeant major as if to correct his stance. "Don't sit now," I whispered. "Someone's watching us."

He glanced over his shoulder and caught sight of the ambling colonel, then straightened his stance. "Thank you, Corporal Park."

Another officer, Lieutenant Lee, who had some experience and great interest in taekwondo, was always asking me questions. More than just fulfilling his required training, he seemed to absorb everything I told him about taekwondo. He became my best student — and my friend. Lieutenant Lee was a graduate of the same military academy I had so longed to attend, and yet taekwondo gave me knowledge he didn't have — and longed for. This irony did not escape me. I was grateful every single day for the world of opportunity taekwondo now opened up to me.

◊◊

A Glimpse of the American Dream

"So what do you want to do after your military service?" Lieutenant Lee asked me one evening after class when he invited me to join him in the officer's club for dinner. The food was much better there, and this surprising treat became a regular occurrence because Lieutenant Lee always wanted to talk about taekwondo. I always looked forward to these meals and our conversations.

The emotional roller coaster ride my recent life had become left me breathless, wide-eyed, and without any idea of what to do next. From the collapse of my grandiose officer dream to the shattering of my hopes for an exciting faraway military assignment, to this amazing opportunity to instruct officers, I couldn't begin to guess what would be next. At 23 years old, and instead of studying to become a general, I was teaching generals, and they were bowing to me!

I said none of this to Lieutenant Lee, of course. "I'm a lucky man to spend my military service teaching taekwondo," I told him instead. As I heard the answer to his question coming out of my mouth, I realized my decision was at last made. "After my military service is over I hope to become a taekwondo master," I said. " Besides helping our military learn taekwondo, this challenge is good experience for me as an instructor."

"Will you open your own dojang?"

"Maybe," I said, thoughtful. "My grandmaster in Pusan has said I can take over his dojang when I'm ready, but we'll see which door opens." My recent experience taught me how opportunity can spring itself on you when you least expected it. I also learned that if I was always ready to step through those unexpected open doors, amazing things could be waiting on the other side.

"Have you ever thought about teaching taekwondo in another country?"

I had not even considered this option. "How would I do that?" I asked, curious.

"Seoul is the headquarters of all branches of the US military in Korea, a place where the US and Korean military work together in many ways," Lieutenant Lee told me, passing me another plate of food. "If you get a chance to go over there to teach, it would be a good opportunity to learn English and work for American GIs. To teach taekwondo at the US military headquarters would make it very possible for you to go to the US to teach. To do this is very difficult, but if you are interested, I will help you the best I can."

"Sure," I said. I knew nothing about America, Americans, or the US military, but his offer touched me. Though farfetched, I agreed with him that the idea was interesting. With a little more than a year left of my military service, I was also content to stay where I was, doing what I was doing, waiting once again for my future to arrive.

◊◊

I had almost forgotten about my conversation with Lieutenant Lee when the letter came from the personnel office of the ROK Military headquarters. According to this letter and the enclosed paperwork, I would spend my last year of military service teaching taekwondo to the soldiers of the US 8th Division Army in Seoul. I was surprised by this sudden reassignment, and even though I knew it was a rare and sought-after opportunity, I was unsure how I felt about it.

"How did you get this assignment?" the others at Non San quizzed me. "Who helped you?"

"I'm not sure — maybe my brother or his friend," was always my answer. Lieutenant Lee never said another word about it, but I was certain he had somehow made this happen. Regardless of who helped me, it was taekwondo that once again opened the door to an opportunity I never could have imagined.

I was as excited as I was terrified as I climbed out of the jeep they sent for me. I looked up at the large concrete buildings, barracks three stories high. I watched the uniformed soldiers hurrying about in clothes that were vastly different from anything I had ever seen before.

I was met by a man who introduced himself as Captain Chapman. Somehow, using the few words of English I knew and the few words of Korean he knew, along with a pointing and gesturing, we got through the basic introductions and entered a dining hall.

I tried not to gape at the sights and smells that surrounded me. I followed Captain Chapman to a long line of tables where a huge amount of food I did not recognize was laid out. He handed me a tray. I took it and, watching everything he did, I did the same. If he took something, I took it.

We each put a glass of bright orange liquid on our trays. Unable to contain my curiosity any longer, I took a sip. The taste was wonderful—nothing like I had ever tasted before. Captain Chapman pointed at a large bowl of orange fruit, and then at my glass. Apparently that was where the orange liquid came from. I had never before even seen oranges, but I knew right then that they were my new favorite fruit.

My mind boggled at the food on my tray. I had never had so much food, and even though some of it looked strange to me, everything I tried was wonderful. If the food on its military base was any indication, life in America must be better than anything imaginable. America must be a very rich country, I thought. How can a corporal eat this kind of food?

When Captain Chapman showed me to my quarters in the huge barracks, I saw that the room I would live in was larger than my entire apartment in Pusan. In the corner was a bed covered by sheets and a blanket. I had never slept on anything but the floor, and couldn't wait to see what sleeping on this softness would be like. Captain Chapman watched me take in my quarters, and I could tell he was trying to imagine what my usual accommodations were like.

I just smiled and said, using my most important new English words, "Thank you."

To me, Captain Chapman seemed very nice, but judging by the intimidated reactions of others, he was a very strong leader who tolerated no nonsense. On my first morning of duty, we walked together across the compound to an empty quonset that had once been used as barracks. It had a concrete floor and the spacious interior was both heated and air-conditioned.

"This is where you will hold your classes," he said, walking through the center of the building. At the end were about seven pri-

A Glimpse of the American Dream

vate offices. He showed me to one of them. This is your office," he said. Sharing this office space were a captain, a lieutenant, several sergeants and a few corporals.

"This is a special division," Captain Chapman explained. He told me I would start teaching him and 4-5 others there. Then in a few days, a class of 15 would come; each new group would appear when it came time in their training rotation for their taekwondo training. Just like at Non San, the emphasis here was to be on hand-to-hand combat techniques and self-defense, so beyond teaching basic technique, we would focus mostly on one-step sparring and one-shot self-defense techniques. Again I felt the weight of the responsibility for teaching our American friends the things that could save their lives if caught without a weapon in the jungles of Vietnam.

During the next 12 months, I began to think more seriously about Lieutenant Lee's advice to go to the United States to teach taekwondo. As I taught American soldiers from all branches who were stationed at their Seoul Headquarters, I enjoyed their eagerness — and how much they wanted to learn what I had to teach. Would American civilian students be the same?

Just as at Non San, my days were opportunities to explore the base, do my own training, to enjoy free time. In the evenings, I taught taekwondo. Through it all, I tried to learn as much English as I could.

After those first five classes, Captain Chapman asked me if I would be willing to also do private instruction for him. He wanted to learn more than I was able to teach the large classes, so I agreed to work one-on-one with him.

After two months, Captain Chapman asked, "Can you teach more students?"

"Yes, Sir!" I said, proud of my English expression of this familiar response.

The next day Captain Chapman ordered his entire company to be trained in taekwondo. Although taekwondo training was not mandatory for all American military, he made it mandatory for his men.

"Can you teach more students?" he asked again a few weeks later.

"Yes, Sir!" After teaching 200 at a time at Non San, no class seemed too large.

So the announcement was made that anyone else on the base — whether Army, Navy, Air Force, or Marines — could come and train as well. As word of this new program spread throughout the base, my classes grew. Group classes, private classes, everyone who came was eager to learn and they all worked very hard.

The first thing I noticed about my American students was that they were all very big. Even though I was still small, even by Korean standards, these students were bigger than any students I had ever taught before. I was also impressed right away with how fast they learned and how sincere their effort. Despite frequent struggles with language, I was gratified by their progress. Because teaching taekwondo lends itself more to demonstration than explanation, my instruction seemed to be communicating with these students very well through my physical examples.

I was quick to discover that English learned from a book in school is far from real English conversation. Captain Chapman knew a little bit of Korean, and he tried to help me with a few basic words and phrases I needed to know. He also gave me a little English to Korean and Korean to English dictionary, and I carried it wherever I went.

Little by little, I learned to communicate with my students. They tried very hard to understand me, and I often asked for their help with pronunciation. I also realized that students from different parts of the United States pronounced words differently, and sometimes even they had a hard time understanding each other. It made me laugh to hear New Yorkers and Southerners and Midwesterners asking each other, "What? What?" Soon we all laughed together over this, and just saying, "What? What?" sent ripples of laughter across the classroom. My taekwondo classes became a great opportunity for me to practice my English, and for any of my students who were interested, I repaid this kindness by helping them practice Korean.

By the end of that wonderful year when I was on loan to the American military base, I was promoted to Sergeant, learned quite a bit of English, and made a lot of good American friends. I was starting to dread my discharge from the Korean military and returning to the realities of my life. Also during that year, to move forward on my plan to be a taekwondo master after my military service was over, I spent my personal training time preparing for my 4th dan test. To be a taekwondo master required a rank of 5th dan or higher, so that much, I knew, was my next step.

As I taught soldiers, both Korean, then American, I continued to strengthen my own training, wondering what my future would hold.

US Independence Day demonstration at US 8th Army Headquarters, Seoul, Korea

Regardless of personal disappointment in my military career, I saw very quickly the doors taekwondo was opening for me.

My first dojang in Seoul was a beautiful dream come true. Here I taught both local Korean students of all ages and American military students who desired more in-depth training.

CHAPTER EIGHT:
Job, Family and Dojang of His Own

It was about a month and a half before my military service ended when Captain Chapman called me into his office.

"Sergeant Park, what do you think of teaching taekwondo here to our GIs?" he asked.

"It's very good, sir," I said.

"Would you like to continue here after you are finished with your ROK military service?"

"I don't understand."

"Would you like to apply for a job as instructor here?"

My dread of the end of this fairy tale existence was growing each day as the end of my time here loomed nearer. Even though I had missed some of my home culture living here on the base, I knew I would miss even more all the wonderful friends, American food and creature comforts that, although once so strange to me, I now enjoyed. If my military assignment became a permanent job, it could offer the very best of both.

"Yes!" I said, "I would like that! How do I do it?"

Captain Chapman explained to me the application process. "I'll go with you when you are ready to apply," he said. "It is a very difficult job to get; there are only a few positions available and many people will apply. Maybe if I go with you and personally deliver my recommendation it will help."

"Thank you, Sir," I said. I still couldn't believe this was happening. I wanted to jump, to dance, to shout. Instead I just shook his hand and in my best English said, "Thank you. I really appreciate your help."

I don't know what was in the letter of recommendation Captain Chapman handed to the clerk in the personnel office, or what he told them during the meeting that followed behind the closed doors of an inside office. He later said he just told them what a good job I did teaching his entire company, both in private instruction and in many different classes, and that he knew personally that I would be right for this job. His recommendation must have been very powerful, because three days later I got a letter that said, "As soon as you complete your military service to the Republic of Korea Armed Forces, you are accepted to begin teaching as an employee of the United States government."

Standing in my room reading that letter, I was overcome with amazed gratitude for this new door taekwondo and friendship had opened in my life. "Thank you," I said out loud, again and again as I danced around the room. I thanked God. I thanked the United States. I thanked Captain Chapman. I thanked my master. I thanked Ung Chik and Young Soon. I thanked my parents, who I knew were smiling down at me from heaven.

I pulled out a piece of paper and sat down at the table that also served as a desk. I wished I could tell him in person, but a letter was better than nothing. I wrote to Master Park, telling him my wonderful news and thanking him for everything he did to make this possible. "Because I had no money and you let me work in your dojang in exchange for training," I wrote, "I am sitting here today, accepting a very good job teaching taekwondo as an employee of the United States of America. Because of how you taught me, I am able to teach others so well that they gave me this wonderful job. Because you believed in me and helped me and encouraged me, I have a life and opportunities I never could have imagined."

◊◊

During a short vacation after I was discharged from the ROK military, before my new job began, I went to Pusan see Young Soon and Ung Chik. Young Soon squealed when she saw me coming up the walk to their house. She grabbed me and hugged me and then she held me back and looked at me, up and down, inspecting my US GI haircut and the western clothes I had bought at the base commissary. I thought about Uncle Ki Hoon as I saw myself through her eyes and how she stared at my shiny western shoes.

"You look so different!" she said. "Everything's different!"

"I went to the USA" I joked.

"No!"

I told her about the abundance and strange comforts of living on the American base — the food, the fresh fruit, and the bed. She was astounded, hanging on each word, struggling to imagine what I was describing.

"And now, I have a permanent job working there," I said. "As an employee of the Unites States military."

"Doing what?"

"Teaching taekwondo to American soldiers," I said, puffing out my chest. It was OK when talking to my sister to allow pride to overshadow humility. After all we had been through together, Young Soon would appreciate this news most.

"America is a very rich country," she said. "You must be a very good teacher to get a full-time job teaching taekwondo to their soldiers."

I had written letters whenever I could to both Young Soon and Ung Chik, and they both knew the story of how my teaching had taken me from Non San to the US military headquarters, but none of us could have imagined that this wonderful job could continue.

I visited Ung Chik next, and his enthusiastic and tearful congratulations were overwhelming in still a different way. He pounded me on the back. "I can't believe it!" He kept saying. "You got a job working for the United States military?" He danced around in a circle. "My little brother is a taekwondo instructor for the US military!" he crowed loud enough for everyone in Korea to hear.

The next weekend we had a big celebration dinner, inviting as many of my friends as we could find. and all my many relatives now in Pusan. It was a big day for my family, a moment of triumph we all shared.

I stood up to make a toast to my brother. I raised my glass. "Because Ung Chik took me in, I was able to go to school. Because he encouraged me when I got beat up over that soccer ball, I found taekwondo. Because of Ung Chik's help and support, I have an education and now, a good job teaching taekwondo. Thank you, *hyong neem!*" I said these things through grateful tears and seeing glow the of pride on my brother's face added a new layer of richness to this unforgettable moment of personal triumph.

◊◊

As a Korean civilian employee of the US military, my life took on a perfect balance between old and new. During the day I worked on base, teaching classes as I always had at Trent Gym. Once my workday was over, I returned to my Korean life.

As a permanent instructor on the US base, I still taught GIs hand-to-hand combat and self-defense techniques, but to these classes, with Captain Chapman's encouragement, I added several more traditional classes for families, children and non-military base personnel. To these I added poomse, sparring, and breaking techniques to our regular instruction.

Teaching three classes of American GIs every day except Sundays, children kindergarten through high school in the late afternoon and entire families in the evenings was a very different experience. My daily military-only classes were still held in the aging Trent Gym, which also housed basketball, weightlifting, handball, and squash courts. Classes for other base employees and their families were in a newer gym called Collier Field House.

Collier Field House was very nice, with new shower facilities and all kinds of family-oriented recreation equipment. It was here that I learned more about real American life. As I got to know the families of the US military, I discovered a different picture of what "regular" Americans were really like. Without exception, everyone was very nice to me; the children liked and respected me, and even the ones who were known to be problems to their parents and teachers gave me no trouble at all.

By always encouraging my young students to show their taekwondo spirit by behaving as respectfully at home as they did in my class, I won the approval of many parents, including several high-ranking officers. With this perfect balance of military and civilian life, I was feeling more and more comfortable in the company of Americans.

◊◊

With Captain Chapman's permission, I often invited friends from a local Korean competition taekwondo team to practice and train with my classes on base. This was enlightening for both my American students and my Korean friends who otherwise would never have seen this world. Units of the ROK army stationed close by were also welcome to join in our conditioning and taekwondo programs. At testing time for the American students, I invited local masters to come in and meet my American students, officiate the test and enjoy a meal in the base cafeteria. This was popular with everyone concerned — another opportunity for our cultures to interact and to share this connection called taekwondo. I couldn't believe my good fortune to be here at this time, in a position to help taekwondo create a special new bridge of friendship between Korea and the United States.

After the excitement of the past two and a half years, my 4th dan test was anticlimactic. Because I lived in Seoul, now the home of the official Jidokwan headquarters and the new Korea Taekwondo Association, I could test as soon as I had the formal recommendation of my master. His reply came promptly, as always, and confirmed that the Korea Taekwondo Association officials now had his official recommendation.

A few weeks later my application arrived by mail from the Korea Taekwondo Association with instructions to complete and return it in person. I would also be expected to present all my testing records to Grandmaster Chong Woo Lee, the new Jidokwan president, and then answer a series of oral questions about my training and teaching experience.

"Your master's recommendation is the best I've ever seen," Grandmaster Lee told me as he signed my application. "You are approved to take your 4th dan promotion test."

I was 24 years old at my 4th dan test, by far the youngest of the 20 or so others testing for this rank. Two older gentlemen were there to test for 5th dan.

The testing requirements were pretty much the same — but at higher levels. Our poomse was specific to the test we were taking, and free fighting was done without pads to show our control. When it came time for breaking, my nerves fluttered for the first time. I was attempting a very difficult break to showcase my increased strength and power from all my weightlifting on the American base. I would attempt a knife hand "speed break" with the outside of my rigid hand through several thin, flat bricks, standing vertically on end. There would be no holders; this break required ultimate precision, speed and power — all concentrated into the exact moment of contact.

I set up my bricks carefully, took a deep breath and with a loud kihap, delivered a fierce knife hand strike to the first brick. The bricks went flying but did not break. I tried again. Same result.

I took a step back and paused, remembering Grandmaster Park's coaching on this break:

"Look at the center of the brick," he had said, standing behind me with his arms crossed, inspecting my technique as I attempted this break in the yard behind his dojang where testing candidates were allowed to do a real trial run of their breaks just before testing. I had traveled to Pusan on the Sunday before my test to go over each section of the test with him as I always did.

"Keep your eyes on the center of the brick until you are all the way through it. And don't forget to breathe," he added for what was probably the hundred millionth time. "You must exhale as you kihap — all the way through the brick. That is why we kihap during breaking. The brick can't hear you." He laughed at his own joke. "But continuing your kihap through the whole break will make sure you breathe through the whole break."

I unleashed a mighty *kihap* and delivered the knife hand strike

Job, Family and Dojang of His Own

again, making my mind visualize my hand going all the way through the bricks. This time the bricks broke cleanly at their centers, leaving a pile of rubble and crumbled cement. I bowed to the judges and to the crowd still clapping. For some reason, it seemed to make a bigger impact that I missed twice and then finally succeeded than if I had broken on the first try. I puzzled over this as I watched the rest of the group complete the physical part of the test.

The written portion of the 4th dan test focused on measuring the shift in our understanding of how to convey our taekwondo knowledge and experience to our students. When I received word a few weeks later that I had passed this rigorous test, I knew I was on my way to becoming a taekwondo master.

◊◊

After so many years of barely scraping by, it was hard for me to get used to the idea that the same job I had been doing for more than a year now produced a salary that was quite high by Korean standards. I considered my options. Should I use this extra money to go back to school and work toward a college degree? Start saving for my own dojang?

My job — and my new life — was in Seoul, making returning to Pusan to take over Grandmaster Park's dojang now out of the question. Since I taught on the base in the afternoons and my private dojang classes were held mostly in the evenings, I could only manage both with my private dojang Seoul. As sad as this realization was to me, the excitement of my new path was greater.

Another issue that required my immediate attention was finding a place to live. After my military service ended, I was no longer allowed to live on the US base. Apartments in Seoul were few and far between, but families with large houses often rented out extra rooms as apartments.

Temporarily I was staying with Young Soon, but I needed to be closer to base. "We have an uncle living in Seoul," Young Soon told me. "Maybe you can live with him."

Job, Family and Dojang of His Own

I followed her direction to my uncle's house. It was large, but already overcrowded. "You can stay here," he said, seeming oblivious to the close quarters. "You can share a room with your cousin."

"Thank you," I said, with a silent vow to keep looking.

My cousin, whom I had met only once, was 17, and in his last year of high school. He was seldom in the room when I was, so this arrangement worked out well. Though closer to base than Young Soon, my uncle's house was still a 20-minute bus ride to the base. My impatience with the herky-jerky old bus and its many stops grew each day, but it showed me parts of Seoul I had never seen.

Within a few months, I met a family with a room to rent within walking distance of the base. They had two sons who had just left for their military service and seemed happy to have some of that empty space filled with another hungry young man. It also didn't hurt that my job provided me with enough money to pay my rent on time. With that important piece in place, I settled in to my new life with a contentment I had never before known.

Remembering what Grandmaster Park said at the completion of every promotion test, it was time to set a new goal. This, I decided, would be opening my own private dojang in Seoul. A little beyond my imagination lingered the idea of one day going to America to teach taekwondo, but my dojang was a concept I could take immediate action upon with every paycheck.

◊◊

My time off was in the mornings and early afternoons, so each morning until just after noon, I looked for a location for my private dojang. I knew it would be a while before I could save enough money, but I knew I needed to give my dream constant focus and attention in order for it to grow into reality. For a few minutes or a few hours each day I put active steps into moving this dream, inch by inch, toward actuality.

I visited Young Soon on one of these mornings to talk about my finances. In our culture at that time there were no banks; instead, we kept money flowing by banking with each other. When I first started my job, Young Soon and I decided that I would cash my paychecks on base every payday and then bring her the money. She would record my deposits in a little notebook with my name on it. She would then make loans she deemed to be good ones to others who came to her, and we would split the interest she was able to earn on my money.

"This is my brother's money," she would tell her customers as she went over her stern set of rules. "Be very careful with it."

On this day when I visited her, I wanted to see where I stood.

"Your money is growing fast, Won Chik," she said.

"Good!" I said. "I am saving everything I can to get my school open as soon as possible," I said, taking a sip of the tea and a bite of the fruit she prepared for my visit.

"Do you have a location?"

"Not yet."

I found several possible places, but none seemed quite right. I walked daily through several neighborhoods in the quiet area surrounding my uncle's house while I lived there. I liked the neighborhoods with a *da bang,* or coffee shop, on every street. The people I met throughout this area were friendly and nice. The houses and buildings were well maintained. This was the area that kept drawing my attention as I searched for the perfect location for my dojang.

The neighborhood da bang was where people gathered every day to talk, where information and gossip changed hands over coffee or tea; you could get to know a neighborhood very well just by visiting its da bangs. The da bang was its own kind of social institution where in addition to information shared, business was transacted, and courtships were conducted.

"Who is the owner here?" I asked one of the servers at one of my favorite da bangs one spring afternoon in 1968.

Before she could answer, a pleasant looking man turned from the group he was talking to and said, "Are you looking for the owner?"

"Yes."

"Why are you looking for him?" he asked, looking very serious. "Is he in trouble?" Then he laughed and bowed. "My name is Sang Kim and I own this place. How can I help you?"

"I am looking for a space to open a taekwondo dojang," I said. Do you have any space available here?"

"Oh, I don't know," he said. He looked up at the ceiling. "A taekwondo dojang would be very loud."

In Korea, land was a premium commodity. When a property owner wanted to expand, it was always upward. Although this building had three floors, his concern was valid. Jumping, running, takedowns, exercising and loud kihaps above his quiet coffee shop could be a problem.

"Do you have space?" I persisted.

"No," he said. "All of my spaces in all of my buildings are full." He peered at me. "But I like you. You've been here in here before." He looked at my American styled clothes. "Are you working at Yong San? Yong San was what the locals called the US Military Base.

"Yes," I answered. Maybe he could help me find someone who did have space in this area.

"What do you do there?"

"I am a taekwondo instructor for the United States military."

"Wow," he said, looking impressed. "How will you have time for a private business?"

"Taekwondo business is usually in the evening," I explained. "My job at Yong San is mostly during the day."

"Will you have employees?"

"I hope so," I said. "When I have enough students for more than one class a day, I will hire an assistant instructor from the Jidokwan Headquarters to help me."

"I see," he said. He began clearing an empty table.

"Do you know anyone who has space in this area?" I asked.

"No," he said. "Do you have any money?"

"Baik Man 1," I said, straight-faced. In Korea at that time, one US dollar was worth about $1,000 to $1,200 in Korean dollars. Baik Man 1 was the Korean expression for $1,000,000 — or any huge amount

of money unattainable by normal people. In Korea, the usual rental arrangement was to pay the entire amount of your lease up front, and the owner acts as the bank and holds the money for you, making your rent payments and then paying you the interest he is able to earn by loaning your money to others while you are there.

He laughed. "Baik Man 1? Wow! You're a rich taekwondo man!"

Now I laughed, too. "Ok, you got me. Maybe not Baik Man 1, but I have a very good job working for the US Government, and I have been saving almost everything. My sister has been helping me, and I think I have almost enough."

He nodded. "If you did have a taekwondo school in this building, what would you do about the noise? Can you do taekwondo quietly?"

I laughed again. "No, I'm afraid that is not possible." I paused. "Maybe there is a way to block the sound."

He considered this for a moment. "I'm not sure how you would do that, but maybe there is a way."

"Do you know a place?"

"Well, yes and no. Are you in a big hurry?"

"I want to open my school as soon as possible," I said.

"If you want to open your taekwondo school here in this building, I will build a top floor for you," he said. "Your taekwondo school can occupy the entire top floor of this building. Maybe it won't be too loud."

I couldn't believe my ears. Built just for my school? With everything set up for taekwondo from the start?

"Sit down," he said, gesturing at an empty table and ordering two cups of tea. He now seemed excited about the prospect of having a taekwondo dojang in his building. "What else do you need?"

"Not much," I said. Then, remembering recent thoughts about logistics, I added, "If possible, I would like to have a dressing room and a shower." By Korean standards at that time, this request may have seemed a bit extravagant, but in my situation, it was going to be essential for quick transitions between base and dojang.

"I can build you a shower and dressing room," Sang Kim said.

"Thank you!" I said.

We discussed the particulars of how and when this would all happen, and when I left the da bang that day I was delirious with excitement. My own dojang was becoming reality.

◊◊

As my personal plans continued to take shape, my job on base became a perfect blend of routine and challenge. The diversity of my students and the different branches of military they represented was interesting to me. Of all branches, it was the intensity, power and quickness of the Marines that I found easiest to mold into taekwondo proficiency.

I stood watching one of my military classes practicing their one-steps one sunny afternoon, smiling to myself as I remembered the first time I taught military officers, wondering if I could train them well enough and quickly enough to prepare them for unexpected hand-to-hand combat. I remembered the day I came to the American base to teach, wondering whether I could teach people whose culture and language were completely unknown to me. It all seemed like a wonderful dream to me as I walked slowly around each group of 10-15 officers from all branches of the US military, watching them practice the same things in the same way my own master taught me. The strength and precision of their technique told me I had succeeded on both counts.

Promotion tests, the best measure of both my teaching ability and my students' progress, had elevated many of my GI students and their family members to advanced levels. Many of these students wanted to train more, to practice every day, to learn more than they could in my class on base. I knew that once I got my private dojang open, many of my American students would want to come there to train to increase their knowledge and experience training in a real traditional Korean dojang.

Because no one knew for sure how long he would stay in Seoul, and many were getting deployed every day to Germany or Viet Nam, my US military students trained hard. They all had the goal of earning their black belt during their time in Seoul.

I went to Sang Kim's da bang every day to check on the progress of the top floor. With no construction experience, I could only ask Sang Kim what I could do to help. Some days there were things I could do, others not, but I hoped that seeing my willingness and my eagerness to help would make him hurry.

Every payday Young Soon gave me an update. My savings were growing with her expert handling, but as my space neared completion, I worried whether I would have enough by the time Sang Kim's top floor was ready.

"What can I do?" I asked Young Soon, hoping that her talent with money might now yield some magic trick for making it grow just a little bit faster.

"I don't know," she said, shaking her head. "You have saved almost everything you have earned, and I have gotten good interest with the loans I have made. You may just have to be patient a little while longer."

This was not what I wanted to hear. I slammed my hand down on the table. She jumped. I was immediately sorry for scaring her. "I'm sorry," I said.

She nodded her acceptance.

"I cannot be patient. I have students who need this dojang now, before they have to leave. They will bring more students and the community will see that I am a good teacher by the students I have already taught. If I wait, they may go back to the US or somewhere else, and I will have to start all over the way all schools do."

I knew from my many discussions with Grandmaster Park and others at the Jidokwan headquarters that it usually takes about three months to get enough students to break even on expenses. But with my classes already established on base, I already had a good base of dedicated students. Even a handful of these coming to my dojang to train would do much to attract local students.

I also believed that mixing my classes in this way would give my American students a rare opportunity to really get to know Koreans and Korean culture — and a way to show my Korean friends and students how wonderful it is to get to know these Americans. As I discovered in my own teaching, in taekwondo class, language and culture are secondary to physical expression and the universal nature of this ancient art. A snap kick is a snap kick, regardless of what you call it, and it looks and works the same in any culture. Human arms and legs all move in pretty much the same way, and I was always amazed at how fast my students' differences disappeared once class began.

"You are right, you must not wait," Young Soon said. "I will loan you the rest of the money so you can open your school as soon as the space is ready."

"How can you do that?" I asked, looking in the direction of the room where her husband sat.

"I have saved a little bit here and there on my own," she said. "For an emergency."

"But this is not an emergency," I said, humbled by her offer, wanting to take it, yet worried that it would take away her emergency savings.

She shrugged. "It's a loan," she said. "You will pay me back." She smiled that coy and mischievous sister smile I always remembered when I thought of my older sister. "With *big* interest."

"Big interest," I agreed, hugging her. "Thank you."

She smiled at me again, this time the warm smile of a mother. "I wish our parents were here to see how well you have done," she said. "They would be so impressed with you." She playfully shoved my shoulder with her dainty hand. "You and your big American job."

Leaving Young Soon's house that afternoon, I knew my own dojang was now within reach.

The next weekend I went to Pusan to ask Grandmaster Park for his recommendation to take my 5th dan promotion test. I was 27 years old, the minimum age for taking the promotion that would earn me the title of Master, another dream fulfilled.

I entered my old dojang, surprised at my emotional response to its familiar smell. It was my first time back since I left for my military service, and to my delight nothing had changed. With all the change that punctuated my life, I took great comfort that in this place, at least, life was constant. Like home.

I bowed to Grandmaster Park, and then our greeting turned into a fierce hug. Not demonstrative by nature, this told me above all else how glad he was to see me back here, where I belonged. It surprised me, therefore, that he encouraged me to open my school in Seoul instead. "Your students are there, your experience is there, your life is there," he said. "I hoped that you would take over my school when I retire, but your best opportunity is in Seoul. So now," he said, his eyes revealing a shift to humor, "I can never retire."

"That's good news for your students," I told him, smiling. "Thank you for understanding and always supporting me."

He bowed to me, then shook my hand. "How could I do anything else?" he asked, eyes glistening.

For the past several months, my letters to my master kept him apprised of my activities and progress, and his responses were always informative and encouraging. Hearing and seeing this support in person, however, affirmed its truth, and I was glad to share my latest news about the loan from Young Soon.

"I also came here today for another reason," I said.

He gave me a playful sideways glance. "I see," he said with mock seriousness. "And what might that be?"

"To ask for your recommendation to take my 5th dan promotion test," I said.

He paused, as if considering this request. Then he smiled. "I thought you would never ask," he said. "Of course you can have my recommendation. When would you like to test?"

"As soon as possible," I said. Hoping not to sound too presumptuous, I added, "By the time my dojang opens I hope to be Master Park."

"Master Park," he said, letting the words roll out slowly. "That has a nice sound to it." We laughed together at his play on our names. "Congratulations on your dojang and good luck on your 5th dan promotion test," he said when we parted.

When I completed my 5th dan test in Seoul the following month,

Job, Family and Dojang of His Own

it was my master's face I remembered through each movement, each poomse, and each technique. Because of his dedication to teaching, what I learned from him formed an indelible stamp on everything I did, everything I was. My only hope for my future as a taekwondo master was that I would be as good a master to my own students as my master was to me.

◊◊

After my children's class one afternoon, as people began to arrive to warm up for the family class that would begin next, an American man dressed in civilian clothes ambled into Trent Gym. "I'm looking for a Won Chik Park," he said.

"Yes?" I said. "I am Won Chik Park."

"We are making a movie about taekwondo," the man said. "At the end of the movie we are doing a short, three-minute feature about how American military and families stationed in Korea are learning taekwondo – and how because of this, taekwondo is now being introduced to the rest of the world. We would like permission to film one of your children's classes."

My class? I thought. *With me teaching it? Wow.* "Did you get permission from my commanding officer?"

"Yes," He said. He handed me a letter and signed consent form.

"Sure," I said. "When?"

"When is your next children's class?"

"Thursday afternoon at four o'clock," I said.

"We'll be here by 2:30 to set up," he said. He extended his hand. I shook it and bowed at the same time. He returned my bow, a quiet connection of our two cultures.

When Thursday came and they arrived as promised, I tried to teach my class just as always, but with this new challenge of holding the children's attention despite the cameras, cameramen and electrical cords surrounding them. "Keep your eyes on me," I told them before class. "Today we are all taekwondo movie stars, and taekwondo movie stars must focus on taekwondo."

Amused at this thought, they tried very hard not to look at the cameras. I did the same.

The movie, called "Il Kyok Pil Sal," meaning "one strike must kill" was shot at several locations in Seoul. When the director told me the title, I thought how often in my training I had heard that expression — how my understanding of it had changed now that I was teaching soldiers. From Wan Kyu's wide-eyed, boyish explanation to the great reverence in my master's voice as he explained this ancient teaching. *"Il Kyok Pil Sal"* means that we must make our kicks and strikes so powerful that if we needed them to defend ourselves against a serious attack, it would only take one kick to disable or kill our attacker. I smiled as I remembered the first time I had stopped the bag with my side kick.

"Il Kyok Pil Sal," I repeated. I smiled at the director. "Good name for a movie!"

"Il Kyok Pil Sal," probably one of the first movies ever made about taekwondo. Even though it was not much of a popular success, it created quite a stir on base. A reporter from *Stars and Stripes* interviewed me, and the movie was shown in Seoul's local theatre. I went with a group of students to see the film on its opening night. When the movie trailer shot in my class began, the first thing onscreen was a big close-up of my face. I laughed right out loud.

The student next to me looked surprised. "What's so funny?"

"My face!" I was laughing so hard now I could barely speak. "My face is right up there on the movie screen! Won Chik Park, movie star!"

He still looked puzzled about why this was so funny to me.

Seeing his confusion, I tried to explain. "My face is up there, so big!" I said, still laughing. "It's funny to see!"

He shrugged and returned to his popcorn.

As my children's class did a kicking exercise on the screen, the announcer said, "US Army instructor Won Chik Park teaches taekwondo to the families and children of US military personnel at Yong San military base, our US military headquarters in Seoul, South Korea."

I elbowed the student next to me and pointed at the screen, "See?" I said, "there's 'Won Chik Park!' I'm a movie star!"

The student laughed then, too, most likely because it was all so funny to me.

◊◊

My rapport with my children's class was automatic. They seemed oblivious to any language issues, because children like to learn by imitation. They also seemed to enjoy my clowning around, but when I raised the intensity and demonstrated correct technique for them, their eyes were big and their efforts sincere. I had never taught young children before, and once I realized the limits of their attention spans, I learned to change activities often and use lots of examples and demonstrations to keep their attention.

While motivating children was far different from working with adults, I was gratified by how quickly they learned, how much detail they retained and how steady their progress.

"I need to talk to you about my son," a well-known Army major said as he entered my office one day after the children's class. His son, a stocky boy, had a very hard time paying attention in class and his father was concerned.

"What's wrong, Major?" I said, wondering why he would speak about his son as if the boy was not standing right there with us. The boy's head was down; he was embarrassed. I looked at the boy and then back at his father. "Is there a problem?"

"I'm very disappointed that my son is not listening to you," the Major said. "He's not paying attention in your class." He looked at his son and said in deep military tone, "Attention!"

The boy, who could not have been more than seven years old, started to cry.

"Don't you understand what that means?" the dad yelled.

The boy cried harder, head still down, even more embarrassed. It was the first time I saw a father talk to his son that way. Being a child

Job, Family and Dojang of His Own

of a high-ranking military officer must be a hard life.

"I understand your feeling," I said, keeping my tone soft and low. "And since you're military, you have big expectations for your own son. But this is a good boy. He tries very hard in my class." I looked at the boy who was still crying and thought of Sung Hoon. Then I looked squarely at the father. "He is still young," I said. "You cannot expect everyone to behave like military soldiers."

I realized I was taking a risk by saying this to an officer. I knew didn't want to risk drawing that anger toward myself, but something within me felt so protective of this boy. I realized I had no idea what it was like to be a father, but by then I had encountered enough children in class to understand that with different levels of maturity it sometimes takes a little more flexibility to teach them what we want them to know. His love for his son was evident, but his approach was misguided.

Hearing my words, the Major softened a bit. "I understand what you're saying," he said, "but I want my son to learn to pay attention. The reason he is here is to learn better self-discipline; he is also having problems with this at school."

"Taekwondo will teach him both discipline and focus," I said. "Please be patient. Continued taekwondo training will achieve the result you are looking for." I looked at the boy who had by now stopped sobbing. "Without yelling."

Sure enough, by the time the boy reached green belt, there were no more bad reports coming from school, and his attention improved in my class, as well. Just after he got his green belt, the family was transferred. I have often wondered what happened in that boy's life, and how his taekwondo training made a difference. I realized with this incident that teaching taekwondo to children was training them for a different kind of combat.

◊◊

In addition to my children's classes, which were a blend of elementary school, middle school, and high school students, another new experience for me was teaching taekwondo to women. With the wives of many army officers now in my family class, I realized that taekwondo was good for women. In fact, because taekwondo relies more on the natural strength of legs than upper body strength, and, as I knew from personal experience, being smaller could sometimes be an advantage, the women in my classes proved to be among my best students.

Having this new mixture of students made no difference to my teaching. I treated all my students and all my classes the same, regardless of their age, level, occupation, race or gender. I began to see how, even though every taekwondo student learns the same techniques, practices the same basics, and builds proficiency step by step, each person's expression of taekwondo's physical, mental and spiritual attributes is as unique as they are. Once I understood this, and putting cultural expectations aside, I realized that teaching women was no different from teaching anyone else. Often, their strength and grit surprised me.

"Mr. Park?" Julia, a 42-year-old Hawaiian woman who enrolled in my family class, was on her way out of Trent Gym after class, and today she was wearing a pilot's jump suit. She was married to an engineer who worked on the base, and both Julia and their son, Peter, were excellent blue belt students in my class.

"Yes?" I said. I liked talking with Julia — it was always a good opportunity to practice my English, and I never knew what the day's topic might be. Often, Julia talked about how much she loved to fly. In fact, she was working on her pilot's license. This amused me. It was not only beyond my understanding how one of those large metal contraptions could ever stay in the air in the first place, but with a *woman* as pilot? Julia was different from any woman I had ever known, and she was very serious about her flying lessons. With each conversation, my curiosity about flying began to grow.

"How do I look?" she asked, turning around in front of me. "Do you see anything different about me?"

I looked at her, up and down. Something was different, but more in her manner than in her appearance. "You look very nice," I said. "What's new?"

"I got my pilot's license!" she said. Her expression reminded me of a little girl, giddy with excitement.

"Congratulations!" I said.

"Now I can take you up!"

"OK," I said. This thought was terrifying to me on many levels, but I could not let her know that.

"Do you want to go today?"

"Go where?" I asked, trying to buy a little time. I took care to keep my face neutral. I didn't want to dampen her enthusiasm, but I was very concerned.

"Oh, just around Seoul," she said gesturing in a big circle in the air around her. "We'll stay close to the base."

She *does* have her license, I thought. *They wouldn't give it to her unless she knew how to fly, would they?* My nervousness began to yield to my curiosity. I looked at my watch. I was finished with classes for the day and didn't have to be back for the night class for several hours. I had planned to go visit Young Soon and stop at the market for some food, but all of that could wait. *I will fly in an airplane,* I thought. *Today.* I also knew that if I didn't go right then I might never do it.

"OK, I can go this afternoon," I said, wondering what I had just gotten myself into.

We arrived at the hangar, and Julia led the way to the plane. I walked all the way around the plane; it was much smaller than I imagined. *Maybe that's good,* I reasoned. *Not so much weight to keep up in the air.* I climbed into the seat, trying tried not to let my anxiety show.

Julia started the engine. As the plane roared to full throttle, my nerves revved right along with it. *What have I done?* I asked myself over and over as the plane taxied into position for takeoff. In any of my life's true perils, I was never as frightened as I was in that moment. I leaned over to look at the ground as the plane started to move forward. Too late to change my mind. I closed my eyes in silent prayer.

"Do you trust me?" Julia yelled over the engine noise.

"Yes, I trust you," I yelled back. *I must be crazy*, I thought.

Once up in the air, Julia began to play, showing me what she could do with the plane. She banked the plane into a steep turn, dived, and then pulled it back up. The engine coughed. My stomach lurched. I tried to think of something else. I wondered if I would throw up. I was glad I had not had lunch. I kept my eyes fixed on a single spot on the horizon in front of me for most of the flight.

"There's the Han!" she said, gesturing.

Please keep your hands on the steering wheel, my thoughts implored. Then I willed myself to take a peek at the winding Han River below us.

The Han River runs east and west, at the edge of our safe zone. As I looked down from this new perspective at the geographic separator between Korea's north and south, I was filled with sorrow. So many people had died there during the war. In 1950, when the South Korean government moved south, the military destroyed all the bridges across the Han in a decisive statement of the permanence of this division. I was glad the plane's engine noise made it too difficult to talk, leaving me alone with my thoughts.

In what seemed like several hours, but was more like 40 minutes, we landed. I quickly unbuckled the seatbelt and climbed to the safety of the ground. I bowed to thank Julia for the airplane ride, and then I shook her hand. The idea of a woman flying a plane was now not so strange after all.

"Did you like it?" she asked, eager to see my reaction.

"Oh yes, it was very nice," I said. "I had a very good time." Inside, all I could think was, *Whew! I am so glad it is over and I didn't die.*

"We'll go again soon!" she said.

"Yes, very soon," I said.

◊◊

Job, Family and Dojang of His Own

As the US Military Force Headquarters in Seoul, Yong San was the center of all kinds of activities involving American soldiers from all its military branches. With the rise in popularity of taekwondo competition, and remembering the excitement and fun of team competition, I wanted to offer the taekwondo tournament experience to my students.

Using the Jidokwan team tournaments I participated in as a model, I wanted to create a competition that included Yong San as well as the many smaller bases throughout South Korea. I approached Captain Sullivan, who was in charge of the 8th US Army Special Service Department, with this idea. I told him of the tournaments I had competed in and how exciting they were, both for participants and spectators.

"I think it would be a good thing for building good relationships between all the US military bases," I said. "People who have been training in taekwondo at all these bases would enjoy this kind of friendly competition."

"OK," he said. "Let's try it. I'll let the appropriate people know that we'll be hosting it here in Trent Gym and we'll let you know what dates are available. You just keep me informed and let me know what you need. Thank you, Master Park. I think this is a very good idea."

The 8th US Army Headquarters sent out a news release about the American Military Taekwondo Championship, and as I had guessed, all of the other Korean base instructors were excited about bringing their American students to the competition to see how they would stack up against the students of other instructors on other bases. It was an idea everyone got behind, including the students who understood that this was a once-in-a-lifetime experience.

Many of the Armed Forces Network sports and entertainment shows talked about the tournament, and Bob Hope even mentioned it in his shows. As the publicity built, I thought, *what have I gotten myself into? Can I really do this?* For the first time I felt nervous about my inexperience at running this tournament that suddenly had gone from just a fun idea to a major event with everyone's eyes on me.

The publicity was effective. We had about 60 competitors in all, and while many of them were my students, there was a good mix of students from all eight states of South Korea. One master I had never met before brought 17 students. We set up just one ring in the old Trent Gym, and we all rotated duties. The experience most of us had acquired by fighting in tournaments served us well. Everyone, from participants and instructors to my Korean friends there to help, seemed to have a good time. At the end of the tournament we all had dinner together in the base dining hall to celebrate what we all agreed was just the first of a wonderful annual event.

Captain Sullivan stood up after dinner and thanked everyone for coming and for participating. "I was very impressed with the quality of this tournament and the hard work everyone did to make it happen," he said. He turned to me. "Thank you, Master Won Chik Park, for your idea to have this tournament and the leadership you provided for this special event. I especially thank you for inviting and letting us get to know the many Korean instructors and masters who helped make the first annual American Military Taekwondo Championship such a success. You have created memories that these American competitors will cherish for the rest of their lives."

When word got out of success of the American Military Taekwondo Championship, it was all the encouragement the Korea Taekwondo Association needed to move forward with plans for their own sanctioned "Foreigners Tournament." Although there had already been some talk of doing this, the Association had been hesitant, unsure of how successful it would be. Now, with such a good result to use as a model and volunteers who were excited to help do it again, the tracks were laid for the KTA "foreigners" tournaments.

◊◊

I was standing just outside my office in Trent Gym, talking with my new assistant instructor, Jin Song Chung. The growth of my classes and the popularity of the Yong San taekwondo program had prompted the assignment of another young Korean instructor here. Just as I had been, Jin Song was sent to Yong San to help me teach and to learn how to teach American GIs. Jin Son Chung was a strong young competitor and was learning to be a good teacher. After only a few weeks, we were already good friends.

The gym door creaked open and a tall, lanky American sauntered in. He bowed to us, and then shook each of our hands. "Specialist Roy Kurban," he said. "I am the new coordinator of Trent Gym."

American military personnel came and went constantly — it was hard to keep up with the changing inhabitants in the back offices where they worked. We nodded.

"Welcome to Trent Gym, Specialist Kurban," I said, smiling. "If I can help you, please let me know."

"Thank you," he said. He continued to stand there, something else on his mind. He cleared his throat. "So," he said, looking at our doboks, "Y'all do taekwondo?"

"Yes," I said. Jin Song said nothing.

"Y'all want to spar sometime?" Specialist Kurban asked, adding, "I have my black belt in Karate."

I felt Jin Song stiffen beside me. His English was not yet good, and he did not yet understand the ways of Americans, so I knew he was considering this a challenge.

I looked at this American and said in a soft voice that I hoped would calm Jin Song down. "Specialist Kurban, maybe you would like to join our class."

"Yes sir, I would!" Specialist Kurban said, bowing, undaunted. "I would like that very much. When is my class?"

"Be ready for class here at 3:00 pm on Monday," I said.

"I'll be there!" he said, "and please, call me Roy."

We watched him saunter back to his new office.

Jin Song glowered.

"It's OK," I told him. "Americans are just different. They don't know Korean culture, and sometimes their manners are not what we expect. We will learn much more about this American in class on Monday."

Jin Song laughed. "I guess I do have a lot to learn about these Americans and their ways," he agreed.

When the GIs lined up for Monday afternoon class, Specialist Roy Kurban was among them. Watching him warm up, I saw that he was very strong and powerful. The precision and power of his movements also told me that he had put a lot of time, discipline and passion into his training. In spite of his American brashness and bravado, there was something about this guy I liked.

"Specialist Kurban!" I called him to the front of the class. "Will you help me with a demonstration?"

He puffed out his chest. "Yes, sir!" he said, ambling to the front of the room to where I stood. We bowed to each other.

"Today we will practice front snap kick, *ahp chagi*," I said to the room full of students. I heard a little bit of muttering toward the back of the class, and it brought back the memory of my own impatience.

Remembering the words of my own master at these times, I said, "Basics are everything. Basics are the foundation, and taekwondo is the house. Upon your basic movements everything else is built. If your basics are strong, your taekwondo will be strong. That is why we work on them every day. Even if you're high ranking, there is always more to learn. Let me show you an example."

"Sparring position please, Specialist Kurban," I said. He complied with a loud *kihap*. *Good spirit*, I thought.

"As a green belt or blue belt, we have a pretty good *ahp chagi*," I said, delivering a solid, medium-paced front snap kick to Specialist Kurban's chest. Standing solid, he didn't even flinch. *Good conditioning, good composure*, I thought.

"Then later, after much more practice and training on this simple, basic kick, *ahp chagi* can look like this," I said, delivering a lightening-fast front snap kick to the same spot on Specialist Kurban's chest. I was careful to check my power at the last second, not allowing my kick to penetrate as I would in a real life, self-defense situation, but he doubled over and gasped for breath, unable to conceal his shock at the force behind such an innocuous kick.

"Basics are everything," I told the class, patting Roy on the back. His color was returning and his breath was starting to flow easier. "Thank you, Specialist Kurban," I said. We bowed to each other and he returned to his place. He never asked to spar with me again.

After class he came to my office. He bowed as he entered the doorway. "I just wanted to tell you, sir," he said, "that I have fought in a lot of full contact, no-holds-barred karate tournaments in the States against some of the biggest, meanest heavyweight fighters on the American karate tournament circuit."

I sat still. I couldn't imagine what he was going to say next.

"I have to tell you that I have never encountered a front snap kick that hard and fast in my life." He smiled and bowed to me again. "I am so honored to be here and I want to learn whatever you are willing to teach me."

◊◊

The telephone rang one morning at about 6:00 am, startling me out of a very sound sleep. It was Ung Chik.

"Won Chik, are you awake?" he asked.

"No, I was sleeping," I said. "It's very early. Is everything OK?"

"It's almost 7:00!" he said, ignoring my question. "Can you meet me at the *da bang* near my house at 7:30? I have something to tell you."

"What's wrong?" I asked, my alarm growing.

"Nothing wrong," he said. "It's exciting news and I have to tell you now. Come meet me!"

"OK," I said, knowing better than to argue. Once Ung Chik got a thing in his head he would not let it go.

When I arrived at the *da bang,* just after seven and he was already there.

"What is it that is so important?" I asked once the waitress had brought our coffee.

"Good news!" he said.

"What about?"

"You! Your life!" He handed me a small picture of a beautiful girl.

"This is my friend's sister, Yunbok. "We have set up your meeting with her."

"You're crazy," I said, handing him back the picture. Most of my knowledge of girls so far was limited to my friends' sisters; I had never dated anyone, and right now, with my dojang about to open and my busy teaching schedule, settling down was the very last thing on my mind.

"I'm your big brother and this is good for you," he said, undaunted. "I know the family and we have already set a time and place for you to meet her. You have to show up."

I sighed. He was not going to let up unless I agreed to meet this girl. I looked at the smiling picture again. She had a very nice face and intelligent eyes. "I suppose I can meet her," I told him, "but I don't have time right now for dating. I am opening my dojang soon and I have no free time."

"I know all that," he said. "Just meet her. If you meet her and say no, I will not bring it up again."

"OK," I said, handing him back the picture. "Where does she live?"

"Inchon"

"Inchon?" I did not have time for a trip out of town to meet this girl.

"It's not that far," Ung Chik said. "Just a few miles from Seoul."

"Seoul's big," I said.

"Just be at this address at 1:00 this Thursday afternoon," he said, writing down an address on a piece of paper.

"That's just two days from now!" I said, searching my mind for something else I had to do at that time. Nothing.

"Why wait?" he said, pushing the piece of paper across the table toward me.

Why wait indeed, I thought, finishing my coffee. Sometimes my brother was too meddlesome for his own good.

◊◊

Precise Korean rules and customs surround meeting, dating and courtship. These were rules I only knew of from hearing my friends

Job, Family and Dojang of His Own

talk. Un Chik tried his best to explain them all to me at once. "The girl's father and brothers bring her to the da bang for the first meeting," he said. "They will introduce her to you and then leave. You will have about two hours to talk to each other, and then they will return to pick her up."

"What will we talk about?" I asked. I had no idea how any of this was supposed to go or what I would say to this girl. Since I was only meeting her to humor my brother I wasn't too concerned — I just didn't want to embarrass him.

"Don't worry," he said. "She is very easy to talk to. You will have no trouble at all. It is a very good family. I think you will like them."

Following Ung Chik's directions, I arrived just before 1:00 pm on Thursday at the small Inchon da bang where I was to meet Yunbok. Soft music was playing, and when she walked through the door with her father and brother a few minutes later, I recognized her right away from her picture. If anything, she was even more beautiful in person.

"I'm Won Chik Park," I said, greeting her father first, and then her brothers, just as Ung Chik told me to do. They seemed pleased that I did this.

In return, they introduced Yunbok. The sound of her voice matched the laughter in her eyes, but again I wondered, what will we talk about for two hours?

As if hearing my thoughts, her father and brothers left. Two hours. Already this was harder than I thought it would be. I smiled at Yunbok. She smiled back. Now what?

With halting awkwardness we chose a table and sat down. She seemed amused at my unschooled ways, and willing to be patient.

We ordered tea, and talked, first sticking to easy pleasantries and small talk, but as I began to see her intelligence and hear her well-spoken thoughts and opinions, I found myself talking with her just like I would anyone else. Soon I forgot that we were on a date, and we began to laugh and talk like old friends.

I was surprised at the depth of her knowledge about so many different things, and she seemed fascinated by my stories of teaching on the US base and my plans for opening my dojang. Even with no knowledge of taekwondo, her grasp of its impact on my life was immediate. Yunbok was so unlike any of the silly, flighty girls I had observed in the distance. Maybe my brother was right. I felt better after spending time with her. And I couldn't wait to see her again.

Before we knew it, our two hours was over. I left the da bang and returned to Seoul to find Kyon Won, my best friend at that time, to tell him all the details about this mysterious girl my brother found for me.

"She was nice," I told him, trying to hide my excitement. "She's very beautiful — and very smart. I really enjoyed talking to her."

He took a step back. "Might be time to settle down?" he said.

"Oh no," I assured him, "I only went to meet her because of Ung Chik."

"Are you going to see her again?"

"Yes."

"I see." He didn't say anything else, but I knew what he was thinking. To my surprise, part of me hoped he was right.

Thanks again to Ung Chik, the next meeting was set — this time with Yunbok's mother and aunt. According to Korean custom, if the father and brothers approved, the women of the family would want to meet me next. If that went well, I would be invited to the family home to meet the rest of the family.

"When can I meet her?" Kyon Won asked. We were having coffee in the da bang below my future dojang. This was an interesting question. Since they already knew my brother and sister and their families, and I had no parents, there was no one else for them to meet. Why not Kyon Won? I valued my friend's objective opinion, and more than that, I wanted to show her off to him.

"You can meet her next week," I said. I wasn't sure how this would fit with tradition, but I told him to come to the coffee shop after Yunbok's mother left, and then to leave right away to meet me later so we could catch the bus back to Seoul together.

At the designated time, I arrived once again at the same Inchon da bang, nerves fluttering much more than the first time we met. This

Job, Family and Dojang of His Own

time I cared.

Yunbok entered the da bang with her mother and aunt. I could see the family resemblance right away. Yunbok's mother was also beautiful, revealing the radiant mature beauty in store for Yunbok in the future. Just like her daughter had, Yunbok's mother put me at immediate ease with her intelligent conversation and easy laughter. Yunbok's aunt was quiet, but joined the conversation and laughter enough to show that this was an easy family to be with. Ung Chik was right, I thought. These are very good people.

"Would you like to meet my best friend?" I asked Yunbok as soon as they left.

"She smiled. "Of course!" Then she looked around. "How?"

As if on cue — and at our prearranged signal, Won Kyon walked through the door.

Yunbok laughed. "What would you have done if I had said no?" she asked, eyes twinkling.

"I would have told him to leave," I said.

The conversation between the three of us was awkward at first, but once again Yunbok's perfect ease relaxed the situation, and before I knew it we were all talking and laughing together. Every time Yunbok smiled she grew more beautiful to me.

"Would you like to come to our home for dinner and meet the rest of the family?" Yunbok's mother asked me as we got ready to leave. She was extending the invitation for the next official step in the courtship ritual. Ung Chik had prepared me for this.

"Yes," I said, bowing. "It would be my pleasure."

"You're a lucky man," Kyon Won said on the way back to Seoul.

"You really think so?" I asked. His opinion no longer mattered. As I returned to base to teach my evening classes I knew I was walking, but I felt as if my feet were floating several inches above the ground.

◊◊

When the work on my dojang began, I checked its progress almost daily. Then, with my activities on the base, the tournament, and my courtship with Yunbok, my checks became less frequent. One day, when a week had passed since my last visit, I entered the da pang and sought out Sang Kim.

"Come and see for yourself, Master Park," he said, leading the way up the narrow stairs.

He opened the door and stepped aside with a grand flourish, inviting me to enter.

The sight before me brought tears to my eyes. It was finished. Looking to be about 1500 square feet of open space, its clean expanse stretched out before me. At the front hung a Korean flag, just as I described.

He bowed. "Do you like it?"

"Oh yes!" I said, shaking his hand, and then hugging him, then slapping him on the back in the way I had seen very happy Americans do. This surprised him and he took a step back.

"Sorry, I said, "I am very excited. Thank you very much for all this hard work. This is beautiful. What now?"

"Inspect everything closely," he said. "If you say it is ready, then pay your rent and open your school."

I walked slowly around the room. On the far left side Sang Kim had sectioned off an area to be used as a dressing room. In it he had put a shower, just as I requested, with several showerheads, just like on the American military base. Working only from a picture I drew for him, he had done everything exactly right. Not only would this make it easier for me to go between jobs, but this would also be a great help when my American students needed to shower before returning to base. This was the set-up they were accustomed to.

My only concern was the concrete floor. Wood floors were much better for taekwondo — not as slick as concrete and, because wood gives a little bit with repeated jumping, easier on feet, knees and ankles.

I turned to Sang Kim. "Everything is wonderful, and I appreciate everything you have done. Do you think it would be possible to add a wood floor on top of this concrete, with maybe a small space between the wood and concrete? Adding wood would make a better surface for taekwondo and an even better sound barrier for your customers below."

Sang Kim thought a minute. "I understand what you are saying," he said, "but I have done all I can. If you want to add wood, that is fine with me, but you will have to pay for it and do it yourself."

While this seemed fair, it posed a problem. Even though I was almost certain that Young Soon would loan me a little more money for the floor, and I could do all the preparation myself, I did not know the first thing about laying a wood floor in a way that would be smooth and even with no cracks, gaps or splinters.

"Do you know anyone who lays wood floors?" I asked Sang Kim. "Do you know where I could get a load of wood shavings?"

"Yes," he said, "I know both. I will be happy to make these calls for you, and then we can work out the details and payment."

For the next several weeks I went every day to my school and worked on preparing the floor. First I built a support frame just as the floor man instructed. when he approved my work, I ordered a load of wood shavings. Bucket by bucket, I hauled the shavings up three flights of stairs and filled in all the spaces between the 2x4's of my frame. When this was done, I called the floor man. "I'm ready for my floor now," I told him, exhausted but exhilarated.

While the floor was being finished, I used two leftover 2x4s to build a *dalyun ki* just like Grandmaster Park had in the corner of his dojang. When I asked him how to build it, he explained that a dalyun ki was actually made of two six-foot-long 2x4s, set with their 4-inch sides parallel, standing on end. There should be a space between them, he told me, wider at the bottom and then narrowing toward the top. In much the same way as the space beneath the floor, this space would give a little bit with contact to create a slight cushion to protect hands, feet and elbows. Two 6-8-inch target areas, one near the top for striking and one in the middle for kicking, should be wrapped in thick rope for extra cushioning and to provide a visual target for focused striking practice.

Once complete, I put my dalyun ki in the same corner of my dojang as my master had his, smiling as I remembered the time when the electricity went out while I was punching that dalyun ki. I looked down at my hands now, still proud of the size of the knuckles that were a permanent reminder of the focus of my practice that day. Once I overheard Roy Kurban tell someone about my "giant knuckles and forearms like Popeye." Even though I had no idea who "Popeye" was, by the awe in his voice I knew it was a compliment.

I used the last of my money to purchase a heavy bag. Since boxing was still a huge national sport in Korea, I had no trouble locating one in a nearby sporting goods store.

"Will it be OK to hang this up there?" I asked Sang Kim when he stopped by to check on my progress.

He looked at the bag, and then at his newly constructed ceiling and roof. "We'll need to reinforce the beam," he said.

"How do we do that?" I asked.

"I will help you," he said. He reappeared a few minutes later with his tools, lumber and more hardware, and together we reinforced the beam and hung the bag.

We stood back to admire our handiwork, and then we looked around the room. Suddenly, in the soft afternoon light coming through its high row of new windows, this space was a real dojang. From gleaming wood to the uniform hooks on the walls, to the heavy bag, dalyun ki, and Korean flag, my dojang was ready at last. Tears gathered at the backs of my eyes. My biggest dream was at last reality.

"If you want to take this wood floor with you if you ever leave here, you can," Sang Kim said.

Jolted out of my reverie, I looked at him, puzzled.

"I like you," he said. "I hope you stay here for a long time. You have worked very hard to make your dojang just right. But since you paid for the floors, they are yours to keep if you ever need them." He tapped the floor with the toe of his shoe. "This is a good improvement," he said. "Downstairs we will not be able to hear all the jumping and yelling."

I spent the next two weeks, every morning before work and every evening after my last class, preparing flyers and advertisements about the school's opening. Master Park and many others warned me not to expect students for about three months, but I knew it would be sooner because of my students on the base who wanted to train there.

I also knew that as soon as I made the announcement on base I would have to be there every day, ready to teach whoever showed up. This immediate activity, plus my advertising efforts in the surrounding neighborhoods would soon attract others. From there, word of mouth would do my marketing for me.

I realized that attracting local Korean students, especially those shy about mixing with my American students, could take a little bit of time. However, with only a few happy locals in my classes, I could share with the Seoul community what I had discovered about Americans and taekwondo — and how the language of blocks, kicks, punches, and poomse is universal.

To market any new business in South Korea at that time, you first had to register it with the local police and pay for a permit. With this permit, registered businesses could put their advertisements on street bulletin boards for one month. After that the business owner was required to either take them all down or renew his permit. With just enough money left for one month's permit, I knew I needed to make my one month count.

Walking Seoul's busiest streets and intersections with an armload of flyers every morning, I papered the entire city with my announcement of the opening of the Won Park Institute of Taekwondo, with a special offer for those who enrolled during its first month. With Sang Kim's permission, I also made a giant sign to put on the outside of his building, as well as posting the flyers in his da bang. As I posted flyers each day, I also stopped in to visit any elementary, middle and high schools I passed that were within walking distance of my dojang. Remembering my visit with my own high school principal, I told these principals, teachers and students about how taekwondo improves focus, discipline, self-confidence and respect.

Even though my paycheck depended on my teaching taekwondo to soldiers, teaching children and teenagers was what I enjoyed most. In them I saw the most dramatic results, the biggest transformation; to bring the benefits of taekwondo into a young life was my greatest reward. Because of all taekwondo meant to me when I was young, teaching children and teenagers allowed me to relive those wonderful moments and training milestones again and again, connecting my past, present and future.

Taking into consideration the differences in attention span and maturity levels I discovered while teaching children on base, I decided to offer more classes, geared more to age than belt level. To do this, I needed an assistant to cover for me at the dojang when I had to be teaching on base. I put the word out at the Jidokwan headquarters, knowing the right person would appear. In answer, the Jidokwan headquarters kept me supplied with a steady stream of young instructors eager for teaching experience and the opportunity to practice English with my American students.

Teaching my first class in my own dojang was a moment I will never forget. I looked at the 20 or so expectant faces lined up and ready to begin, and I felt a wave of goose bumps. I did it! Between the base students and local interest from my flyers and school visits, I managed to fill my classes from the very first day. I thought of all the people who had made it possible for me to be standing here. I thought of the all the miracles in my life and how, no matter what had happened, there had always been one or two people who had reached out to help me, just as those unseen hands had lifted me over the side of the boat on that fateful day that started my unexpected life's journey. I fought back a surge of happy tears. I am a taekwondo master, I thought. This is my school. My dream has come true. My next thought was of Yunbok. Now a new dream can begin.

◊◊

Job, Family and Dojang of His Own

Dinner with Yunbok's family went just as well as our da bang coffee dates. From the moment I had entered their very traditional Korean home, I felt complete ease — a far cry from the feeling I remembered all too well when I entered Ung Chik's future inlaws' home on that pivotal, hungry day that seemed several lifetimes ago.

As I did then, I removed my shoes and entered the house, feeling all eyes on me. But this time I met these eyes and smiled. Scurrying and giggling behind an ornate screen told me more eyes were inspecting me from there. This was a very big family that I loved in an instant.

Following Korean custom, Yunbok's mother entered with a tray of fruit, followed by a tray of tea. Yunbok's sister came in first and introduced herself. Then, one by one, family members came in and introduced themselves to me. As their warmth surrounded me, I knew that they liked me as much as I liked them. We shared a wonderful meal and by the time I left, any trace of doubt was gone.

"When are you going to make a decision?" Ung Chik asked early the next morning in another impatient wake-up call.

This time I didn't argue with him at all. I was too happy to be annoyed.

"Yes," I said. "My decision is yes." I had no idea how I was going to add marriage to my already overcrowded life, but I knew I wanted Yunbok to be in my life always. I thanked God for sending her to me and asked Him to help me figure it all out. I knew He would, because He always had.

Our engagement party came next. Following tradition, Ung Chik and Young Soon, acting as my family, first met with Yunbok's family to plan this important event. Yunbok and I were there, too, and everyone's opinion was considered. The date and location was set and plans transformed into action. Before I knew it, the party date arrived.

We invited about 100 people — friends and family from both sides to the small restaurant we selected. We followed the prescribed order of our ancestors: the announcement of our engagement, a ceremonial meal, then Yun Bok and I bowed, first to the group gathered in our honor, and then to each other. As we knelt facing each other, Ung

Job, Family and Dojang of His Own

Chik and Yunbok's father, each speaking as head of our respective families addressed the two of us to share their thoughts and words of advice. Then it was time for us to exchange engagement gifts.

I had chosen for Yunbok a beautiful ring and necklace. Ung Chik told me that when the time came I was supposed to put the necklace on her. He said I should practice, but I had not taken the time to do this. How hard could it be?

Yunbok stood facing me and I held the necklace up to show my gift to her. The beautiful dance in her eyes told me how much she liked it. Putting on the ring was easy. Then she tucked her head slightly to allow me to put the necklace on her. I tried to put it on over her head, but it would not go over her hair. She started laughing, and then everyone started laughing. Except me. I felt embarrassment creeping up my neck, but when our eyes met, I started laughing too.

"Unclasp the necklace!" someone shouted from the back of the room. Then everyone joined in, some including miming hand gestures to show me how. Still laughing and to much applause, I managed to get the necklace on her. In return, she gave me a ring, which she placed on my finger.

With formality that rivaled most weddings this ceremony announced to the world that I was about to be married. I watched Yunbok through the entire evening in complete awe. I was overflowing with gratitude that good fortune had smiled on me once again in such a remarkable, unexpected way.

◊◊

As my wedding plans progressed, the Korea Taekwondo Association announced new plans of its own — to host and sanction its long awaited Foreigners Taekwondo Championship in Seoul's enormous Jang Chun Gym where basketball championships were held. This tournament, announced to all military base and civilian schools, would be open to all military and embassy personnel and their families.

Job, Family and Dojang of His Own

The registration information said the tournament was open to competitors at all levels, including black belt. Because it was strictly a "foreigners tournament," no Korean nationals were allowed to enter. My students were very excited about this, and knowing my background in competition, clamored for more tournament-focused training.

"Master Park, I want to fight in this tournament," Roy Kurban said to me one day after class. He had been training very hard, every day, and even came to my private dojang for extra training. Still somewhat hotheaded and a little too full of himself, Roy was nevertheless doing well, and most of the time he complied with my instructions and corrections without question or resistance. His patience with my continued emphasis on basics had improved, and his practice was diligent and focused, even when he became bored with the repetition. Even he could see that the resulting improvement to his basic technique made his advanced technique as solid as it was spectacular.

"Good," I replied. I was looking forward to seeing the result of his concentrated work in the competition arena.

After a few weeks of increased intensity in our classes, with special emphasis on conditioning and sparring much like the special training we did in my masters' dojang in Pusan, I knew my students were ready. Roy trained with such dedication and focus that I knew he was setting his sights on winning the Foreigners Tournament.

The two-day event was competition on a much larger scale than any of my students imagined. I watched their faces as they entered the vastness of the Jang Chun Gym, and I delighted in their awe and excitement, remembering my own first big tournament at Chang Kyong Won Park in Seoul. That, too, seemed like another lifetime, and I was proud to now be the master, taking my students to competition and exposing them to this new taekwondo experience.

Several hundred competitors were wandering about on the convention center floor. Most of these people were military, but the group also included a fair number of civilians who worked for the military bases or embassies and their families. Spectators had already begun to fill the stands, and excitement rippled through the air. I could see that my students were nervous, and I gathered them around me to repeat the lesson I had learned from my own master long ago.

"Breathe," I told them, "slow and deep. When you are nervous and not paying special attention to your breathing, you may hold your breath." I looked around me at the faces attuned to every word I said. "When you hold your breath, you cannot keep your balance. Your kicks will be low and you will get tired faster." I paused and let this information sink in.

"OK, everybody," I said, taking a step back from the group huddled around me. I lifted my arms "Breathe in."

They did.

"Breathe out." I dropped my arms slowly with the exhale. They matched my movements exactly. I repeated this several more times, extending the length of each breath until I could hear the relaxation in their breathing.

"See?" I said. "Make sure you keep breathing and you will have nothing to worry about. You've worked hard; you deserve to do your best. You cannot do your best if you don't breathe."

With that, I turned and walked away from them, just as my own master had always done after making an important point.

As an employee of the US army I was acting in this tournament as their representative, so I could not be involved in running it. I was glad for this, because it gave me the opportunity to focus only on helping my students, coaching them through their first major tournament experience. With 15 students participating, this was a job that kept me running back and forth between rings to make sure I was there for at least part of each round my students fought.

I marveled at this transformation in my thinking as I put my mind and my energy to helping each student figure out how to fight their best possible fight. I found myself in a new dimension of taekwondo — a place I never knew existed. As someone who had only seen tournaments as a competitor, the view from outside the ring showed me a new kind of challenge — and a new exhilaration. As I spent that day encouraging, supporting, analyzing the dynamics of each fight, and

Job, Family and Dojang of His Own

thinking of each student's best strategy based on his own strengths, I slipped easily into this new role. It surprised me most to discover the same surge of adrenaline outside the ring, supporting and coaching my students, that I once felt inside the ring.

I jumped straight up in the air when one of my women students took first place in her division. My heart pounded as one of my high school students missed winning his final round by one point, but still won second place. In each division, a new coaching challenge unfolded. Some of the competition that day was very good; some was terrible. Due to many training differences, there was great inconsistency of style and technique. I was proud to be able to stand back and look across the floor at several fights going on simultaneously and to recognize my own students by their form and technique.

The final round of the open black belt division was announced, and Roy Kurban, who had fought very well all day, stood ready to take home the highest prize in the Foreigners Tournament. His opponent was tough — I had watched parts of his past few rounds and knew Roy had a big challenge on his hands. But, judging from his earlier rounds, it was a challenge Roy was more than equal to.

The final round began, and as Roy's coach, I tried to help him to see opportunities think of new strategies when what he was doing stopped working. For the most part, however, I just encouraged him, cheered him on, and felt the vicarious rush of adrenalin with every kick he landed. At the end of three rounds, the score was tied, but the other young man was starting to show fatigue. With his conditioning giving him the advantage, victory for Roy was just seconds away.

Then, without warning, Roy's earlier karate training rose to the forefront. Closing in on his opponent, he grabbed him, held him and punched him. This technique, although legal in a karate tournament, earned a penalty point in a taekwondo tournament. The tie was broken. The fight was over. In that one moment of lapsed concentration, the tournament's biggest title slipped away.

"What are you doing?" I heard myself screaming, jumping up and down as I saw Roy grab his opponent's dobok. After the decision, as

Job, Family and Dojang of His Own

Roy left the ring I was still screaming. "You had it won! You were going to be the champion of this tournament. Why did you grab him?"

I grabbed Roy's uniform just as he had grabbed his now grinning opponent's. "What were you thinking?" I shoved Roy backwards, still holding onto his uniform, still screaming.

Roy's eyes were huge with surprise. "I don't know, Master Park," he said, moving backward. "I guess I just got too excited. I wanted to win, and my brain went back to my earlier training." He looked miserable. "I'm sorry to let you down."

I let go of his uniform and took a step back from him. "You must learn to control your brain," I said in the most even tone I could muster. Then I turned and walked away before I said anything more. It was just so unbelievable to me that, so close to winning, he did such a stupid thing. I was angry with Roy, disappointed for Roy, and now, very embarrassed about my reaction.

"Master Park?" a young man with a notebook hurried to catch up with me. I was still seething with anger, but the insistence in his voice made me turn around. "I'm a reporter with Stars and Stripes, and we are doing a story about your students and your taekwondo program at Yong San. Can we take a picture of you and your students and their trophies and do a short interview?"

I struggled for composure. "Of course," I said. Of my 15 students competing, six won trophies, and all performed well. I couldn't let Roy's outcome put a damper on their jubilation. We lined up for the photo. I was in the middle and at the other end, a sullen Roy Kurban. After asking me questions about the base training program, taekwondo and its benefits, and each student who placed in the tournament, the reporter told us the story would appear in the next issue and he would make sure we all got copies.

A man with a microphone walked up and said he was with KBS, the Korean Broadcasting System. They, too, wanted to do a story on this little band of American taekwondo students who had taken home more trophies than any other single group. I obliged with another interview, wondering as I did what I was going to say to Roy.

"Roy?" I said as we began walking toward the bus that would take us back to the base.

Roy said nothing. He did not even look at me.

"I am sorry I lost my temper." I had never had to apologize to a student before. I never remembered my master apologizing — or having anything to apologize about. I was ashamed. I realized that I, too, still had a lot to learn. "Can you please forgive me?"

"Yes, sir," he said, "I forgive you. It was a stupid thing to do and you were right to get mad at me. I am just as angry with myself as you were with me back there."

"Maybe so," I said, "but I shouldn't have lost my temper."

Roy laughed. "You scared me, Master Park! I thought you were going to kill me!"

"I did consider that," I said with a very serious face. Then I burst out laughing. "You should have seen your eyes!"

Roy looked at me for a moment then he started laughing, too. We laughed all the way back to the bus.

At the next class period for every base class was a party. We lined up our six big trophies in the front of our training area and celebrated what *Stars and Stripes* called "an amazing sweep."

"Congratulations," I told them, raising a glass to their victory. "I am very proud of you and all your hard work." I was surprised to discover that I was as proud of those six trophies gleaming beside me as I had ever been of any I won myself.

◊◊

By the day of my school's grand opening, I already had 35 students enrolled. Only about 20 of them came from the Yong San, and the others were from surrounding neighborhoods. Some came in response to my flyers, some by word of mouth, and some observed a class as I once had, and then came back, bringing friends.

For part of my Grand Opening I decided to hold a demonstration at the elementary school nearest the dojang, hoping to attract more of its students. I approached the principal of this school to ask his permission to hold our opening demonstration there.

"Why do you want to do your demonstration here?" he asked.

"Because taekwondo is good for children, good for families," I said. "I want to show your school's children and their families and friends what they can learn at my dojang." I paused. "For parents, teachers, and community officials, I want to demonstrate how taekwondo builds improvement, not just in individual practitioners, but in the whole community."

"You have chosen a good area for your school," he said.

"Yes, sir," I said.

"I would be honored to host your demonstration," he said. He thought for a moment. "I will put up a big tent for your spectators, and if you will bring more of your advertisements, I will have a few of our students pass them out for you during the demonstration. I am glad you and your dojang are here."

"Thank you, sir!" I said, shaking his hand with vigor. "After the demonstration, we will have a big grand opening party at my dojang with lots of food. Please come and bring the school's faculty, families and friends."

"I will look forward to seeing your dojang," he said.

I didn't know much about running a business, but I began to realize that anything that was good for my school, good for taekwondo, good for the community and good for me was the right measuring stick for business decisions. After that, everything about being a business owner seemed easier.

I asked Roy and a few other of my top students to plan a good grand opening demonstration that would include breaking, one-step sparring, poomse, self-defense and a little bit of controlled sparring. They worked on this demonstration every day after class, and from what I observed, it was going to be very good. I appreciated the care they were putting into planning every detail, thinking about what kinds of things would most impress the spectators. I knew it would be a wonderful show.

Almost everyone offered to bring food, drinks, and flowers. One student from the base said he knew how to set up a sound system for music, and another offered to make two giant signs, one for the demonstration site and the other for the outside of the dojang. I had more flyers printed, and these offered a "Grand Opening Special."

My master sent word that he was not able to attend, but wishing me a successful opening. He also made a call to his friend, Grandmaster Chong Woo Lee, who at that time was the president of Korea Taekwondo Jidokwan Association. Grandmaster Lee agreed to come to my grand opening and make a speech. Although I was disappointed that Grandmaster Park would not be there, I was surprised and honored that Grandmaster Lee himself would be there to say a few words at my dojang's Grand Opening.

The day of my Grand Opening arrived with beautiful weather. The large tent my students erected created a perfect venue that transformed the bland schoolyard into an impressive demonstration arena. People arrived early, then more and more people came, then there was standing room only in the tent and a large band of spectators gathered around the perimeter, straining to see what was going on inside. My Grand Opening flyers had done their job. My heart fluttered with nervous joy and anticipation.

There were chairs set to face the crowd in the front of the tent. These were reserved for all the masters, Grandmaster Lee, and the school principal. After thanking the principal and welcoming the guests, I introduced Grandmaster Lee. Whispers in the crowd confirmed that they, too, were impressed that the president of Korea Taekwondo Jidokwan Association would be here to help open my school.

Grandmaster Lee rose to speak. To my surprise, he had spoken with my master and knew all about my life and accomplishments. In his speech, he laid out the milestones of my life, end to end, telling the crowd a story that was amazing even to me. I felt all the eyes of the crowd on me, and I was humbled by Grandmaster Lee's praise and kind words.

He explained to the crowd some of the history and development of taekwondo, as well as its significance to our culture. I had petitioned the Association to make my school an official Jidokwan branch school, and, as an affiliate of Jidokwan, this meant that no other Jidokwan schools would be allowed to open in my area. Grandmaster Lee's presence here confirmed that this status had been granted. He explained this to the crowd, who responded with applause.

When it was my turn to speak, I stood and thanked him for his kind words, for being here to help make a wonderful Grand Opening. To the crowd, I said, "Thank you for being here today, for supporting the opening of Won Park Institute of Taekwondo. I am very glad to be here and to bring taekwondo training to this area." I paused and looked around at the gathering, taking in the rapt attention of the sea of faces listening to what I had to say. "I promise to do my very best to create a strong taekwondo family in our community."

I felt the tears coming, so I made a quick shift to introducing my demonstration team and telling the crowd what they would be watching. Then I sat down, relieved beyond measure that my speaking part was over. *Breathe, Won Chik,* I reminded myself, smiling as I thought of my master and wishing he were here to share this day.

The demonstration team moved with precision from one-step sparring to poomse to free sparring. I was proud beyond measure of their flawless performance. If there were mistakes, I didn't see them. I couldn't stop smiling.

Another reason I couldn't stop smiling was that Yunbok and her family were there in the front row. I was so proud that they were here to share this moment with me, to hear the words of Grandmaster Lee, to see my beautiful dojang, and to realize the importance of what I was doing. After that day Yunbok's family knew for sure that I could take good care of her.

Just before the demonstration, we had stopped together at the dojang to check on party preparations there. Yunbok seemed impressed with what she saw. "My future husband," she kept saying, " is a taekwondo master with his own school. Wow." Even she knew that in those days, very few masters had their own schools.

Roy and the seven other black belts that made up the demo team were just about finished. As I watched the faces of the crowd and listened to their whispers, gasps and applause, I knew our demonstration was the success we hoped it would be.

Then Roy and Jin Song faced each other. This, I supposed, was the secret grand finale they told me about. When Roy slipped two ping-pong balls in his pocket before we left, I asked him what they were for.

"It's for our grand finale, Master Park," he said. "Just wait. You'll see." The twinkle in his eye told me they were up to something, but they seemed so excited I didn't want to ruin the fun by making them tell me what they were planning.

Jin Song grabbed Roy as if choking him. Roy stomped near his instep, made a fast pivot and executed a groin grab-and-pull technique from one of upper level poomses. Reaching toward Jin Song's groin, Roy made a fist and then stepped back fast, raising his fist, elbow at a right angle, fist up high near his head. Then he opened his fist to drop the two ping-pong balls on the stage and before they could bounce, stomped them with his heel, letting out a loud *kihap* as the balls crunched under his heel. The crowd gasped, laughed, and then applauded. Roy looked around, as if surprised that anyone was watching. Everyone laughed louder, still clapping.

I glanced at Grandmaster Lee. He was doubled over with laughter. Relieved, I joined the laughing and clapping, shaking my head at Roy as he bowed and walked off the stage.

"What are you teaching these Americans?" Grandmaster Lee asked when he could speak.

"*That* American is one of a kind," I told him, shaking my head. "That was their idea, not mine."

He laughed. "It was a good demonstration," he said. "No one will ever forget it!" He walked away, still laughing.

The spread of food my students and their families had laid out at the school was an outpouring of generosity. There, surrounded by my family, my future family, students, friends and neighbors, I felt like the luckiest man on earth. If its grand opening was any indication, the Won Park Institute of Taekwondo was going to be a big success.

◊◊

There have been only three times in my life when I was literally too nervous to breathe. During the first two, Grandmaster Park reminded me to breathe. But no amount of breathing could stop the jitters I felt on November 7, 1970. It was the day of my wedding.

By Korean standards ours was a big wedding, and to accommodate our many guests, Yunbok's family rented the entire second floor of Seoul's Yesick Jang wedding hall. Decorations and flowers were everywhere — it was like a beautiful dream. As guests continued to arrive, the butterflies in my stomach danced in time with the beautiful music that filled the hall.

I closed my eyes and tried to picture Yunbok's face. It was not the marriage or our life together that made me nervous. It was the wedding itself, a daunting hurdle that we must clear — in proper Korean style — between this day and our life together.

I watched the arriving guests from behind a curtain. Family and friends from both sides took their places, including my family, my taekwondo students and classmates and their families, many Jidokwan friends, the students and families from Yong San, and a few old friends from Pusan who had made the journey here just for my wedding. I looked at the grinning face of Roy Kurban, towering above the crowd and considered what a good friend he had become. He was nearing the end of his military service, and I dreaded how much I would miss his antics and friendship. I wondered if I would ever see him again.

Rousing myself from thoughts too somber for such a happy day, I returned to my survey of the room, silently greeting and saying "thank you" to each person there who had played a part in my life.

Then the guests were all seated and I was prompted to begin my walk to the front of the room. We had practiced this procession the day before, and to the beautiful music we chose, I began my walk through the doorway to a new life.

"Is it Korean custom to walk that fast?" I heard Roy's unmistakable whisper as I passed him.

"No, Roy, Won Chik is just very nervous," answered a Korean voice I couldn't identify.

Somehow, after my fast entrance the ceremony proceeded from there as if in slow motion. It was a magical dream, with Yunbok's radiant beauty at its center, around which all else revolved. "We are gathered here at this hour to witness . . ." in just a few short minutes the traditional words of the *ju rea,* the officiating minister, transformed Won Chik Park and Yunbok into husband and wife.

From there the ceremony moved to another room. Now wearing ceremonial clothing to honor ancient Korean wedding tradition, we stood at the front of the room, facing our guests. Just as we practiced, I kneeled and then touched my forehead to the floor in a Korean ceremonial bow of salute, first to my brother and sister, and then to Yunbok's parents, sisters and brothers. Then Yunbok and I kneeled and bowed to each other.

A basket of chestnuts was in the center of the room. One by one, each guest took turns taking a handful of chestnuts and, attaching a specific wish to each one, tossed them in our direction. It was a literal shower of good wishes from our friends and family, each wish represented by the chestnut that carried it.

In a third room, laid out in grand style, was a big feast. As our guests ate and mingled, we circulated through the crowd together, greeting everyone as husband and wife and thanking them for being there. The celebration would last for days, but at the end of the feast Yunbok and I were free to leave for our honeymoon.

We spent the next three days at On Yang On-chon, a popular honeymoon spot for Seoul couples, just an hour and a half away. With its hot springs and big, fancy hotel and the knowledge that this beautiful girl was now my wife and partner for life, On Yang On-chon was nothing short of paradise.

While most of the traditions surrounding a Korean wedding are observed during the courtship, engagement and wedding ceremony, there are several other customs designed to ease the transition from honeymoon to new life together. The first thing a newly married couple must do upon their return from their honeymoon is to visit the wife's family. When we arrived, the party was already waiting for us, a continuation of the wedding reception with more food, special music and a houseful of Yunbok's extended family. As custom also prescribed, we spent the night there, marking Yunbok's last night in her family home, spent there as a married woman.

The next day, we visited my family. We went to Ung Chik's house, where likewise all of our cousins, uncles and extended family were waiting with another giant spread of food, music and celebration. We spent that night at Ung Chik's house, to mark my last night in my family home, spent as a married man. The following morning, at long last, we went to our new home together.

The home we chose for beginning our life together was an apartment on the second floor of a nice house we found near the base. It had its own private entrance, and the owner lived below, happy to lease the entire second floor as our apartment. With my ample salary, we were able to furnish and equip our little home with everything we needed. Yunbok's delight in our apartment showed in her eyes, and I knew our home together, wherever it was, would always be in good hands.

Once settled into our apartment, the last Korean wedding custom to observe was to invite all of our friends to continue the celebration in our home. Several of the 11 Club who had made the trip from Pusan for the wedding had stayed over to wait for us, and five or six of Yunbok's friends came, too, all bringing food, laughter and more good wishes to complete the celebration.

Then we were alone, and another beautiful journey began.

◊◊

With a good job, a new wife and thriving dojang, my own life settled into a blissful normalcy I had never known. Meanwhile, changes in taekwondo were a swirling reflection of ideas and events focused on moving taekwondo from ancient martial art to competitive sport.

In an interesting side effect of war, as soldiers returned to their home countries, they took with them whatever knowledge of taekwondo they gained in Korea. As taekwondo began to spread throughout the world, its leaders recognized the need for a central governing organization that would reach beyond Korea and the Korea Taekwondo Association to the entire world.

At the same time, taekwondo competition was becoming more organized and more refined. Changing to rules, scoring systems and tournament formats made competition stronger, and better with each passing year.

I visited with Grandmaster Park as often as I could, traveling to Pusan to visit with him and see my old friends, and whenever he was in Seoul, he would come to see me. We always discussed what was happening in taekwondo, the future of its competition, and the taekwondo organizations now taking root throughout the world. He told me what the old grandmasters were saying, sharing their hopes, dreams, and concerns for the future of taekwondo.

During the next two years, life was good in Seoul. With friends, family, and the birth of our bright-eyed baby girl, named Suyun, my personal life continued to be more than I had ever dreamed it could be. Still, another idea, planted long ago, was tugging at the back of my mind.

1970 This was my engagement picture just before my wedding to the beautiful Yunbok. By this time I was a full-time employee of the United States military, a professional taekwondo instructor, and a local business owner.

November 7, 1970 My wedding to Yunbok was one of the happiest days of my life. Here we are dressed in our ceremonial wedding clothes, sitting before the table of traditional wedding items including the chestnuts guests tossed our way, each, according to Korean custom, carrying a good wish for our future together.

1968 The Grand Opening of my first dojang in Seoul was a huge celebration held on the grounds of No Ryan Jin elementary school, Seoul, Korea. Pictured left to right as indicated: Roy Kurban, Young Joon Jang, Master Won Chik Park, Jin Suk Byun, Master Jung In Kim, and Jin Song Chung

1970 My first school's classes were a blend of local Korean students and American GIs who desired more training and a more authentic experience. This picture was taken after my first official belt test. Pictured left to right as indicated, Sang Kim, building owner, a very proud Master Won Chik Park, my friend, Master Kyong Yeon Won, and instructor Jung In Kim

1970 U.S. 8th Army Headquarters 2nd Annual Foreigners Taekwondo Championship. It was in this tournament that Roy Kurban (front row, far right), within minutes of winning the championship, reverted to his earlier Karate training and punched his opponent, causing him to lose the match. The heated exchange between us over this was something we would laugh about for years to come.

1970 Jidokwan team demonstration at the US 8th Army Service Center

1969 As my American students learned taekwondo from me, there was much I learned from them. During this time, fast friendships were made that opened my eyes to new possibilities for my life. I was humbled by how hard they worked and how taekwondo was its own form of communication.

1969 Despite injury, John won the first place trophy at the Korea Taekwondo Association's 1st Annual Foreigners Championship at Chang Cheun Gym, Seoul's largest venue. Seeing my American students excel in taekwondo competition brought a new excitement to me I could never have anticipated.

Leaving for U.S Aug 20, 1972 As excited as I was to have the opportunity to go to America to teach taekwondo, leaving behind my wife and our baby, eight-month-old Suyun, was the hardest thing I have ever done.

CHAPTER NINE:

Opportunity on the American Horizon

One of my US military students, a big guy named Douglas Stanford from Eugene, Oregon, was always talking to me about the United States. He worked for the forestry service, fighting fires with helicopters. He described trees so large that even with his considerable wingspan, his fingertips wouldn't even touch if he wrapped his arms around their trunks.

"Master Park," Doug said, "when you stand in a forest of these giant trees and look straight up, you can't see the sky."

I wanted to see trees this big.

"Come to Eugene, Master Park," he'd always say. "I'll be your sponsor. If you don't like Oregon, you can go somewhere else, but you can start there and I will help you."

"Oh I couldn't," I'd reply. "I am very happy in Seoul. I have a wife and a baby and a good job here. But thank you for offering."

"OK," he'd say, "but if you ever change your mind, I will help you. You can live with me and my wife until you decide where you want to go."

"Thank you," I'd say.

As hard as I tried to dismiss this idea, part of me kept remembering what Lieutenant Lee told me long ago: "If you get a chance to go to the US, you should go." I also remembered Captain Chapman's encouragement: "If you get a chance to go to America, Mr. Park, take it. With your teaching ability, your opportunity to teach taekwondo there will be tremendous." I knew of many masters who had gone to the US to teach, mostly to the east or west coast. Student after student had asked me if I would ever go, but Douglas was the only one who offered to sponsor me, a place to live, and real help in making this unimaginable transition.

I told Yunbok of Douglas's offer. We had talked often of the possibility of going to America if we ever had the chance. She knew of my dream to go there and teach.

"It would be a good opportunity for our future," I told her. "Everyone wants to go to the United States."

"Going there to teach would be a big accomplishment," she'd say.

"There are bigger dreams there," I'd say. "Better education, more freedom, and everyone is rich."

"Everyone?"

"I think so," I said, wondering if this was true.

Since Suyun was born, I began to think even more about Doug's offer. I wanted to provide the best life I could for my family, to make sure Yunbok and Suyun always had a nice life.

"This is the right time," Yunbok told me one night. She had been giving it some thought, too. "If you were older, we couldn't do it. If you want to go to the US to teach, the time is now."

The next day I told Douglas I had decided to take him up on his offer.

"That's great, Master Park!" he said, excited. His tour of duty had ended and he would be going back home within the week. "When I get home, I will contact you with all the information you will need."

"OK, thank you," I said, hoping I had not made a mistake. I went home that evening with the biggest mixture of emotions I had ever experienced. Already I was having second thoughts. Everything was good here. My job, my dojang, my home, my family, my friends. Why would I want to leave all that for something unknown?

Suyun crawled up to me and held up her tiny arms. *"Apa! Apa!"* she squealed her name for me. She snuggled into my lap, happy as always to be with me. Having a child was more delightful than I imagined it would be. My heart ached with love for this tiny little being who already looked so much like her mother.

As I held her, my mind turned this decision over and over. Things were good in Seoul for us now, but what if I let this opportunity slip away and things got worse here again? Being a parent myself now gave me a whole new appreciation of what it must have been like for my father that night he sent us away. I remembered the starving children on the streets of Kun San, and felt a new ache for the parents unable to save them. The stark reality of growing up in a country in turmoil shaped my fear as a parent. While life in America could also be hard, taking my family to America while I had the chance seemed like an opportunity too good to pass up.

Because going to the United States was both expensive and uncertain, Yunbok and I agreed that I would go alone and send for them when I got settled. She and Suyun would be safer and better cared for here with family and familiar surroundings while I was exploring our options. We also agreed that if I got over there and decided it wasn't the right thing to do, I could come back and we'd just continue as we are now.

I looked at my beautiful wife and the sleeping baby in my lap. Am I crazy? I wondered. How can I leave them just for the chance to go to the United States? Is this really the right thing to do for my family? Or is it just something I just want to do that I will someday regret?

For the next three months I fell asleep every night, wondering and worrying. By day, I got my paperwork in order, applied for a visa and composed my letter of resignation to the US Military. My hand shook as I wrote this letter — to give up such a good job was almost unthinkable. Yet the pull of opportunity was strong. I said a prayer, finished the letter and put it away. And then I waited. When there was still no word from Douglas, I felt a little relieved and decided to just go on with my wonderful life and see what happened.

◊◊

On a day when I had all but forgotten about my decision to go to the United States, Yunbok met me at the door with a letter in one hand and a plane ticket to the United States in the other. I could tell she had been crying, but the smile on her face seemed genuine. That was exactly how I felt. The flight left in three weeks.

I hugged Yunbok. "I'm going to the United States," I whispered, as if saying the words too loudly might break the spell.

"I know," she whispered back. Tears glistened in her eyes, mirroring my own. Happy, sad, excited, scared — the emotions tumbled between us too fast for individual recognition.

Then next day I turned in my resignation to the US Military and then made a trip to Pusan to share my news with Grandmaster Park. As always, his support was solid and genuine despite his personal sadness that I would be so far away.

"It's time for your 6th dan promotion test," he said, getting down to business. "It would be good to go to the US as a 6th dan — you would be one rank above most of the masters already there."

I saw the logic in this thinking, and there was not much preparation required for 6th dan. I knew the poomse already; the self-defense and sparring were free form; and with a little bit of studying I could be ready for the written portion, which mainly centered on teaching philosophies and numbers of students. Having opened my own dojang alone would earn more than enough points to pass the written exam.

"Is there time? I asked.

"There is a promotion test next week," he said. "Is your poomse ready?"

I showed it to him.

"You must test now," he said after I completed my poomse and also showed him the breaking and self-defense I planned for my test. "I will make the recommendation now and you may go to the Jidokwan headquarters to apply," he said. "I will send a special letter to Grandmaster Lee to make sure he will allow you to test before you leave."

"Thank you, sir," I said. "Thank you for everything." We both knew it could well be the last time we saw each other, and I wanted to say it to him one more time.

"You are most welcome," he said, bowing to me. "You have made me very proud, Master Won Chik Park."

◊◊

My 6th dan test came and went in late December of 1971 without much fanfare, lost in the frenzy of parties, celebrations and endless goodbyes. The US Military named Jin Song Chung as my replacement, and I spent my days preparing him to take over as head instructor. My evenings were spent preparing my assistant instructor at my dojang to take over my school, and every spare moment in between was filled with family, friends, Yunbok, and especially, Suyun.

"*Apa! Apa!*" Her only two words were my name. I carried her almost everywhere I went those last two weeks. As if she knew something was up, she wanted nothing to do with her mother — only me. I'll never forget her cries and her arms reaching out to me as I walked away from her, suitcase in hand, toward the plane. Looking back one last time before I ducked through the airplane door, I saw the faces of everyone I loved streaked with tears, smiling, waving and encouraging me. I felt as if my heart was being torn into two pieces, and I was leaving the bigger part of it in Korea.

◊◊

When the plane's wheels bumped onto the runway in Hawaii, it jolted me from a light and fitful sleep. While not as terrifying as the small plane, flying was still an uncomfortable sensation, and I could not stop wondering how a thing so big with so many people in it could stay in the air for so long. I was sitting as far from the window as I could.

As my thoughts bounced between the improbability of the airplane, the crying faces I left behind, and the big uncertain future that lay in front of me, I felt a strange assortment of excitement, sadness and apprehension. My dream of going to America to teach was coming true, but at what a price? Would America be everything I imagined?

Focusing my gaze on the gray upholstery of the seatback in front of me, I had decided to meditate. If I couldn't give my body sleep, then maybe I could at least give my mind some rest. I was not sure when my meditation drifted into sleep, but now the lights were on, the pilot was talking, and people were beginning to stir. All my thoughts and worries came rushing back into place, filling my quiet mind like a flock of squawking birds.

"Welcome to America," the pilot had said. I let those long-awaited words soak in, but strangely, felt nothing. We would be here for one hour for the plane to refuel, the pilot announced. Everyone around me got off the plane; I stayed in my seat, wondering what Yunbok and Suyun were doing.

Refueled and refilled with passengers, the plane at last took off for Los Angeles. I drifted in and out of sleep until the bumping wheels told me my long journey was over. I paused at the doorway of the airplane, letting the awareness wash over me that I was taking my first step into a strange new adventure. What new dreams would I find here?

Kwang Jo, my old 11 Club friend from Korea who had moved to LA a year earlier for an engineering job, was supposed to pick me up at the airport. I planned to stay with him for two days to see LA, and then fly on to Oregon where Doug would help me settle into my new life there.

I looked around me at the sea of unfamiliar faces, suddenly feeling very small, lost and unsure of what to do next. My English was good when it came to teaching taekwondo and communicating with my students, but in this new arena, I realized how little I really understood. I collected my suitcase and got in line as directed to go through customs.

"Mr. Park?" a strange American voice said.

I couldn't see the face that belonged the voice, but he kept repeating my name. At first I ignored it. How could someone in this big place know my name? Then I felt uneasy. Is there a problem? What could this person want with me? The voice got closer, still saying my name. I did not turn around. It must be another Mr. Park he was calling.

"Are you Won Chik Park?" the voice was now right next to me. I spun around to see a face that looked vaguely familiar, but this stranger was wearing the uniform of a customs officer.

"Yes?" I said.

"Do you remember me? My company trained with you in Korea!"

I looked at him closer, searching my mind for a match for his face. Then it registered. Blue belt. Long legs. Second row. Tuesday Thursday evening class. Once connected, the memories came rushing in. "Yes!" I said, relieved on many counts. "I do remember you!"

"I work in customs here," my former student said. "Let me help you through. Is this your first time in the States?"

"Yes," I said, still overwhelmed that out of all these people and all this confusion, this one student I barely remembered was here to help me. More taekwondo magic.

"Come this way," he said, guiding me toward a counter. He introduced me to his supervisor, "This is Master Won Chik Park, my taekwondo master from Korea." The pride in his voice humbled me.

The agent behind the counter nodded. "It's very nice to meet you, sir," he said. Then he opened my luggage, inspected the contents, and then closed it. "If you will go with this young man, he will show you the way to the parking lot. Is someone here to meet you?"

"Yes," I said. "He said he would meet me in the main terminal outside my baggage claim. His name is Kwang Jo and he is very tall."

Before we parted, my former student took a card out of his pocket and wrote something on the back of it. "Here is my home phone number," he said, "if you need anything while you are here, please call me!"

"Thank you very much," I said, bowing and then shaking his hand. "I am so glad to be in your country — and so glad you were here to greet me!"

"I'm glad, too, sir," he said. "And please call me once you get settled if you decide to stay here," he added. "I married a Korean woman who is a very good cook — and we would love to see you any time!"

I thanked him again and put the card in my pocket.

He directed me down a long hallway and at the end of it, Kwang Jo, was there waiting. "Welcome to the United States!" he said. "How long did it take you to get here?"

"All my life," I said. Then I laughed and told him the details of my trip. It was a wonderful to share this moment with my old friend, a familiar face in a strange new world.

Kwang Jo's studio apartment in LA was very small, with everything in one room, reminding me of my apartment in Pusan. The refrigerator was stocked with food and beer, and I was especially impressed with the oversized cans of beer.

Kwang Jo laughed as he watched me examine the can. "It's beer, called Coors," he said. "You like beer, don't you?"

"Of course!" I said. "But it's so big!"

"Only in California!" He said, "Have one!" Kwang Jo was still laughing as he went to a large door in his wall. He grabbed a handle and pulled down a full-sized bed.

"Wow," I said. Then I looked around. Where would I sleep? Was there another door?

Kwang Jo laughed again. "Your bed is here," he said, answering my silent question. He pulled out an army cot from the closet, along with pillows and blankets. It wasn't comfortable, but it was a place to sleep.

I called Douglas the next morning to let him know I had arrived, and would be flying up to Portland on Saturday. He was ecstatic. "I'll be there to pick you up!" he said. We made arrangements where to meet in the airport, which he said was much smaller than the one I flew into in LA. From there he would drive me to his hometown, a place called Eugene, Oregon. "Just wait till you see it, Master Park!" He said. "You're going to love it."

Eugene, Oregon was a small town on the outskirts of Portland, surrounded, Douglas told me, by a total of 41 mountain summits and peaks. As we drove through the area where Douglas worked, I was astounded to see that the trees really were as big as he had said they were. "Let me show you," he said, pulling off the road. We walked up a short path to a small clearing surrounded by giant trees.

"Look up, Master Park," he said.

I looked up. Nothing but green and brown as far as I could see. No sky up there at all. "Wow," I said.

The sky, it turned out, was rarely visible at all anywhere in Eugene, Oregon. How can there be fires to fight when it rains all the time? I wondered. And when it wasn't raining, it was overcast and cloudy.

The first week Douglas showed me the sights of Eugene — the ranger station where he worked, and the various highlights of quiet, small town living. It was a new picture of American life, far different from what I had seen in LA.

The next weekend, Douglas and I made a trip to Portland, which he called "the big city." While bigger than Eugene, Portland was no match for the excitement of LA. From Portland we traveled up to Washington State, spent one night in a motel by the ocean, and explored the area by day. Everywhere we went, from Eugene to Portland to Washington State and the Northwest Coast, I saw a different picture of American life. Then we returned to Eugene and Douglas had to go back to work. I walked around Eugene for the next few days and tried to imagine myself living there, opening a dojang and sending for my family.

Although seeing the Pacific Northwest was a big adventure I would always treasure, I knew I could not stay there. The constant rain was depressing and the giant trees, while beautiful, made me claustrophobic. I was so grateful to Doug for bringing me to the States, and I hated to disappoint him, but I longed for the LA sunshine, activity, and excitement.

I confessed my true feelings — and my gratitude — to Douglas the next week. True to his word, he said, "It's all right, Master Park," he said. "I understand." He tried to hide his disappointment, and I wished there was some other way to make both of us happy. But Douglas loved his life in Eugene, and I needed a different sort of place for my new dojang — and our new life.

"Master Park, I am very glad I was able to help you get here, and wherever you go from here, I will help you," Douglas said. "When I asked if you wanted to come to America and teach, of course I wanted you to come here. But that was not a condition of my helping you. My intent was to help you get to the United States and open a taekwondo school. My offer to help you means that of course you are welcome to stay here as long as you like, but, you are free to settle wherever you'd like."

Douglas's generosity of spirit brought tears to my eyes. "Thank you," was all I could manage to say.

◊◊

The wrinkle in this change of plans was that if I went to another state, Douglas couldn't be my sponsor. So, with just a six-month visa and no sponsor, I had less than five months to find another sponsor, go back to Eugene – or return to Korea.

I made a call to Master Ho Young Chung, another friend from Seoul who came to America before me and now lived in Detroit, for advice. After I told him my story, and he was thoughtful. "If you really like LA you should stay there and give it a try," he said, "but LA is very competitive, and it may be difficult. If you have trouble, please call me. If you want to come to Detroit, I can help you here."

"What about my sponsor?"

"Don't worry about that," he said. "I have many black belt students, and I am sure I can arrange for one or several of them to sponsor you."

I hung up the phone from that conversation greatly relieved. At least I had a back up plan. The lure of LA sunshine was strong, but if I couldn't work it out, at least I didn't have to give up and go back to Korea.

I returned to LA and met, through Kwang Jo's network of friends, Master Yong Kim. Master Kim had a well-established taekwondo school in LA, and he had also just opened a branch school in Thousand Oaks. I had known of Master Yong Kim in Korea, but had never met him. When Master Kim asked me if I would like to help him open his second school in Thousand Oaks, I said, "Sure!" I had no idea where Thousand Oaks was, or how I would get there, but if it was a branch school, it must be fairly close, I reasoned.

"In return, I can teach you how to run a taekwondo school in America," he said, "as well as some of the things I have learned about teaching over here, opening a new school, and finding students."

"I'll be glad to help you," I told him, "those are all things I need to learn!"

"Do you have a car?" he asked.

Not only did I not have a car, but at 31 years old I didn't really know how to drive. At the insistence of the US military I had gotten my driver's license in Korea, but with no need and no access to a car, I had barely driven at all. In Korea, there were no highways. I marveled at LA's eight-lane thoroughfares and how fast people traveled. How do you have time to think? Change lanes? Make sure you were in the right lane to merge, veer, exit, any number of strange possibilities I had never seen in a road before? I was so glad not to be driving; now it appeared that if I wanted this job with Master Kim, I must learn.

"Not yet," I told him. "But I will have one very soon."

By then I was staying at the Korean Culture Center, a two-story building where Korean college students could rent rooms inexpensively. My room there was small, clean and comfortable, and with the steady stream of people coming and going from there, it was fairly easy to get a ride just about any direction at any time. Up until Master Kim's offer, having a car seemed unnecessary.

"We need to find you a car," Master Kim said.

The next time I talked to him, he had found a car for sale, a 1968 Buick Skylark for $800. I walked around and around this car, impressed with its size. In Korea, cars were very small and had little power. This monster had an 8-cylinder engine and more power than I imagined could be in just one car. With the money I brought with me, "just in case," I bought the Skylark.

"I'm so lucky," I told Master Kim as we left the dealership with him driving. "Now all I have to do is learn how to drive!"

"It's will be easy," he assured me. "No stick shift!"

I hoped he was right. But looking at the ant bed of LA traffic all around me, I couldn't help but worry. We stopped on the way back to my apartment to get license plates and a learner's permit. To my surprise, the driver's test was available in the Korean language because there were already so many Korean people in Los Angeles. I showed the clerk my Korean driver's license, and she handed me a study guide for the State of California drivers' test and a learner's permit. I was on my way. Later that evening, I went out and walked around and around my Skylark. This was too good to be true. And too frightening to let myself think about too much.

Learning to drive, I told myself, was just another skill. I must learn so I can drive to Thousand Oaks to teach. I imagined Yunbok's smiling face, saying, "I know you can do it!"

As I kissed Yunbok's picture goodnight that night, I asked God to please watch over her and Suyun — and me as I learned to drive. I couldn't believe how much I missed them.

◊◊

When discussing where I should practice driving, Master Kim said, "You need a map."

"A map?"

"Yes," he said, "If you get a map and study it, you will learn your way around."

This made sense. I began practicing my driving on the quiet streets surrounding Master Kim's neighborhood, and each day I ventured farther and farther out. I consulted my map as I went and made notes on it so I could remember some of the landmarks that would help me. After a week or so, I felt fairly confident, so I decided to range a little farther out.

I planned what would be, according to the map, about a 20-mile drive. As I got onto my first highway, I checked my mirrors just the way it said to do in the book. I took a deep breath and felt myself relax a little bit. Here I am, driving my own car on the LA freeway, I said to myself. I wished my friends in Korea could see me. I smiled as I imagined Yunbok smiling proudly at me. "I knew you could do it," I could almost hear her say.

A large sign bearing the name of the street I was looking for loomed above me, so I signaled and took the next exit, only to realize it was one exit too early. No problem, I thought. I'll just go down this side road to the next exit. Wrong. The exit I took was a one-way street headed straight for downtown LA.

I felt panic rising. What do I do now? I thought, searching all around me for a place to turn or stop. No luck. The road spiraled up, up, up — until I was afraid to look down. When I did steal a quick glance to the right, downtown LA sprawled out — on the opposite side of the road than it was supposed to be. This is wrong, I thought, remembering the map. Cars were honking and stacking up behind me, and there was no place to stop and look at my map. With both hands gripping the wheel, I kept going.

About a half-mile further down the road, there was a rocky driveway that led into a construction site. Moving about the site were men wearing yellow hard hats. In Korea, only MPs wore hard hats, so I assumed these were some kind of law enforcement officers. I was torn. Would they help me or would I be in trouble for driving without a real license? I was supposed to have a licensed driver in the car with me, but everyone I knew worked during the day. I pulled into the driveway and waited for a reaction.

At first, no one even looked my way. Then one man in a hard hat started walking toward my car. My heart pounded.

"Can I help you?" he asked. His nice face and helpful tone told me that arresting me was not his intent.

I showed him my map and told him where I was trying to go.

"Well, you're in the wrong place," he said. "And there are two ways to get back to where you want to go." He pointed back over my shoulder. "Through downtown is the short cut."

"I don't want to go downtown," I said.

"The other way is the highway," he said, pointing in the other direction and making a circular motion with his finger.

I thought about the fast moving cars I had just encountered on the highway. I didn't like the way his finger circled around. "I'll go through downtown," I said. "The highway is too fast."

The man in the hardhat laughed. "Well, just be careful of one-way streets," he said, waving me off. "Good luck!"

"Thank you!" I said as I backed the Skylark into the street and headed toward downtown.

After making several turns, including more than a few onto one-way streets in the wrong direction — I found a quiet place to park. I pulled out my map and studied it. I was still just a few miles from where I left; I had been traveling in circles the whole time. I plotted a new course and somehow made it back to Master Kim's house without further incident.

"I'm never driving again," I told him over dinner. I showed him my insidious loop, marked in pencil on my map.

He laughed. "Don't give up, Won Chik," he said. "Today was good experience. Next time you will be fine. Until you are comfortable driving to Thousand Oaks by yourself, my wife will drive with you."

The first day I was to start teaching at Master Kim's school in Thousand Oaks, Mrs. Kim arrived at The Korean Culture Center to pick me up.

"It's a 45-minute drive," she said, "but there are some tricks to it. I'll show you a few times before you try it on your own."

After a few days, Mrs. Kim said, "You have your license, now, right?" she said we walked toward the car.

"Almost," I said. "I do have a permit, and I am practicing every day for my test."

"Good!" She said, handing me the keys. "You drive."

This made me a little nervous, but Mrs. Kim assured me that since it was 9:30, well after rush hour, it would be easy. It wasn't. For one thing, I had never driven as fast as the cars whizzing around me told me I should be going. Big trucks blew by me, and fear tightened my grip on the wheel until my hands ached. "I cannot go this fast," I told Mrs. Kim.

"Slow down, then," she said, laughing.

Finally, in exactly 45 minutes, we arrived. My legs wobbled as I climbed out of the driver's seat. It reminded me of the airplane ride, and yet this was an experience I must repeat twice daily if I wanted this job.

"Want to drive again tomorrow?" She asked.

"Yes." I heard myself say. Although it terrified me, I knew I was gong to have to do it by myself soon. And, just as Master Kim told me about learning my way around with a map, it was good experience.

When I took my driver's test two weeks later, I passed with nearly a perfect score.

◊◊

Unlike the flat barrenness of LA, Thousand Oaks was hilly and dotted with beautiful trees. This, I supposed, was how it got its name. Students who enrolled in Master Kim's school were affluent, and different in attitude from the military families I had taught. Everyone was very friendly, though, and seemed eager to learn. I worked hard on improving my English so that I could ask them more questions and better understand their answers.

Master Kim's school was in what Mrs. Kim called a "shopping center," with a huge parking lot shared by all its stores. In Korea, the shopping experience was generally confined to one store with many departments; these American "shopping centers" and "shopping malls," on the other hand, offered many different stores, all grouped together and connected by the big parking lot. This was important, Master Kim told me, because it assured that we were seen by lots of traffic that passed by there each day, and anyone in the parking lot could see his sign.

During my informal American apprenticeship at Master Kim's school, I learned many important details about managing an American taekwondo school that were completely different from running a private dojang in Korea. From what to charge, how much rent to pay, and how to advertise, this was a different world.

Of special interest to me in this strange new world was a place across the street from Master Kim's new school called McDonald's. We walked into this brightly lit and colorful restaurant, but instead of sitting down to order, we stood in front of a counter.

Mrs. Kim pointed to a list of items and pictures hanging overhead. "Just point to what you want to order," she told me.

I studied the menu and the pictures. "That one," I said, choosing a hamburger.

Every day after that, for the rest of the time I was in Thousand Oaks, I went to McDonald's for lunch and had a hamburger.

1972 Family and friends all gathered at the airport to see me off and wish me well.

1972 One outstanding student, Doug Stanford, from Eugene Oregon, made it possible for me to come to the United States. His generosity and hospitality gave my American life its start.

Won Park Institute of Taekwondo, Detroit Michigan, circa 1974.

CHAPTER TEN:
Detour to Detroit

After three months passed, my concern again began to grow. Despite many visits with other LA masters, I still had no sponsor that would keep me in LA. Master Kim and his wife were happy to help me learn the ropes of running a school in exchange for my help teaching, but they were in no position to sponsor me.

The clock was ticking on my six-month visa, so despite my love for the LA sunshine, I made the difficult decision to call Master Ho Young Chung in Detroit to see if his offer still stood to help me find a sponsor there.

"Yes! Come on!" he said without hesitation. So I packed my belongings back into the same beat-up suitcase I had arrived with, sold my beloved Skylark and with the money, purchased a plane ticket to Detroit.

I called Yunbok to tell her of this change of plans. Just hearing her voice say, "I miss you" just before we ended our brief call brought a lump to my throat and a heaviness to my heart. Calls were expensive, and something reserved for emergencies and to convey time sensitive information, but I just wanted the call to go on until neither of us could think of another thing to say.

I had written her a letter almost every day, telling her everything that was happening. Every few days I received a letter back from her. These became my lifeline; I measured the worth of each day by whether the mailman carried a letter from home. About once a month, Yunbok sent me pictures and updates on Suyun. She was growing so fast. It was almost unbearable to me that I was missing all this, but I focused instead on the life I would be able to provide for her later, the only balm for my sadness.

Detour to Detroit

◊◊

After a four-hour flight, the plane landed in Detroit. From the moment the dark, icy air touched my face, I knew I was in a completely different world from the one I left. Detroit in November was as dark and cold as LA was warm and sunny. While the contrast was shocking to me, I was excited at the prospect of helping Master Chung strengthen and develop his school.

"We'll work together and have fun," Master Chung promised in our last phone conversation before I left LA. "We'll make a strong school here in America that will show people here what a true dojang is like. Then, when you are ready, I will help you open your own school here."

Master Kim became a good friend in the short time I was in LA, but Master Chung was an old friend from Korea. We had already shared many experiences, from our first meeting at a 1959 Jidokwan competition to our parallel tracks as taekwondo teachers on US military bases. Like me, he had followed the opportunity gained by working on a US base to come to the States to live and teach Americans on their own soil. Best of all, since Master Chung had lived in Detroit for quite some time, he could teach me a lot about living and working in America. It would be so good to see him again.

Master Kim could not imagine why I would leave the warm sun of LA for the dark, cold, snowiness of Detroit.

"It seems like the right decision," I told him, while a part of me begged silently to stay in LA, I knew my opportunity to stay in the United States was wrapped in this difficult decision.

My first observation, once outside the terminal with my luggage, was that I needed a much heavier coat — and warmer clothes. Even though I was wearing all my warmest clothes, the cold Detroit wind cut through them as if they were gauze. Winter in LA rarely gets below 65 degrees, Master Kim reminded me on the way to the airport in a last ditch effort to change my mind. I thought about this now and hoped I made the right decision; if this first blast of cold was any indication, it could be a long, miserable winter.

Master Chung was there to meet me as we arranged; it was good to see my old friend and I felt better about my decision within minutes of getting into his warm car. On the way to Master Chung's apartment, I looked out at the large, old and sprawling home of the American auto industry city, whose industrial smokestacks reminded me of the smokestacks Young Soon and I fixed our eyes upon when we still hoped our parents would come to join us on Yeon Pyong Do. I shook my head. Such a long time ago, in a life I could have lived without ever knowing the smokestacks of Detroit even existed.

◊◊

Ten days after arriving in Detroit, on that wonderful American holiday called Thanksgiving Day, Master Chung and I were invited to the home of one of his black belts, a man named Scott who had agreed to be my sponsor. I had celebrated Thanksgiving on the base in Seoul, so I understood the concept, but experiencing this holiday in a real American home was quite a different matter.

We got out of the car and I stepped off the driveway into snow up to my knees. A big storm had just dumped the season's first full load of the cold stuff, and I had never seen so much snow in my life.

"Now, tell me again why I left LA?" I asked Master Chung as we slogged toward the house. "It was so beautiful there — sunshine all the time." I waved my arms at the white blanket that covered everything in sight. "It's always warm there!"

"Because of me, Won Chik," he said, smiling. He was right. My new friends in LA were wonderful to me, but it was good to be back with my old friend — even in all this snow.

As we walked into Scott's home, the first thing I noticed was the blazing fireplace. With friends gathered around it, laughing and talking, and the smell of good food wafting through this beautiful room, it was a picture of America I will never forget. To my right, an enormous dining room table was set with beautiful dishes, gleaming silver and crystal, and a centerpiece of fresh flowers and candles.

Following a time of introductions and pleasantries, we gathered around the big table for the blessing, to which I added my own special silent prayer of gratitude. Scott's father carved the turkey with a big carving knife and everyone began passing around steaming plates of food. I tasted everything, and everything tasted good.

Stuffed, we all returned to the room with the fireplace. Looking around me, I thought, this is the most beautiful house I have ever seen. My gaze came to rest on the crackling fire and the beautiful mantle and hearth that surrounded it. *If I ever own in a house in America,* I vowed to myself, *it will have one of these.*

◊◊

"Won Chik, when do you want to open your own school?" Master Chung asked me one day as we finished our last class. Master Chung had two schools. His original dojang was very nice, with showers and beautiful wood floors; it reminded me of my dojang in Seoul. Master Chung had also just opened his second school, and he wanted me to keep his main school running smoothly while he put his time and attention to work on developing his new branch school. This arrangement was good for him, good for me, and it had lasted all winter.

"Oh, probably in a few more months," I said. Detroit was such a different place from LA, I knew I needed a little more time to make good decisions about opening my dojang.

"Take your time," he advised. "Detroit is a big city, full of opportunity. When you are ready, I will help you find the right place. There is plenty of room here for both of us."

◊◊

In exchange for my teaching, Master Chung provided me with room and board and transportation, but no pay. Even though I had no real expenses, I was getting concerned about my dwindling cash reserve, when someone from the Federal Bureau of Investigation called the main school and asked if I would train 25 of their agents in hand-to-hand combat in their own private class. Someone who trained with me in Korea had given him my name and recommended me for this job, he said.

I asked Master Chung if I could use his school during vacant times to teach this class. It was his school, but it was me they wanted to teach the class. He agreed that I could use his school to teach them and keep the money I made for the start of my own school. On the first day, when they walked in with huge overcoats and concealed weapons strapped all over their bodies, I understood why they needed a private class. The guns and ammo alone in that locker room would have been enough to open a small munitions supply.

Up to that point, I had only heard of the FBI from television and the movies. I had never actually seen or met an agent, nor did I really know what they did; nevertheless, I was glad to teach them. These men were already well trained, but mostly in weapons. Their conditioning made them powerful and fast, with very quick reflexes. Charged with teaching them to use their hands, feet and elbows as weapons, I trained them exactly the way I had trained the Korean and American military.

"*Il Kyok Pil Sal*," I often reminded them, remembering with an inward smile the movie of the same name. "One strike must kill."

I began this class in early December, and once again, each week I watched my money for my own dojang begin to grow. I just wished Young Soon were here to take care of my money and help it grow faster.

◊◊

One bitter cold night in March, as I was finishing up the last class of about 10-12 students, the back door opened, and a large man came in and slammed the door behind him. The sudden noise made the entire class look his direction as he came down the narrow hallway, past the office, past the locker room and up to the edge of the training floor.

"May I help you?" I asked, annoyed at his rude intrusion.

"Yes!" he said, still a little too loud.

Everyone in the room was still and silent, all eyes on him.

"Man, you know what?" he said, coming closer.

This was not a question and I did not like the look in his eyes. I said nothing.

"I want to fight you."

"You want to fight with me?" I asked, now confused. "Why?"

"I'm a kung fu black belt and I'm here to challenge you — and taekwondo — to see who is best."

I laughed. "Get out of here," I said, waving my hand toward the door. "I don't want to fight you."

"You're scared of me."

I felt the blood begin to rise in my face. I turned to face him, looking him right in the eye. "I am an instructor. You are interrupting my class," I said. I knew he was trying to embarrass me in front of my students to provoke me into fighting him. I had dealt with this before. Inside, my thoughts parried against one another. *If I fight him, I give him what he wants. If I don't fight him, my students will think I'm scared of kung fu. He'll leave here and say a taekwondo master is scared of kung fu.*

Then, my decision made, I stepped toward him, looking as menacing as I could. "You really want to fight me?"

"Yeah, man, I want to fight you."

"OK," I said. "Then we will fight." I turned to my students, "I'm sorry," I said, "I have to fight him. Please sit down." I gestured to the edge of the training floor usually reserved for spectators.

Excited to watch a real showdown, they sat, faces expectant.

"Would you like me to show you to the dressing room or will you fight in what you're wearing now?" I asked, keeping my voice polite, as if he were an invited guest. I looked up and down at his heavy boots, jeans and leather jacket.

"Just a minute, man," he said. "I need my uniform."

"I'll wait for you," I said.

As I stood waiting, I considered my options. It was clear to me that, much like my previous classroom challenge, back in Pusan High School, I needed to make my point quickly and clearly. This time, however, I would have to be very careful.

I heard some of the masters in LA discussing the difficult position a master is in when attacked, even in his own school. Even though this boy came in here to challenge me, as a taekwondo master I could be held legally responsible if I hurt him. With all these students' watching I couldn't very well ignore this challenge, either.

The young man emerged from the dressing room, dressed in his kung fu uniform. He came to the center of the room where I was standing. "First we bow to each other," I said.

"Yeah, I know that, man," he said.

We bowed to each other. Then he stood staring at me.

"I'm ready," I said.

He did a series of motions with his hands.

"What are you doing?" I asked, puzzled by all the arm waving. I heard my students laugh. It was all I could do not to laugh with them.

"OK, you attack me," he said. More motions. "Come on!"

"Why would I attack you?" I said, keeping my tone even. "This was your idea. You attack me."

He charged at me and, just as before, I stepped 45 degrees to one side and landed a roundhouse kick in his solar plexus with a loud *kihap*. Even though this was the simplest of all one-step sparring techniques, it is also the very most effective when someone is rushing right at you. Meeting your attacker's momentum head-on with correct speed, timing, distance and a well-focused aim at your target, the solar plexus, creates a powerful, decisive answer to a straight on attack. Often, it is the only answer you need.

He doubled over, sputtering.

I leaned in close to his head, but spoke in a voice loud enough for my students to hear. "I'm sorry," I said. "I thought you said you wanted to fight, kung fu against taekwondo."

He said nothing.

I looked at my students and shrugged — a comedic American

gesture I had discovered useful in conveying confusion.

They laughed.

Slowly, he straightened up.

"How are you feeling?" I asked.

"Embarrassed."

"Say 'Sir.'"

"Sir."

"Are you ever going to walk into someone's dojang and challenge him again?" I asked him, looking at him hard.

"No, Sir."

"Get out of here."

Word spread. For the next couple of months, everyone kept talking about it, retelling the story again and again. When I realized this talk also brought in a whole crop of new students, it seemed like a very good time to open my own school.

As my reputation grew as a master, and my Detroit students became very tough competitors, I realized the opportunity and responsibility I had to be a positive influence on their developing competitive spirits.

CHAPTER ELEVEN:
Competitive Edge

When I told Master Chung I was ready to open my own dojang, we began driving around in different parts of the city, looking for the right location. He knew Detroit well — and where a taekwondo school might flourish without being an immediate threat to his own school. Master Chung's dojang was on the east side of Detroit, so we concentrated our search on the west side.

"Taekwondo across Detroit!" we'd shout out together.

After several days we discovered a promising "For Lease" space that looked to be about the right size in a slightly run down shopping center surrounded by several good neighborhoods.

Master Chung consulted his map and saw that there were also two schools within walking distance.

Cupping our hands against the dirty windows, we peered into the large empty space. It needed a little work, but looked to be about 2000 square feet — a perfect size. In a quick blur of phone calls and signatures, I was a leaseholder. I stood in the center of the big, empty space and smiled. My own American dojang was on its way. Looking out through the same dirty window, I saw the street sign. Joy Road seemed like a good place to begin.

I squatted down to examine the red industrial carpeting that covered the floor of my space, remembering my Seoul dojang's beautiful wood floors.

"Wood is better," I said, running my hand across the carpet.

"Yes," Master Chung said, "but this is America. Americans like carpet. You can always add wood floors later if you still want them."

"No shower, either." I said, looking toward the restroom. The tiny restroom in the back of this space offered just enough room for the toilet and sink. I tried to stop thinking about my Seoul dojang.

"Most US schools don't have showers," Master Chung said, following my gaze. "Just make a changing room. It's nice to have showers, but American students usually go back home to shower and change."

Master Chung introduced me to a friend of his who lived near my new school and would allow me to rent a room once my school opened. This, he said, would give me a convenient place to stay until I could afford my own apartment. Meanwhile, he took me to my dojang every morning to work and picked me up in the afternoons to continue teaching for him until I had enough students to pay rent. I was very grateful for all his help. I had not even considered where or how I would live once I opened my dojang. "Thank you." I said to him, again and again.

◊◊

I walked to the nearby lumber store Scott told me about with a list of what I knew I needed. As Scott predicted, someone who worked there helped me find everything on my list, as well as a few things I had not thought of.

After I paid for my purchases, I looked at the pile of lumber and tools on my cart and tried to estimate how many trips it would take to carry it all back to my school. "I'll be right back," I told the clerk. "Please hold all this right here."

I remembered an old car I saw for sale on one of the streets I explored when I was getting to know my neighborhood. I hurried along, hoping it would still be there. It was. Very old, somewhat dilapidated, and covered with bangs and dents like so many battle wounds, this old green station wagon looked to be the perfect solution.

"Can I help you?" said a voice behind me. The voice belonged to a small black man who had just come out of the house.

"This car is nice for me," I said, searching my growing vocabulary for car buying words. "How much?"

"$200."

"Do you think lumber will fit in the back?"

"Yes, I think so," he said, coming closer. "These cars are very popular because they haul like a truck."

That was good. A truck would be better, but too expensive. To be able to buy a car for just $200 surprised me. Having only between $2,000 and $3,000 left, I had to guard my cash. I remembered the Skylark with longing.

One of the students at Master Chung's school had recommended that I buy an old used car with cash.

"How else would I buy one? I asked, puzzled.

"With credit, you can buy things without cash," he explained. "Then you pay it off little by little, with an extra fee, called interest, added in exchange for the opportunity to have what you want right away."

I had never heard of such a thing. "How do you get credit?" I had asked.

He explained that to establish credit, you have to start with small things and pay them on time; then, once you have a good payment history, you can get credit for bigger things like cars. But I needed a car now, and my cash was dwindling fast.

"What is the condition?" I asked.

"Good!"

I didn't know much about cars. "Guaranteed?" I remembered this word from a radio car commercial. It seemed like a good term to use in this negotiation.

"No guarantee," the man said. "It runs now, but I don't know for how long."

"That's OK," I said, still circling the car. I really just needed for it to run until I got my dojang finished and open. Once I lived in this neighborhood, almost everything I would need was within walking distance. If it would just run for a few months, that would be enough. "OK," I said, taking the bills carefully out of my wallet. "I'll take it."

As I chugged away with my purchase, I looked in the cracked rear view mirror to see that smoke was pouring out of the exhaust pipe behind me. What I also saw in the mirror was the smile on my face. I had a car.

I returned to the lumber store and, with the help of a pimpled teenager, got everything loaded. Even though I couldn't see out of any windows except the driver's side and the windshield, I hauled everything back to my future school in one trip.

Elated and singing to myself, I unloaded everything into a huge pile in the center of the big open space. When this pile is gone, my school will be ready, I promised myself. I strapped on my brand new tool belt, filled it with hammer, nails, measuring tape, and level, just the way the man at the hardware store had showed me, and turned to face my project.

For the next two months, I worked every day getting my school ready to open. After much construction trial and error — and many rumbling, coughing station wagon trips back to the lumber store for advice and more materials — my crude walls were in place, with doors that more or less opened and closed, and mirrors hung. It was far from the beauty and perfection of my finished Seoul dojang, but in some ways, as I stood back and looked at it on the day it was finished, my satisfaction was even greater. In the front of the room, hanging side by side, was the paired Korean and American flags that my students on the base in Seoul presented to me as a gift at my going away party. My American dojang was ready; I just needed students.

As if it knew its job was done, the day after I pounded the last nail into place, the old station wagon died. Coughing more than usual and now making a new sound I had never heard before, it stopped right in the middle of the road and sputtered into silence. I managed to coast into the driveway of a nearby gas station and then just left it there with the keys in it. If someone wants to fix it, they can have it, I thought.

Repeating my Seoul marketing plan, I spent every day walking the area neighborhoods, passing out flyers, and visiting schools and local businesses. It was hard to be patient, but I reminded myself every day that it usually takes three months to fill classes. The immediate results I enjoyed in Seoul were because of my job on base, the students I already had there, and the big public demonstration they were kind enough to do for me. I had none of that to draw on here. For the first time since I came to America, I wondered if I would succeed at all.

After teaching my last few classes and exchanging goodbyes and gratitude with Master Chung's students, I moved in as planned with Master Chung's friend in a drafty old apartment building near my dojang. It was a two-bedroom apartment, and I shared a room with his two sons, sleeping on the floor. It was a second floor apartment and not well insulated. At night, cold air came through the floor and chilled me to my bones. I longed for the warmth of the *ondool* in Korea. More than anything, I missed my family and friends; and my new life was losing its charm. I was grateful for the exhaustion that brought immediate sleep each night, before I had a chance to dwell on how much I missed my beautiful life in Seoul.

◊◊

Even though the old station wagon had been an awful thing to drive, it surprised me how much I had come to depend on it. I called Master Chung to ask for his advice. He knew many people in Detroit; maybe he would have an idea. He did.

"You need to find someone to co-sign with you," he said. "If you pay on time and pay it off, you will have credit of your own."

"But who would do such a thing?"

"Let me ask my black belts," he offered.

The next afternoon Master Chung called. One of his black belts, a doctor, had offered to help me. "His name is Dr. Brockington," Master Chung said. "He said he would be glad to help you. You must make certain to make all your payments on time," Master Chung said. "Because he knows you are my friend he is willing to take a risk, so please be careful."

"I will," I promised. "Thank you, Master Chung."

Dr. Brockington arrived the next afternoon. "Let's go find a car!" he said.

I decided I could manage a $300 down payment and a payment of $100 per month. We approached row after row of shiny new cars, but soon realized that with this budget the car I could afford would most likely not be one I would otherwise choose. At the Pontiac dealership, there at the end of the first row was the ugliest car I had ever seen, a bilious green, but brand new, Pontiac Ventura. To my great chagrin, it also happened to be the cheapest car on the lot, and by far, the cheapest one we had seen all day.

Dr. Brockington laughed at the look on my face. "Remember, Master Park, you just need reliable transportation."

"If you say so," I said, dubious. I looked longingly at some of the other cars.

"Next time," Dr. Brockington laughed, following my gaze. "Want to drive it and see what you think?"

"OK," I said, trying not to grimace.

He summoned the salesperson, who tried not to show his surprise that I was considering this car. But once inside, it wasn't so green. Its new-car look and smell filled my senses, and driving it was nicer and smoother than anything I could have imagined.

"It's fine," I said to the now-eager salesman when I returned from my test drive. I tried not to look at it. "I'll take it."

We signed the papers that very day and I left the dealership with my first brand new car, a note for 24 payments, and my genuine promise to Dr. Brockington to make each payment on time to protect his credit and build my own at the same time. With profuse thanks I shook hands with him and the salesman to cement my first major American purchase — a brand new car for just under $2,000.

It had been less than a year since I left Korea and already I had my dojang open and a new car. Once I had a few students and an established business, home, and credit, I could apply for a permanent visa — the first step for bringing Yunbok and Suyun to America.

◊◊

Yunbok sent me an audiotape of Suyun's birthday party, and while I was glad to hear the sounds of her party and the voices of our friends and family, missing this special day was one of the saddest moments of my adult life. Again and again I listened to the familiar sounds of this very special Korean celebration — picturing it all in my mind with tears streaming down my face — the singing, laughing, and dancing. On the tape each person at the party took turns talking to me, telling me everything was fine, that everyone was doing well, and that they were all taking good care of my family. I could almost smell the wonderful food I knew was being served. My heart ached as I imagined beautiful Yunbok and precious Suyun opening gifts and eating her birthday cake without me. I put the birthday pictures that accompanied the tape in my office and kissed them each day, wondering again and again if I had made a terrible mistake.

To save money and to get out of the drafty cold and relentless noise of Master Chung's friend's apartment, I made a little apartment out of my office at the dojang. I did not, of course, tell Yunbok about this, and, because of my dojang's commercial zoning I was careful not to let anyone know I was living there. This was easy enough to do; I was accustomed to sleeping on the floor with only a blanket, and I ate mostly hamburgers and pizza. I fashioned a makeshift shower in the small bathroom from a few plumbing supplies I found at the hardware store, and just like in the military, I kept all my personal belongings in a wooden box in my office that also served as my table.

◊◊

At last, my relentless marketing started to pay off and, first one at a time, then in small groups, students began to enroll as word spread. By the end of the year, all my classes were full and I began planning, as Master Chung had done, to open a branch school in a different kind of neighborhood.

I began searching the more affluent neighborhoods on my side of Detroit in my spare time. Since my first school was in a lower to middle income area, I wanted my new school to be in a more populated area, to attract a higher income group.

I was very proud of how my students were progressing in such a short time. Almost all of them were becoming extremely good fighters, and many were already asking about tournament competition. I worried about some of these students, glad for the time they spent training in my dojang instead of getting into trouble on the rough streets of Detroit. I told these students often about getting beat up in a street fight trying to show off my taekwondo skills as a green belt. I hoped they listened, and for the first time I understood the concern my master must have had about me.

At last I found just the right location. In easy walking distance from several affluent neighborhoods and schools, this space was on Grand River Avenue, a very wide street of commercial buildings. The space, once a clothing store, was larger than my first school. With dressing areas, restrooms and a water fountain already in place, it would require minimal set up. My second school was up and running in just a few weeks from the day I signed the papers on a lease I negotiated myself.

This time, with students from my main school to help with a grand opening we were able to stage a demonstration that brought in a respectable group of onlookers from the surrounding neighborhoods. My students canvassed the neighborhoods and, with owners' permission, left flyers on doors, on community bulletin boards and in store windows. This promotion plan worked. Again offering a "Grand Opening Special," as I did in Seoul, many signed up after the demonstration, and within the months, my classes were filling up nicely. Going back and forth between these two locations to teach a packed schedule of staggered classes, I was again too busy to think about missing my family, and when I did, I had only to look at the rapid accumulation of my savings to realize we would be together again very soon.

◊◊

With two schools now open, and what seemed like miles of carpet to clean each day, I decided that rather than the ratty broom I was using to sweep my training floors clean, I needed a vacuum cleaner. Remembering the advice of Dr. Brockington to establish credit to support my petition for a permanent visa, I decided to see if I could get a credit card and buy a vacuum cleaner using credit. With a perfect payment record on my car loan, I hoped to parlay that good payment history into a second form of credit. To do this, my friends had advised me to go to our local Sears department store and apply for a credit card. Not only would this be a good credit card to have, they explained, but Sears is very well known for their good appliances — and everyone needs appliances!

When I entered the store, my mouth fell open at all the merchandise and choices that stretched out before me as far as I could see. I asked three different people for directions before I found myself in the vacuum cleaner department, standing before a row of shiny new vacuums. So many choices. I inspected each one, and then chose the smallest and least expensive. Even the least of these would be far better than that old broom.

"How do I apply for a credit card?" I asked the smiling clerk.

"Right here, sir!" she chirped, handing me a form to fill out.

My approval — and my new credit card — came in the mail the very next week, and I went the same day to purchase my new vacuum cleaner from the same clerk. As I walked out of Sears as a proud new vacuum cleaner owner, I felt on top of the world. In just six months this $300-dollar vacuum cleaner would be mine. The best part was that I could take it with me and vacuum both schools that very day.

Despite my rapid forward progress, time seemed to slow down. I still listened to Suyun's birthday tape every night, and each morning as I worked out in the little back room of my second school, I sang "Cago Pa," an old Korean Folk song that, for me, always touched a sentimental chord that echoed back to the family I lost as a young boy, the friends who were like family to me, and now, my special love for the wife and baby I left behind. "Cago Pa" was also a favorite of many Korean opera singers, and I had learned to mimic this delivery quite well. I pictured the faces of the people I loved as I worked out and sang this sweet song. The more I sang, the more I cried; the more I cried, the louder I sang; the louder I sang, the better I felt. It was a kind of therapy for me, a way to let my feelings out in private and to keep my family in my heart and mind every single day. I was tired of being patient. Now I just had to be strong.

◊◊

I stood at the mailbox on the street corner in front of my school and took a deep breath. At last it was over. In the letter I was about to send to Yunbok were pictures of my new school, the two-bedroom apartment I had just rented for us, and the car I had almost paid off, well ahead of schedule. It was time, I told her, for her and Suyun to join me in the United States. I kissed the letter and dropped it in the slot. The hard time was coming to and end.

With between seventy and eighty students in both schools, I had officially established a business. With my own apartment, driver's license, car ownership and credit established, I had fulfilled all the requirements to start my immigration petition and the paperwork to request a permanent visa. Once that was granted, I could bring my family.

"Once I get my permanent visa," I wrote to Yunbok, "you can apply for your visa in Korea." I could almost hear her joyful laughter, and I imagined her dancing with Suyun as she told her it was almost time to go to Apa. I had no idea how long this mysterious process would take, but just the thought that it was beginning put my spirits in a much better place.

"I have found a good Asian food market in a neighborhood near our apartment," I told Yunbok in my letter. In anticipation of our return to home life, I eagerly stocked our pantry with Korean foods, and I started to enjoy coming home to the apartment every day, imaging that she and Suyun were already there, waiting for me.

◊◊

"When can I fight in a tournament?" became one of the first questions a student asked as soon as he or she passed the first color belt test. As the concept of taekwondo competition and tournaments spread across the United States, my students became more and more eager to try fighting in tournaments.

To oblige this interest and excitement, I began to teach them to compete. To my surprise and delight, several of my color belts were natural fighters. I could feel my own excitement growing right along with theirs as they began to win first a few rounds, and then a few tournaments. Soon, each tournament outing was stronger than the last one. A few who joined in the early days of my first school were starting to prepare for their black belt test, my first black belts trained on American soil.

Because Master Chung's school was so well-known for its solid, well-trained fighters, it naturally became my students' goal to beat Master Chung's students. I remembered many of these students from my time teaching in his main school, and I welcomed the opportunity for my newer students to compete against such seasoned competitors.

"Remember the spirit of good competition," I told them when their competitive edges got a little too sharp. "Competition is good, but Master Chung is my friend, and we must always be respectful to him and to his school."

Just as my master had done for my taekwondo classmates and me, I took only my best fighters to major area tournaments, sometimes ranging as far as Ohio and Chicago. One of my heavyweight students, a 16-year-old named Richard Plowden, was one of my first students. He was still very young, but I recognized his natural love and ability for tournament fighting.

Richard made me realize what my master must have felt when he watched me compete. The poetic combination of Richard's flawless technical ability and strong taekwondo spirit made me proud to be his teacher. If I had not come here, this American boy might never have had this experience, I marveled as I watched him warm up before winning his heavyweight championship match in the United

States National Taekwondo Championship tournament in Chicago. Just a few hours later, another dream came true for both my young student and for me. My young American student was now the United States National Taekwondo Grand Champion. Richard had not only won his heavyweight division, but he then went on to beat all the other winners of all the other divisions to become the US National Grand Champion.

I thought my heart would burst with a kind of pride I had never felt before as I watched Richard go up to receive his six-foot trophy. *I trained the United States National Grand Champion,* I said to myself, over and over. I smiled and shook his hand, then hugged him and admired his trophy. It was the first of many he would win, both as a student and, later on, as a professional fighter featured many times on the cover of *Black Belt* magazine. But I knew even then that this was a victorious moment I would cherish for the rest of my life.

◊◊

I waited for the mailman, as I did every day for the past three months. When I applied for my permanent visa, the man at the immigration office said it would take three to six months. In my mind, every day after that first three months crawled by. When all six months passed, I could wait no more. My patience was shot.

"I'm sorry, Master Park," he said. "Nothing today."

The disappointment was bitter in my mouth. After my initial elated preparations, time became dead weight. Now what? I went in my office, not even bothering to close the door behind me, and sank into the chair, staring into space, completely dejected.

"Master Park?" a familiar voice was at the door. "Is everything OK?" It was David Sankovich. Since the first days of my dojang, any time I had a problem, large or small, David was always there to help me find the answer. Not only was he one of my best students, he had become a good and trusted friend.

"Come in," I said, "and please close the door." I had always kept my personal struggles and disappointments from my students, but now I needed help.

"What's wrong?" David was alarmed by my tone. He had never seen me upset.

I slammed my fist on my desk. "No." I said, in belated answer to his first question. "Everything is NOT OK at all. Six months I have waited. Nothing. Still nothing."

"Waited for what?" David asked.

I explained the situation to him and to my relief, he offered to help.

"Don't worry Master Park," he said. "I'll help you find out what the problem is and what we need to do." David was the sales director at our local TV station, and he knew a lot of people.

After a few phone calls he said, covering the receiver with his hand, "You need to go to the US Representative's office."

"Where is that?" I asked.

"I don't know," he said, "but I'll find out." After a few more conversations, he wrote the address and directions down for me. "Do you want me to go with you?" he asked as he handed me the paper.

"Yes, please," I said, "I need your help." My English was much better, but in this emotionally charged situation I was not certain that my mind could process what I was hearing fast enough to ask the right questions and fully understand the details of the answers.

On the way to the US Representative's Office, I told David about Yunbok and Suyun. As the floodgates of my closely held personal information burst, I told him about my apartment, ready and waiting for them for six long months — about how much I missed them and how hard it was to be away from them for so long, and how many times I thought about packing up, spending what I had left on a plane ticket and going back to Korea. As strange as it was to pour my heart out, to say these things out loud, it was a relief just to tell someone. I had never until that moment let myself realize how lonely I was or how much I needed a friend I could confide in.

"Something must be wrong," the official said when David explained my situation to him.

"That's why we're here," David said. I have talked to several different people here, and someone recommended we come see you."

"I'll personally look into this matter to see what the problem is," the official told David. "I'll trace the documents and I should have an answer for you within two weeks."

"Good," David said, nodding. "Thank you."

On the way back to the school, David turned to me and said, "Don't worry, Master Park. They will find out the problem and then we'll fix it." Earnest sympathy filled his face. "We'll get your family here. You've waited too long."

My eyes filled with tears. "Thank you, David," was all I could manage to say.

A little more than two weeks later, a letter came from the US Representative's office with an explanation and directions for what to do next. I showed the letter to David.

After reading the letter he said, "We need to make an appointment with the immigration office," he said.

"Why?"

"I don't know, but that's what it says to do, so let's do it!" He picked up the phone and made an appointment for the next morning.

The Detroit Immigration Office looked to me like the police stations on television, a parking lot of desks where people were sitting and typing on clattering old manual typewriters. I watched the carriages all across the room, clicking together, yet separately, working their way across their individual pages until a small bell sounded. Then, without breaking rhythm, each typist would reach up and push the lever to return the carriage right back where it started, then continue typing. What words are they typing? I wondered. What documents are they working on — and whose life is on hold, waiting for them to arrive?

Finally someone called. "Won Park?"

"Yes," I said. David and I were ushered into a smaller inner office where we were asked to wait yet again. "The investigator will be right with you," a pleasant looking woman said.

"Investigator?" I said to David, alarmed. "Investigating what?"

David just shrugged. "We'll see."

I settled back in my chair, trying to remain calm as my anxiety escalated like a train leaving the station. What are they investigating?

"I was unable to trace your document," the investigator said as he entered the room, dispensing with formalities to pick up the conversation somewhere in the middle. "When did you apply?"

I told him. The date was stamped on my brain.

"I'll be right back," he said.

When he came back, he had a folder in his hand. "I found it," he said. "Somehow, it got put in the wrong stack and set aside until someone could figure out why it was there." He paused. "I'm so sorry," he said. "I have already re-sent your application to the correct office and asked them to expedite it. As soon as they can get it processed, you will get another letter asking you come in for an interview and to answer a few questions."

Less than three weeks letter, David and I were back in that same office so I could answer in person the questions I already answered on the application.

"We'll be in touch," they said again as we left.

I thought of the typewriters, feeling as if my carriage had just been returned to its starting place. Even though it was hard to keep waiting, it was easier now that I knew the process was moving along and I could return my attention to my students and my school.

Two months later, the mailman came in smiling.

"Here's your letter Master Park," he said, handing me the answer to my prayers. "Is this the one you've been waiting for?"

I ripped open the envelope and read the letter. The words, "Your petition has been granted," jumped off the page at me. It didn't matter to me what else the letter said, although I would read it, over and over, every single day until they came to make sure I hadn't missed anything.

One long year after I dropped that first letter in the mailbox to Yunbok saying it was time to come to America, the wait was now, truly, over. I mailed the enclosed petition and two plane tickets to her the day I got it and began a new countdown to the time when we could be a family again. This time when I looked at the smiling pictures of Yunbok and Suyun on my desk it didn't make me sad at all. Today the sight of their faces made me happy beyond measure.

◊◊

My family arrived in the United States in February of 1974, just a few months ahead of my 34th birthday and nearly two years after I opened my Detroit school. I arrived at the airport early, allowing extra time for weather and traffic. I laughed at my own excitement, my days of frenzied cleaning and shopping. I wanted everything to be perfect.

Yunbok had told me Suyun's favorite food was bananas, a rare delicacy in Korea, so I had put a large bunch of them in the back seat as a surprise for her, along with candy, soft drinks, gum — every American treat I could think of — and there was more back at the apartment.

My family is coming — we'll be together again soon. The thought played like sweet music, over and over in my head, all the way to the airport. I could not stop smiling. Of all the things I had waited for in my life, this was the most dear, most treasured, and most anticipated moment I had ever known.

The plane landed, then taxied slowly to the gate. I thought I would burst. One by one I searched the faces until I saw the two I was looking for. I ran to them. Suyun shrunk back and held tightly to her mother's leg. Yunbok and I hugged and kissed and cried. Suyun stared at me as if I were some insane stranger.

Undeterred, I opened my arms and knelt down so she could run to me the way she did when she was a baby. She stood, silent and staring, clinging to Yunbok's leg. I tried to hide my crushed disappointment, but Yunbok patted my arm.

"It's OK, *Yeo Bo*," she said, using our favorite Korean term of endearment for each other. "she only knows you as a voice on the phone. Just be patient. She'll remember everything soon."

We got their luggage and found the car. Yunbok smiled when she saw the car — I had warned her about the color. "It's beautiful," she said, "and even more . . . green . . . than I imagined."

I laughed and hugged her. "It's an ugly color, but a good car," I said.

I showed Suyun her bananas, hoping to help my case. "These are for you," I said.

She shied away and refused to look at the bananas.

"Don't you want to take it?" Yunbok asked her, trying to intercede in this painful exchange. "Apa brought you bananas!"

Suyun reattached herself to her mother's leg, ignoring the bananas completely.

"It's OK," I said. It wasn't, but what could I do?

I watched Suyun in the rear view mirror. So beautiful, and already three years old. Two of our years together, lost forever. Would it be worth it? Time would tell. I smiled at Yunbok. "I am so glad you're finally here."

"I am glad, too," she said, returning my smile. Then she looked out at the dark, cold Detroit cityscape.

"What do you think of Detroit so far?" I asked, realizing it was not a fair question.

"I don't know yet!" she said, laughing. "But what I like about it already is that you are here!"

"I'll show you everything," I told her as I studied her face. My smile overflowed into laughter.

"What's funny?" she asked. Now it was her turn to study my face.

"Not funny," I said. "Just wonderful."

I showed them every corner of the apartment, taking pride telling them every detail of my preparations. Suyun, still hanging close to her mother, refused to even look at any of her toys. I showed them to her anyway. I pulled out my box of letters and pictures, worn from re-reading.

"You kept all those?" Yunbok asked, surprised.

"Every one," I said, "It was all I had here of you and Suyun."

The stack of letters represented the past two-and-a-half years of our letters, week by week, and sometimes day by day, that we wrote to each other. It was a monument to our love and patience — and to our belief that the sacrifice we were making was good for the future of our family.

That first long awaited evening, as I at last sat on the sofa with Yunbok, Suyun stared at me from across the room. At first we tried to persuade her to sit beside me on the sofa, which then evolved to putting her between us, but even then, she wouldn't look at me.

Despite our best efforts, Suyun was also afraid to sleep in the room I made for her. Each night for those first few weeks, we'd let her fall asleep in our bed, and then we'd move her to her bed. If she woke up, she'd start screaming.

"How long will this go on?" I asked Yunbok, my patience wearing thin.

"Give her time," she'd always say.

How could the little baby who had been so attached to me in Korea not remember me at all? It broke my heart to think that this little person whom I loved so dearly now wanted nothing to do with me. What made matters even worse, not only did she not want to get near me, but she didn't want her mother to get near me, either.

"Suyun, I like him," Yunbok would say, smiling as she patted my shoulder. "This is your Apa. He loves you so much. Please be sweet to him."

In reply, Suyun would just stare and then start to cry. Sometimes she'd plant herself between us and push me away from her mother. The truth was obvious. Suyun did not want to share her mother, and she missed her home and friends. She was angry, she was sad, and she was jealous. When she looked at me, she saw that I was the cause of all this trouble.

Of course I understood, and I felt sorry for the upheaval I caused, not once, but twice in her short life. I tried to be patient, but my heart ached when I carried her to her bed at night. After tucking her in, I'd sit there for a moment, looking at her delicate features and stroking her hair, wondering how long it would be before she'd let me get this close to her when she was awake.

1973-1977, Detroit, Michigan
As my Detroit students excelled in their training, they became eager for competition, winning many titles and showing me that American taekwondo was much more than just a passing fancy.

After more than two years of hard work, saving, and frustrating delays, my family at last came to join me in Detroit.

As my students continued to reach new heights, competitive tension with an old friend caused me to rethink my future in Detroit

CHAPTER TWELVE:
Challenges and Choices

At the next National Taekwondo Championships in Chicago, Yunbok and Suyun were there with me. It was a proud moment to introduce my family to everyone there, particularly to Master and Mrs. Chung. We had all known each other in Korea, and as we ate dinner together the night before the tournament, we laughed together and shared stories of home, then marveled that we were together again, but now in the United States.

The next morning, as my students squared up against their competition from all over the country, I could tell from their conversations and demeanor that they were especially intent on defeating Master Chung's students. More than the usual banter between competing dojangs, I realized with growing discomfort this rivalry had escalated more than it should have. I gathered my students and took them outside.

"I hear how you're talking in there and I don't like it," I told them with American bluntness I knew was the best way to get my point across with these students. "Master Chung is my good friend, so we must always keep competition with his dojang friendly. Is that clear?"

"Yes, sir!" they chimed in unison.

I could tell by their expressions they didn't understand the gravity of what I was saying. "Part of your taekwondo training is to be respectful and humble," I said. "Your job is to discipline your mind to concentrate on your technique and the best fighter will win." I looked at this eager young group, remembering what it was like to be so young and so charged with adrenalin and testosterone. "As much as you can today," I said, staring hard at each of them, one at a time, "try to keep your mouths shut."

"We're still going to beat them!" I heard one of them whisper as I walked away.

I shook my head, understanding for the first time what my master meant when he described an impossible situation as, "like trying to stop a waterfall." Of course, I, hoped they would prevail in this competition. I just wished they'd let their taekwondo training do the talking instead of their loud mouthed, teenaged egos. I also hoped with all my heart that Master Chung would see this for what it was and not hold their careless words and actions against me.

When all the final rounds were fought, and all division winners were celebrated, Master Chung and I were pretty evenly divided on our division champions. This would be, I reasoned, a great time to call it a day. No such luck.

This tournament was trying out a new concept — one I wasn't sure I liked. The champions of each division would now fight each other in an open draw to arrive at a National Grand Champion — the champion of all champions. After several hard-fought rounds, Richard Plowden was once again in the finals against Master Chung's number one student. This fight between our very best students would determine the United States National Grand Championship title. After a good, clean, tough fight, it was again Richard's hand the referee raised as the clear winner.

After gleefully congratulating Richard, I went over to shake Master Chung's hand, master to master. He turned away, pretending not to see me, talking instead to the students and spectators behind him.

I followed him down the hallway to the dressing room, hurrying to keep pace with his escalating stride. "Ho Young, why won't you speak to me?" I said.

He said nothing, looking straight ahead as he walked even faster.

"Competition is competition — and friends are friends," I said, determined to provoke some conversation that might clear this problem up. "Why are you getting it mixed up?"

"It's OK," he said. "No hard feelings." He turned and went into the dressing room, leaving me standing there in the hall.

"No," I said to the empty hallway, "This is not OK."

Challenges and Choices

◊◊

After several months in Detroit, and with both dojangs doing very well, we began taking family drives around Detroit, dreaming of the home we would buy once we could afford more than our small apartment. Our dream was a house with a fireplace on a corner, tree-covered lot.

There was one part of American life in particular that both Yunbok and Suyun both embraced with such enthusiasm it always brought a smile to my face. Pizza. Every Friday night after my classes ended it became our tradition to go out for pizza.

Then Yunbok told me that in November someone else would be coming to live with us.

"Who's coming?" I asked. "From Korea?" I wondered which relative had decided to join us.

"Not from Korea," she said with a mischievous smile.

"From where?" I asked, confused.

She patted her belly. I had noticed that it was getting a little bigger, but I attributed this new growth to her newfound love of pizza.

A new baby. I thought my heart would burst with joy.

◊◊

We moved to a bigger and better apartment to prepare for our new arrival, a place with more families, more children, and a safer play area for Suyun. Even though the new neighbor children spoke only English and Suyun spoke only Korean, they played well together, oblivious to cultural differences. Watching this, we smiled. As I discovered when I first started teaching taekwondo to Americans, sometimes clear communication has no need for language.

Soon Suyun began to copy the English words and phrases she heard from the other children. By the time she started school, Suyun had learned to express herself well in both Korean and in English.

Challenges and Choices

One dark, snowy night, November 16, 1976, Yunbok informed me that it was time to go the hospital.

"November is a big month for us!" I told Yunbok as I drove to the hospital. "We were married in November, Suyun was born in November, and now this baby is also coming in November. November will always be a big month at our house," I laughed.

"Big and cold," she agreed, trying to get comfortable. She was right. It was one of Detroit's coldest nights so far this year, and we were on our way to the hospital with fresh snowflakes swirling around us. "Be careful!" she said when the car's wheels slid sideways over a patch of ice. She grimaced. "But please hurry."

"Don't worry Yeo Bo," I said, patting her. Yeo Bo was a term of endearment I always called Yunbok. Once Korean people marry, they seldom, if ever, call each other by their first name. Instead they find their own special term of endearment for one another that no one else in the world will call them. Since we were married, I had called Yunbok "Yeo Bo," something akin to the American term, "honey." Taking a deep, slow breath to quell my rising panic, I forced myself to focus on the road rather than on the nerve-wracking combination of "Be careful!" and "Please hurry!"

When Yunbok told me we were going to have another baby, the first person I called was Dr. Brockington, my good friend, and the black belt who co-signed my car loan. Staying in touch with him even after the car note was paid, I knew he was now an obstetrician in Farmington, a suburb of Detroit. It required a longer drive to the hospital, but I was glad to have a trusted friend take care of my wife and new baby.

We arrived without incident, and standing alone in the hallway after the doors closed behind Yunbok, I asked God to please take care of her and the baby. For the first time in a long time, I felt alone and vulnerable.

I paced back and forth, sat in first one chair, then another, and then, when I could stand it no longer, I asked the woman at the window, "Any news yet?"

"Not yet, Mr. Park."

What was taking so long?

I tried to remember how long it took for Suyun to be born. Everything was so different in Korea, where babies were born at home, with midwives, and the father-to-be was attended to by the family and friends gathered for the event. But here, in this American hospital, I was all alone. I tried not to worry.

Suyun was staying with friends as planned, but I wished for her company, to remind me that everything was going to be OK. Babies are born safely every day, I told myself again and again.

The double doors opened and a nurse came in. I leapt to my feet. She laughed. "No baby yet, Mr. Park," she said. "But soon!"

I resumed my pacing for what seemed like hours. Then the double doors opened again and this time, it was Dr. Brockington himself coming through the doors. I held my breath.

He threw his arms up in the air. "Master Park! You got it!"

"What do you mean? I got it?"

"You got it!"

I jumped up and ran to where he was standing. "What do you mean? Got what?"

"You got a boy!"

I grabbed him, hugging him, jumping up and down, laughing and crying, all at the same time. Relief and excitement all tumbled into this emotional celebration. "Everything's OK?" I asked when I could finally speak. "Why did it take so long?"

"It was a difficult birth," he said. "We had to do a C-section because the baby was too big," he said. "We had a little bit of a hard time, but everyone is OK now."

"Can I see them?" I asked.

"Give us just a little while longer," he said.

As Dr. Brockington disappeared again through the double doors, my knees grew weak and I had to sit down. I knew without another word from Dr. Brockington that if not for this wonderful hospital with its modern technology and a specially-trained doctor to take care of Yunbok and the baby — if this baby had been born in Korea

Challenges and Choices

— the result could have been very different. I said a silent prayer of thanks to God for this baby and Yunbok's safety.

Dr. Brockington returned a short while later. "Mr. Park?" he said, grinning, "are you ready to go meet your son?"

My smile said everything.

He laughed. "Let's go!"

He led me down a winding hallway to a row of glass windows. Behind the window on the end was a small bassinet tagged "John Park." I beamed, first at my new son and then at Dr. Brockington.

"I have a son," I almost whispered, still trying to get used to the sound of those words and the miracle they carried. It was like a wonderful dream to be standing here, in an American hospital, looking through the glass at this beautiful baby boy — my son.

His Korean name, we decided, would be Sae Jun, which in English translated as "John." Our Korean friends explained that choosing a Korean name with a clear English equivalent would make it easier for our child in American schools. Using this same logic, we decided that Suyun would be called Susie when she started school. When the time came to apply for Suyun's citizenship, we changed her name officially to Susie to make it easier for her later on.

I entered the room a little further down the hallway where Yunbok was sleeping. I stroked her hair and whispered, "We did it! One girl and one boy!"

She would sleep for a while, Dr. Brockington told me, and it would take her longer to recover because of the C-section, but she was going to be just fine. I stayed there all night until she woke up. When she opened her eyes, I hurried to her side. "We got it!" I said, repeating the news just the way I had heard it from Dr. Brockington.

"Got what?"

"A boy!"

She nodded. The she closed her eyes again.

"Good job!" I persisted.

She smiled and patted my hand. Then she went back to sleep.

"Sae Jun." I said his name over and over. Another dream come true.

Challenges and Choices

◊◊

Detroit was getting rougher, it seemed, and even the nicer neighborhood where I my second school still thrived had declined to become more like the first. When the area surrounding my first school became so dangerous I decided to close that school altogether, I realized I was happier concentrating my efforts on just one school.

These changes in Detroit's population were causing an exodus out of the city, Dr. Brockington had explained; it was no longer safe to live in even the best parts of Detroit. That's why he had moved his family and his practice to the suburbs. I began to worry about my family's safety, and Yunbok and I discussed this often.

Do you think we should move somewhere else?" she'd ask.

"I don't know," I'd say. "Where would we go?" The trouble with that idea was that I was now well established, had good students and a good business here. To go somewhere else would be to start over from the very beginning — an idea I didn't relish. Still, as an industrial, factory-dominated city, Detroit's economic ups and downs often affected my business. Would another kind of city's economic climate be more balanced? What was the best choice for the future of my children?

◊◊

From the time she was three years old, Suyun watched my taekwondo classes with an enthralled interest that reminded me of my own. Even before she decided whether she liked me, she loved taekwondo.

I often watched her little body trying to mimic what she saw in my classes. Her memory and concentration amazed me. Her enthusiastic and patient practice mirrored my own early days of taekwondo, yet she was less than half the age I was when I started. If she asked me, I helped her, but I noticed that she learned just as fast by watching my classes. By the time she was four years, she knew most of the color belt forms.

"When can I start class?" she'd ask.

"Not yet," I'd say.

"Why?"

"You're too young."

"When will I be old enough?"

"Soon."

The truth was, I had never seen a child as young as Suyun with such an aptitude, interest and concentration. I wasn't sure what to do with her. To appease her, I bought her the tiniest dobok I could find and helped her practice at home.

She wore it proudly — all the time.

"I know all the forms," she pointed out one day when she looked up to discover that I was watching her practice.

"Yes, I can see that," I said.

"Why can't I join the class?"

She had a point. I finally agreed to let her come for the first 30 minutes and then Yunbok came to escort her off the training floor. In 1978 at age five, Suyun began her training in earnest.

Just in time for Suyun to start school, we bought a house in what we determined to be a safe, suburban neighborhood where we could raise our children. After many days of driving through neighborhood after neighborhood, we found a house that matched our dream — a 1300-square foot house with a fireplace on a big corner lot with trees that reminded me of my childhood home.

My business was thriving, my credit was perfect, and before we knew it, we were moving into this house that we dreamed of since the day we first talked about coming to America in our tiny apartment in Seoul. I looked at my family on the first night in our wonderful new home and tried to remember those dark days when I wondered if I had made a mistake.

"Everything is perfect," I told Yunbok.

She smiled back at me, and then at our children. "Yes," she said. "Perfect."

The neighborhood school where Suyun would start kindergarten the

Challenges and Choices

following fall was very close, and every time we drove past it, we pointed it out to Suyun, saying, "That is where you will go to school next year."

One day, after one of these excursions past her school-to-be, Suyun asked, "Who will take me?"

This posed a problem we hadn't considered. To get out of Detroit's urban decay, we had moved quite a ways from my taekwondo school. I looked at Yunbok. "You can take me to work and keep the car here," I said, "and then when you pick Suyun up from school, you can all come to the dojang. After the last class we can all come home together."

"I don't know how to drive."

"I'll teach you. It's easy."

Yunbok looked skeptical.

For about a month we went out every day for Yunbok to practice driving. We went to areas without much traffic and to large open parking lots. One thing I realized very quickly was that knowing how to do a thing well does not necessarily equip you to teach it. And likewise, knowing how to teach one thing does not necessarily qualify you to teach something else.

"No, no, no!" I'd say, clutching the dashboard in front of me. "Watch out! You're going to hit something! Slow down! Stop! Go! Hurry! Wait!"

Seeing the look of terror on Yunbok's face as her small hands gripped the steering wheel, I remembered my own panic as I learned to drive on the LA freeways. Realizing how scared she must be, I softened. "Teaching taekwondo is not like teaching driving," I explained. "If you make a mistake here, we die."

"Then I don't want to learn to drive," she'd say.

"How will the children get to school?"

"You can take them."

"It's up to you." I said. "If you want to just stay home all day and never go anywhere, I guess you can."

She thought about it for a few days. Then she got angry. She stood before me in our kitchen and said, with her hands on her hips, "I am ready to learn to drive." As always, her clearheaded reason won out. Even though the days that followed were not among our best, Yunbok practiced driving every day until we both knew she was ready to take her test. She passed with nearly a perfect score.

"I should have gone to driving school," she said on the way home from taking her driving test. We never spoke of driving lessons again, but I couldn't help but notice how much she seemed to enjoy this new sense of freedom and independence, getting out, taking the children to school, and going to the market on her own. The freedom a driver's license brought was a different kind of milestone in each of our American lives.

◊◊

Weary of the dark, never-ending chill of the Detroit winters, our discussions of leaving Detroit started again in earnest after a family vacation to LA to visit friends and to enjoy a respite from the cold. While the warm, west coast sun beckoned, I knew that making a living there would be difficult at best.

We took in the sights and the sun and indulged our fantasies of living there, but a quick survey of prices, cost of living, and the competition I would face brought to bear the stark reality. We didn't have to stay in Detroit, but we couldn't stay here. Where else could we go?

Yunbok's answer to this question was always, "Somewhere else that will be warmer, maybe?"

I laughed as I hugged her, grateful once again for all the ways my smart, beautiful wife made any challenge I faced seem conquerable. Above all, she understood how important friendship was to me, how many times in my life my friendships saved me. We both knew that friendships were more important than locations, and staying in Detroit would be the end of the friendship that gave our life its real start in this country.

"You're right," I told Yunbok. "It's time to go. Somewhere warmer!"

◊◊

When I confided in David Sanovich our plan to leave Detroit, explaining the situation with Master Chung, his shocked questions and protests gave way to understanding when he saw how upset I was about leaving, but how I also knew it was the right thing to do to save a dear friendship.

As I knew he would, he rose to the occasion. "How can I help?"

"I need to find a good new location for my new dojang," I said, spreading out on my desk the brand new map I just bought that morning. "Somewhere warmer."

He pored over the map. "California?"

"No," I said. This time, I decided, I want to go somewhere I don't know anyone. I didn't want to risk another friendship.

David ran his finger across the bottom section of the map. "I have an idea," he said. "Let's just take a drive through the South — there are a lot of warm places there."

"Do you have time?" I asked, incredulous that he would offer to do such a thing.

"I do," he said. "I've got some vacation time I need to use, and I've been wanting to go someplace I haven't been before." He tapped the map. "A road trip south looks like just the thing for both of us!"

*Detroit 1973-1977
Demonstrations of technique
and power set good examples
for my students and kept
me in prime condition as a
practitioner and as a master.*

The warmth and new possibilities of the South was a welcome change from Detroit's long, cold winters. Here my young family explores Dallas on a vacation here to visit our old friend, Roy Kurban and attend his annual tournament. After this trip, we decided this area would be our new home.

CHAPTER THIRTEEN:
Land of Warmth and Possibility

We set out a few days later, car overloaded with food, and we followed David's map, due south. We drove all night before pulling into a restaurant that looked inviting in Birmingham, Alabama.

"Just sit anywhere," the waitress said without looking up. We ordered and ate and when it came time to pay for our food, I could feel all the eyes in the restaurant follow us to the cash register. I looked around the room and realized with a start that everyone in there was staring at us. It was like being back in Ung Chik's in-laws' living room, and just as uncomfortable.

"What are they looking at?" I whispered to David, whom I noticed was watching this exchange.

He said nothing, but paid the unsmiling hostess behind the register, then turned and walked through the door and out to the car. I followed him, puzzled as much by his response as the stares.

When we got in the car, David said, "Master Park, welcome to Alabama. There are still some places in this country, mostly in the South, where black people and white people still don't get along. I think we were just in one of them."

He started the car and looked around the parking lot before putting it into gear. I could see that he was nervous, and as long as I had known him I had never seen anything that intimidated him.

"So why were they staring at us?" I said. "We're not black."

"That's true, sir," he said, "But it looks like being Asian — or anything different from them — may be a problem around here. Some parts of the South are going to be OK for you, but some areas just still don't like any kind of minorities very much."

"Minorities?" This was a word I had never heard before. "What is that?"

David looked at me and tried not to laugh. Why was this so funny?

"In the South, minority pretty much means anyone who isn't white," he explained. "But technically, the word, 'minority' means a group that is smaller in population and power."

David checked his mirrors again, then signaled to get back onto the highway. "In some places in this country, if someone is different, they automatically don't like him," he said.

"They don't even know me," I said. "How could they already not like me?"

David burst out in raucous laughter. "Hard, to say, Master Park," he said, "But at least we know that the two of us walking in there together for breakfast this morning gave those folks something new to talk about!"

The idea of being a minority was a strange concept to me. Everyone who lived in Korea was Asian. Most of my students in Detroit were black, and between them and the Korean community, I interacted with very few people who were white. LA, too, was so racially mixed it never occurred to me that it wasn't this way everywhere. Oddly enough, I had never even thought of people in terms of color before. "They should come to Detroit," I said. "Then they'd be the ones on the hot seat."

David looked at me sideways, amusement dancing in his eyes. "The hot seat?"

"Isn't that what you call it?"

"Well, yes," he laughed, "I suppose it is!"

We laughed all the way to Mobile. Then, driving through the streets of Mobile, we saw lots of poor people, visibly hungry, down and out, living on the streets. With a pang of compassion I remembered exactly what that felt like. I looked into the eyes of hungry children as we drove past, seeing the same hopelessness that I once felt and saw in all the eyes around me.

I said nothing to David about this, but watched them silently, saying a prayer of thanks and gratitude that my life had taken me out of this desperation. I wanted to tell them, "Just hang on. Keep trying. Your life can be different, — you must never give up."

We drove past a run-down karate school with a "For Lease" sign in the window.

"There's one," David said.

What if I came here and helped those children just as my master helped me? I wondered. Then I remembered the expressions on the faces in the Birmingham diner. I would never want my family to endure those kinds of stares. "I cannot live here," I told David. "Let's keep going."

We continued on through the South and explored several smaller towns. While I was glad to see this part of the country, and much of it was very beautiful, I knew it wasn't the right place for raising a Korean American family. We returned to Detroit, tired and discouraged. This wasn't going to be as easy as I thought.

It was difficult to know that my decision to leave was made, and yet to have no idea where to go. Somehow, I knew the answer would come, just as it always did. I just didn't know when, or what to do in the meantime.

◊◊

It was nearly two months after my ill-fated trip south that a letter arrived from Roy Kurban to invite me to a tournament he was hosting in a place called Arlington, Texas. Somehow, Roy found me through friends and acquaintances, and he wanted me to come to his tournament. In the earnestness of his letter I could almost hear his voice.

"Do you remember my American friend named Roy?" I asked Yunbok when I told her about the letter. "He was at our wedding."

She looked puzzled. Our wedding day was a long time ago and a world away.

"He was also the one with the ping-pong balls at my Seoul Grand Opening."

"Oh yes," she said, smiling. "How could anyone forget that?"

I waved the letter. "He found me," I said, excited at the thought of seeing my crazy American friend again. "Roy wants us to come to

Land of Warmth and Possibility

Texas to visit him and attend his tournament."

"All of us?"

I looked at the letter again. "Yes! He says 'bring your family!'" I looked at Suyun and Sae Jun. "We can make a 'family vacation' out of it and see some famous American sights on the way."

Yunbok shook her head. "I don't know. It's a long way — and so much money for all of us to go," she began. "Do you want to go alone?"

"No, I want all of us to go," I said. I paused for a moment. "Besides, I've never even considered Texas. It's supposed to be sunny there. Maybe it would be a good place to move."

This got her attention. After our decision to leave Detroit for a warmer place, all progress stalled after my trip through the South.

"Isn't Texas in the South?" She asked. She was still getting her geographical bearings in this giant country.

"Yes," I said, "but it's a little different than the rest of the South." I only knew about Texas from TV, but in this case some information was better than none. "Let's go see!"

I called Roy to let him know we were coming. "Roy?" I began, as if we had spoken just last week.

"Yes?"

"This is Master Park."

"Master Park! How are you?" Roy's personality came charging through the line to bring a smile to my face. It would be so good to see him again.

"I am fine," I said. "I was very glad to receive your letter. I would like to accept your invitation to bring my family to visit Texas and attend your tournament."

"Master Park, that is great news," Roy said. "When can you come? Can you stay for a while after the tournament to see some of the sights around here?"

"We will leave Detroit tomorrow," I said, "but we are driving so we can see more of America on the way. We're making this a 'family vacation' trip, so yes, we can stay a little while after the tournament." The term, "family vacation," was a new concept to me, but I liked the sound of it.

"That's a great idea, Master Park!" Roy said. "You will see quite a lot of America on the way here." He laughed as if imagining our wide-eyed, open-mouthed wonder at some of the strange new things we were likely to see between Detroit and Texas. "Have a safe trip and call me when you get here!"

We mapped our journey through Memphis, Tennessee to see Graceland, home of Elvis. This was Yunbok's special request, and I pretended to be jealous, but in truth I wanted to see it, too. We used a travel guidebook to plan our stops in several states I knew nothing about, to arrive in Arlington, which we had determined to be somewhere in between Dallas and Fort Worth, just in time for Roy's tournament. It was the end of June, and as we drove south, the warming temperatures were welcome relief from Detroit's lingering chill.

"The sun feels so good," Yunbok, said, letting it shine on her face every chance she got. "Everything is so bright and beautiful!"

I soon realized that a "family vacation" was a wonderful thing — it was so nice to focus only on laughing and playing with my family instead of trying to do ten things at once. Suyun was nearly seven and Sae Jun was nearly two. I loved seeing America through three different perspectives besides my own.

Following Roy's directions and our worn map, we found our way to his tournament, held in Fort Worth's huge convention center. Expecting around 900 competitors, Roy said it was biggest turnout he ever had, with some of the nation's very best martial arts competitors.

After he left Korea, Roy's competitive career had skyrocketed. Now, after earning 127 national championship titles and being honored as one of Black Belt magazine's top seven fighters of the 1970s, Roy's own school — and annual tournament — was thriving. With many outstanding black belts and champions now to his credit, Roy's accomplishments and those of his students reflected his dedication as a teacher, tournament director, coach, referee and promoter.

Roy's tournament, called the Fort Worth Pro Am Championship, had a very different atmosphere from the mayhem I was accustomed to in other tournaments. It was very quiet, very well organized, and as I walked among the rings, there was no complaining or yelling. But underneath this quiet was what captured my attention most. Bubbling beneath the surface of quiet, respectful order was a proficient competitive intensity that was most impressive. These "crazy cowboys," as Roy laughingly called them, were very good fighters.

Roy himself had changed very little, and over the next several days, I realized how much I had missed our good times and conversations. I also liked what I saw of this small part of what I now realized was a huge state called Texas. Saying nothing to Roy about my decision to leave Detroit, we explored the Dallas/Fort Worth area a little each day during the week after his tournament.

At first I was attracted more to Dallas, remembering how I loved LA. But there was a "little big city" charm to Fort Worth and its suburbs I liked; and with its proximity to Dallas, living in Fort Worth could offer the best of both. Fort Worth was also far enough from Arlington to not impinge on Roy's territory, but close enough that we could see each other often.

"What do you think, *Yeo Bo?*" I asked Yunbok as we prepared to return to Detroit.

"I think you will make the right decision," she said, smiling at me. "I do like it here. "It is very warm and pretty and the people seem nice."

"Everywhere you look, new buildings," I mused. "Everything is growing, and that means there is also plenty of money here." I looked at Yunbok, still so beautiful, still so full of love and support, and then at our children, playing quietly in the backseat. "I think Texas would be a good place for us," I said.

"I think so, too," she said.

Although the particulars were far from settled, our decision to move to Texas was made in that instant. The next morning, as we said our goodbyes to Roy, he became serious. "Master Park, I don't know what your situation is in Detroit, but I will tell you that everything is better here. Better economics, better opportunity — and better weather! If you ever want to move down here, I would be honored

Land of Warmth and Possibility

and delighted to help you find the perfect place for your dojang."

How could he have known that those were the exact words I needed to hear? "I'd like that very much, Roy" I said. I looked at Yunbok, then back at Roy. "We like it here, and we've talked about making a change while our children are still young. I would greatly appreciate your help!"

"Consider it yours, Master Park," Roy said, beaming. "When can you come back so we can start looking for a place?"

We decided to begin the search the very next week. Driving straight back to Detroit, I stayed only long enough to check on my students, make sure my black belts were taking care of my classes, and repack for the return trip to Arlington.

Once there, day after day Roy and I explored the Dallas/ Fort Worth area, looking for good school locations and as well as nice neighborhoods for my family. Wherever we went throughout this sprawling but beautiful Metroplex, one thing was certain. With its widespread, boundless growth, anywhere I chose here would be a good place for a new beginning.

The specific location for my dojang, however, was more elusive. After ten days of searching and no solid prospect for my school yet in my sights, I rented an apartment in Arlington, centrally located for further exploration once my family got there.

"No use getting in a hurry," Roy had said. "The right place will show itself in time. Just come on down and we'll find it."

The calm reason in his words made me smile. Where did all this patience and wisdom come from?

The day after I got back to Detroit, I called the realtor who sold us our house. "I want to sell my house," I told her. "I am moving to Texas."

"Why? What's wrong?" She acted as if she couldn't believe her ears.

"Nothing's wrong," I assured her. "We are just moving to Texas — right away."

"Not right away," she cautioned. "It will take a while to sell your house. Did something happen?"

"Yes," I said, "a better opportunity!"

After a short argument that she soon recognized as futile, the realtor agreed to list the house. Less than three weeks later, she brought me a contract.

"Mr. Park, I can't believe your house sold so quickly," she said. "I have never had a house sell so quickly."

"See?" I said. "Good opportunity for everyone."

◊◊

A few days after I gathered my black belts together and told them of my decision to leave Detroit, George Opalski, one of my strongest Detroit students, both physically and mentally, stopped by my office. "Master Park, my friends and I will help you move," he said. "It will be our thank you gift to you. What day do you need to leave?"

On moving day, George and several strong friends arrived with a gigantic U-Haul truck and loaded our belongings faster than I imagined possible. He knew the best route, he said, so we followed the immense truck in our car, stopping only for restroom breaks, food and sleep. Our first glorious Texas sunset welcomed us at the edge of Dallas. With shades of red, orange, pink and gold none of us had ever seen in the sky before as our backdrop, we entered the next phase of our life in complete awe.

Our Arlington apartment was within easy walking distance of both the elementary school Suyun would attend and an Asian market where Yunbok could walk to buy our food. The two-bedroom apartment was not big, but it was adequate for our young family — and a reasonably priced home base until I made the more permanent decision of where to locate my dojang.

George and his friends spent the night with us in the Arlington apartment. After unloading the truck and then consuming a staggering amount of pizza, we all slept on blankets on our living room floor, all together in one room as only I remembered from times past.

The next morning, as the truck lumbered out of sight on its way back to Detroit, I turned to Yunbok in an unexpected moment of realization. Our world had once again become very small; were starting all over again with only each other to lean on and no idea what new challenges we were about to face. Another surprise to me in that moment was that this time I felt no fear or worry, just calm, happy understanding that our decision was good and right. It was a new adventure together, and I greeted it with open arms.

"Welcome to Texas," I said, hugging her. Then I laughed. "We are now living in a state more than three times the size of North Korea and South Korea combined, and we don't know anyone here but Roy."

She nodded, thoughtful. The she laughed, too. "If we only know one person, I'm glad it's Roy," she said. "He is a good friend."

Later that same day we all walked down the street to the Asian market to buy some food. We were absorbed in gathering the items on our list when a woman came up behind us.

"Yunbok?" she said.

We both wheeled around. Who could know her name here?

Recognition lit up Yunbok's face as she recognized Yum Buk, an old friend from her high school in Korea. They, too, were living in Arlington and her husband worked for the nearby Winn Dixie grocery store.

"Now we know two people here," Yunbok said on our walk back. We smiled together at a world so full of good surprises.

◊◊

For the next two months, I left the apartment every morning around 8:30 to search for the right location for my school. Some days I went alone, some days with Roy, and some days with Yunbok and Sae Jun while Suyun was in school. We found plenty of good places, but each had a drawback that eliminated it from consideration.

When Roy told me about an abandoned kempo karate school for lease on Fort Worth's west side and offered to take me to look at it, I hesitated. I remembered this area, and it was surrounded by pasture. And cows. Accustomed to locating my school in a densely populated neighborhood within walking distance of several schools, I wondered, where will the students come from? How will they get there?

Roy laughed as he saw the doubt on my face. "Let's just go look at it," he urged. "If you don't like it, you can always say 'no,' but I promise it would be a very good location for your school."

As I stood in front of the empty 1600-square-foot space that was once a Kempo school, I was not impressed, but as Roy also predicted, the price was right. He pointed to the vacant spaces on each side of the school. "As your school grows you can rent more space," he said.

One advantage of this space was that, unlike every place I had rented before, it was ready to go as a martial arts school — all I would have to do was change the sign and I would be ready to open my doors.

"You could always try it out for a few months and see what you think," Roy said. "If you still don't like it you could move."

His logic made sense. Looking around me, I wondered where the students would come from.

"They'll come," Roy said, as if reading my thoughts.

Circa 2002 In a news article published by the Cho Sun Daily News in Korea, Great Grandmaster Chong Woo Lee, who served as the second President of Jidokawn and Vice President of the World Taekwondo Federation, gives his unique and powerful perspective on Taekwondo history and Taekwondo's entry into a new era.

In taekwondo, the purpose of breaking is to show that you can focus the energy within you to defeat physical barriers. In life, this same technique also helps overcome many other kinds of obstacles. Speed Breaking Demonstration, circa 1975.

CHAPTER FOURTEEN:
Walking Tall in Fort Worth, Texas

I signed the lease and ordered the sign for what I had decided to call the Won Park Institute of Taekwondo. It was December of 1978, and I was 38 years old, opening my dojang once again in yet another new city.

Despite the reports of mild Texas winters and warm, sunny Christmas Days, it seemed to get colder each day as I drove to my school from our Arlington apartment. Then, on the day after Christmas, which wasn't sunny at all, a little bit of rain turned the streets to what Texans called "black ice." In six years of icy, snowy driving in Detroit, I had never encountered such a strange, slippery phenomenon.

Certain that it couldn't be as bad as everyone said — I came from Detroit and knew how to drive on ice — I went to the dojang as usual that day. I was planning a New Year's Day Grand Opening. I arrived without incident, smug in my ice driving skill. But getting back home that evening was another matter. Cars all around me slithered off the road as their drivers' helpless faces stared through the windows. Others sat in one spot, stuck on nothing with tires spinning. Still others, at first moving forward, took a sudden move sideways before sliding diagonally into a roadside ditch. Size and weight didn't seem to matter — I watched a large truck jackknife, then slide, just as helpless as the cars, to block the road and give cars something to slide into. I inched past the truck, somehow managing to avoid skidding into a ditch myself. On my usual half-hour drive home that stretched to more than two hours, I lost count of the abandoned cars and trucks, strewn askew beside the road like beached whales. I did, however, count myself very fortunate not to be one of them. I would never try to drive on this "Texas black ice" again.

Despite the setback of weather, my Fort Worth dojang was open by early January. I printed up and distributed my flyers, visited area schools and began again the task of filling my classes with new students. Students came slowly, a few at a time, and I wondered how long it would take to have a full enough class that I could pay our mounting bills.

◊◊

"You and your school must leave here," said the scrawl on a note I found taped to my dojang door less than a month after it opened. I removed the note and looked around me. The parking lot was empty, and not a person was visible in or around any of the other stores or businesses in the shopping center. Trying to dismiss my uneasiness, I went inside, locked the door behind me, and threw the note in the trash. For the rest of the morning, I tried not to think about it. I had been threatened before. *No big deal*. I told myself, again and again. Or was it?

I called Roy and told him about the note. "What do you think?" I asked, eager for any advice he had to offer.

"Master Park, they are just trying to scare you, to make you give up," he said. He paused, then laughed. "They just don't know who they're messing with!"

"So should I just ignore the note?" I asked.

"I think so," he said. "These are probably just bullies, trying to intimidate you and run you off," he said.

I told him the story about the young kung fu man who came into my Detroit dojang and challenged me.

Agreeing with the masters I heard talking about this in LA, Roy said, "It happens all the time, Master Park. There are just a lot of punks out there who think they can make a name for themselves by challenging a master in his own school. You just have to stand up to them and if you can, teach them a lesson."

I knew this all too well, and I had dealt with bullies before, but this time seemed different, and I was a little bit worried. The next day, and each day for three days after that, notes with increasingly insulting and vulgar messages were there to greet me when I arrived.

On the fourth day, glad for a reason not to go to my dojang, I went to Dallas to have coffee with Master Dae Sup An. He was a good friend of a Detroit master who suggested I call him when I got to Texas.

"Are you getting settled in Fort Worth?" he asked. "How is your dojang?"

"Fort Worth is fine," I began, taking a sip of my coffee and wondering whether to tell him about the notes. "It is a nice city and I am already getting students."

"But?" he said, seeing the doubt I was trying to hide.

"But I also keep getting these bad notes taped on my door," I said, shoving the latest crumpled note across the table.

He read the note. After what seemed like an hour, he said, "You need to get out of there."

"Why?" I asked. "What do you think will happen?"

"I don't know," he said, "but if I were you, I wouldn't want to find out. This same thing happened to another master in Fort Worth."

"What did he do?" I asked, leaning forward to hear Master An's hushed tone.

"He left," Master An said, taking a sip of tea. "He closed up and got out of there."

"But I just got my school open," I protested, giving voice to the argument in my head. "I signed a lease. I moved my family here." I hadn't mentioned any of this to Yunbok — it would make her crazy with worry.

"Why do you want to be over there, anyway?" he asked. He looked genuinely puzzled. "It's full of cowboys."

"I haven't seen any," I said, amused at his ironic stereotype.

"They don't like anyone who is different over there."

"How do you know all this about a place you've never been?" I teased. "I really like Fort Worth. The people — except for these — have been very nice to me."

"Any idea who it is?"

"No," I said, leaning back in my chair and scratching my head. "I always look around when I find a note to see if anyone is there. I've never seen anyone. I don't know if they put the note there at night, or just before I arrive. I always imagine that they are hiding somewhere out there, watching me and laughing — wanting to see if I am afraid."

"Bullies." It wasn't an opinion; it was a pronouncement.

"Yes," I said, finishing my coffee and standing to go. "And I know how to deal with the bullies you can see. It's just these bullies you can't see that make me wonder what to do."

"Just be careful," he said again. "Do you have a gun?"

I shuddered. I had had enough of guns in Korea. "No."

"You might consider getting one."

"I will," I lied. "Thank you for your time and advice. It was nice to meet you."

Despite my misgivings, I stopped on the way home at a sporting goods store to look at guns. On the way back to the gun counter, a display caught my eye and I had another idea. The week before, I saw the movie, "Walking Tall." The main character, a sheriff named Buford Pusser, wielded a baseball bat like a samurai sword, striking terror into the hearts of his foes. I picked up a baseball bat from a revolving rack and swung it over my head the way Buford did in the movie. I liked the feel of it in my hands. Powerful. I thought about the Kempo sword techniques Lieutenant Lee showed me in Korea. Effective. Scary looking. Perfect. I thought as I paid for my new weapon.

Back at my dojang, I felt better already. I leaned the bat up against the wall of my office, just behind the door. After what Master An told me, I wasn't going anywhere. Cowards who would not show their faces were not going to intimidate me into closing my new school. If they did show their faces, I was ready.

I told Yunbok about the threats the day I bought the bat. "Please be careful," she said, unable to hide her fear and worry.

"I will," I promised. "Bullies are nothing more than cowards." Then, to reassure her, I added, "But I do look around outside very carefully every time I leave."

Walking Tall in Fort Worth, Texas

I told her about the bat. She saw "Walking Tall," too, so she understood — and couldn't help but smile at the image of this small Korean man "Walking Tall."

"If they come after me," I said, "I'll be just as scary as he was in the movie." I made an imaginary twirl of my samurai bat over my head and let out a fierce kihap.

She laughed. "You scare *me*," she said.

"All they're trying to do is scare me," I said. "So if those cowards put even one foot in my school, "Buford Pusser" Park will give them a taste of their own medicine."

◊◊

As if answering that challenge, they came in a few days later. I was in my office doing paperwork when I heard the door open, then shuffling footsteps that sounded like trouble. Without making a sound, I stood up, got the bat from behind the door and, bat tucked out of sight by my side, stood in the doorway of my office.

There were three of them, big and tall, wearing cowboy hats and boots.

"May I help you?" I asked, putting my most pleasant expression on my face. The first look at them told me these were the cowards who had been leaving notes on my door.

"I don't need your help," the biggest one said. "I'll just look around."

He walked over to a picture I had hanging on the wall in the training room near my office. I got up and followed him, leaving plenty of distance between us. The bat was still tucked by my side.

"Is this you?" he asked, jabbing a dirty finger at the glass.

"Yes," I said, keeping my tone even.

He flipped the picture off the wall. When it hit the ground, the glass shattered the frame split in two.

"Oh dear me," he said. "Did I break you?"

I ignored him, turning my attention to the other two who were now walking around the training floor in their boots, making a point to touch everything on the walls.

"Hey," I said, pointing at their feet. "Please take off your shoes."

"I don't want to," one of them said, not even looking at me.

Anger rising, I gripped the bat tighter; I wondered if they were armed — and with what. "Are you guys here to cause trouble?" I asked them as if offering refreshments. As I talked, I moved toward the biggest one, still keeping the bat hidden by my side.

They said nothing, watching me.

"Because if you guys are here to cause me trouble," I said, raising the bat over my head, then screaming like a samurai warrior, "I will kill you!"

I ran right at the biggest one then, swinging the bat as if I intended to take off his head. Adjusting my swing at just the last second, I knocked off his hat instead.

"Oh my God! You're crazy!" he screamed, running for the door, leaving his hat where it landed. His friends followed, and I followed the three of them out into the parking lot, screaming and swinging that bat as hard as I could, buzzing within inches of their retreating bodies so that they could feel — and hear — how close I was to making contact.

"Yes! I'm crazy!" I screamed after them. "And if you ever come back here to bother me again, I will break your head like a watermelon!"

They ran across the parking lot. People came out of the surrounding businesses to see what was going on. "What's the matter?" someone shouted. "Did they steal something?"

"Everything's fine," I called out to my neighbors as I smiled at my beautiful samurai bat.

When I told Roy my samurai bat story, he laughed until tears rolled down his face. "Good for you, Master Park!" he said, slapping me on the back. "Good for you!"

I thought about it later and the reality of the situation hit me. Although I took a big chance with that bat, it was the right choice. If I had bought a gun and they started acting that way, I might have shot them in fear. If I had used taekwondo against them and hurt them, I would have been in trouble with the law. But as far as I knew, there was no law against waving a bat, screaming like a crazy person and scaring troublemaker cowards away.

In the movie, Buford had actually hit people with his bat. As terrible as that was, it worked to my advantage. The boys didn't know that I wasn't going to hit them. And they did understand the bat.

Then I began to worry. Would they come back with guns? Would they follow me home? Would they try to hurt or scare my family the way I had scared them? I was alert for trouble from them for a long time after that, but I never saw or heard from those young men again.

Raising a family in America offered opportunities and experiences they never could have had in Korea. Still, it was very important to us that we teach them to love and honor their Korean roots along with their American life.

My son, Johnny, was powerful and strong as a fighter and in his breaking demonstrations, as shown here. I always smiled when I watched him compete. Just like me, he never backed up.

Fort Worth Texas, circa 1982
Watching my daughter, Suyun, whose American name became
Susie, compete and win in forms competition was a delight
I never considered. I glowed with pride when I heard people
whisper in awe, "That's Won Park's daughter!"

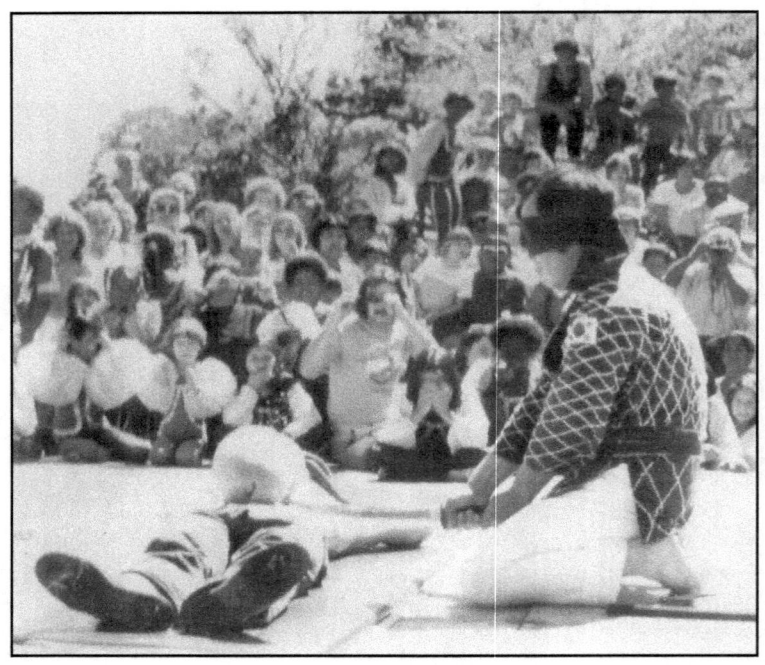

Fort Worth Mayfest, circa 1980
Here, as the grand finale to my students' demonstration of kicking, self-defense and breaking, I sliced a watermelon with a Samurai sword on top of a volunteer's abdomen. It had very little to do with taekwondo, but the crowd seemed to like it — as did the local media.

CHAPTER FIFTEEN:

Magic in the U.S. Media

Even though my classes were not filling up as quickly as I hoped, one of my new students, a doctor, scheduled private lessons for himself and his son three times a week. Since I charged more for private lessons, this helped a little bit. Then, as others learned about private lessons, they asked for them as well. This was funny to me, because I had no other students anyway, but this way they could choose their class time, rather than adhere to my class schedule.

Hoping to eventually fill regular class times as well, I kept those times blocked off, even when there was no class to teach. By the end of February, I had seven students taking private lessons, but my classes were still empty for the most part. I was sitting in my office, wondering what I could do to get more students, the phone rang.

"Master Park?" The voice on the other end of the line was somewhat familiar, but I couldn't place it.

"Yes?" I answered, then asked, "Who is this?"

"Griffin," he said. "I was a green belt at your school in Detroit."

"Oh!" I said, picturing the face right away. "How are you? How did you get my number?"

"From a friend who lives in Plano and met you when you were there looking for a location for your dojang," he said. "I live in Fort Worth, too, now, and I work for Channel 8 in their advertising department. Can I come visit you?"

"Yes! I'd love to see you!" I said.

"Tomorrow?"

"Sure!" I said. "Please, come have lunch with me. It will be wonderful to see you."

When Griffin arrived the next day, we ate lunch, caught up on each other's lives, and then he came to the point. "I can help you get new students with some TV advertising," he said.

I had never considered TV advertising because I assumed it was very expensive. Griffin explained his plan. If I purchased one 30-second spot, he would also use it to fill in, anytime there was a gap, mostly late at night.

"In late night programming, we always need advertising to fill these small spaces in our schedule," he said. "When I discovered you were here, I thought it might be a perfect way for you to get a lot of good exposure."

Griffin explained that while prime time commercials could cost as much as $3,000 per run, these late night slots could be as little as $20 each. Griffin said that because he was the one who scheduled them, he could make sure my commercial ran as often as possible and in the best spots available.

It was an interesting idea, and I knew I had to do something different — my usual marketing plan was just not working this time. So every night for the next two months, Griffin put a 30-second advertisement he created for Won Park Institute of Taekwondo in at least one, and sometimes two, of these available spots. And to my surprise, people saw them, even in those strange late night slots. Master Lee called me from Midland to say he saw it; then a lady in the grocery store recognized me.

"You're a celebrity!" Yunbok teased.

Even though few if any students joined right away because of my TV spot, Griffin assured me that the $2,000 I ended up spending on this advertising would be worth it over time. He was right. When the movie," "The Karate Kid" came out the same time as my TV ads began, new students began arriving every single day. Often, they came in groups, then each new student brought friends, their friends' friends, and sometimes, their parents. Within two months, every class was full and my desk drawer was stuffed with signed contracts.

Unable to contain my curiosity any longer, I went to see this movie that, just by happening to coincide with my TV ad, changed my future. While the physical technique in the movie was not that strong, the relationship between the master and the student gave me great insight. Judging by the appeal of this movie, American people seemed to be inspired by this time-honored relationship so familiar to Asian cultures in which both master and student invest their utmost respect and discipline to create a unique exchange between them in which each gives even as he receives. "Taekwondo gives human beings a powerful opportunity to transform ourselves," my master had said the day he placed his own black belt in my hands in tribute. ". . . to share this opportunity with others is both our gift and our responsibility."

Not only had I personally witnessed the power and transformation of this amazing bond in my own life as a student, but now, as a master, I was starting to see the other side — how sharing this knowledge with others was transforming me yet again. What was especially interesting to me was how closely the touching relationship between the main characters of Karate Kid mirrored my relationship with my own master, and now, more often than not, I felt that kind of connection with my own students. Americans want to experience this transformation in their own lives, I realized with excitement. Once again I was amazed that taekwondo had placed me in exactly the right place at exactly the right time, and what's more, given me an important gift to share.

"What do you teach here?" they always asked first when they came in to meet me and see my school. Then came the next question, "Is this the same stuff we saw in The Karate Kid?"

"What impressed you about the movie?" I'd always ask. "Was it the championship?"

"No," they'd most often say. "It was the philosophy — the discipline and the respect."

"Yes," I'd tell them, "the way I teach is similar. The karate tournaments and training styles are different, but the basic martial arts philosophy is the same."

Understanding their motivation and interest didn't change anything I taught, but it did give me a few good opportunities for "wax on, wax off" jokes. While Karate Kid was mostly about getting ready for a tournament, I understood that my job was to teach them how to apply what they learned as student of taekwondo to get ready for life.

◊◊

With the wonderful reversal of fortune that resulted from my burgeoning enrollment, and after driving back and forth between our apartment in Arlington and my taekwondo school in Fort Worth for nearly a year, we bought a house on the west side of Fort Worth and moved in just in time for the children to start school there in the fall of 1979.

In 1980 Yunbok, Suyun and I became official American citizens. To make life a little easier for us, especially the children in school, Yunbok and the children took American names as we planned when Sae Jun was born. Yunbok became Julie, a beautiful name I picked out for her. Suyun officially became Susie, the name she was already using in school anyway, and Sae Jun was, of course, Johnny.

By that time, Suyun had become an excellent taekwondo student, showing tremendous focus and concentration in class. She excelled at poomse, with grace that reminded me of Young Soon when she danced. However, to the same degree Suyun loved poomse, she hated fighting.

"Daddy, why do we have to fight?" she would always ask.

"It's good for your confidence," I would tell her.

"But I don't like it."

The class was mostly boys and she was small. I knew she was worried about getting hurt.

"You need to practice fighting for self-defense," I told her.

She understood and did her best to acquire "good enough" fighting skills, but she never developed the love for it I had always felt. Putting her heart instead into her poomse competition, she won nearly every tournament she entered, collecting more than 20 first place poomse trophies by the time she reached 2nd dan.

"That's Won Park's daughter," I would hear people whisper as they watched her perform in tournaments. I just smiled, remembering how she learned all the color belt forms just by watching, before she was old enough to be allowed in class.

When Johnny turned five years old, he began his taekwondo training. Shy like his mother, Johnny preferred to sit back and watch, analyzing every movement before trying it the first time. With both children now practicing taekwondo, it was fun to see their very different temperaments expressed in their fighting styles. Susie, the more outgoing, was more aggressive in her sparring — despite her disdain for it. Johnny, the more reserved, always waited, keeping his distance until others committed, then moving in close and never backing up, just as I always do.

Since Johnny was so quiet, I could never be sure what he was thinking. He was very strong inside, but he kept his thoughts to himself. As a young child, he never wanted to order his own food at McDonalds. Assuming this was because he was too shy to speak up, I always chided him, "You need to do this — you're getting to be a big boy."

Still he refused.

Then one day, when I kept on about it, saying, "Why can't you order your own food?"

He looked at me with a level stare that reminded me so much myself it almost made me laugh. "I can," he said. "I just don't want to."

Korean culture teaches parents to be firm in the discipline of their children. However, having seen that idea taken to the extreme among American military families, I also tried to temper my firmness with understanding and listening. Sometimes I was successful at this, sometimes I was not.

"You're being too strong with them," Julie would say to me privately in those less-than-patient times.

"I'm not."

"Yes, you are."

With very little memory of my own father, I had little to go on when it came to knowing how to act as a father and husband. In Korea, family roles are spelled out very clearly, but in America, parenting styles vary with the individuals involved. I saw these styles reflected in the discipline — or lack of discipline — in my taekwondo students, and as I danced back and forth across these cultural lines with my own children, I struggled to be firm in my discipline, according to my roots, yet kind and supportive as I had seen the best American parents to be.

As part of the Fort Worth community, my taekwondo school participated in a citywide celebration known as Mayfest.

Soon after my Fort Worth, Texas dojang opened, the movie, The Karate Kid, propelled martial arts training for children into the national spotlight. As my reputation for working well with children and teenagers grew, so did my enrollment.

Adult classes also filled quickly, partially with parents joining their children in training, creating several key "taekwondo families." As the health, exercise, self-defense, and stress relief benefits of taekwondo became apparent to these adult students, they began to bring friends.

Beginning with a collegiate tournament in 1981 to show my TCU students the excitement of intercollegiate team competition, the now legendary Fort Worth International Tournament laid the groundwork for uniting an influential group of Texas taekwondo masters.

CHAPTER SIXTEEN:
Visionary Connections of Old and New

In the fall of 1980, I decided to visit the two colleges in Fort Worth — Texas Wesleyan College and Texas Christian University — to offer to teach a taekwondo class as part of their physical education program. After speaking with the appropriate people at each college and explaining my background, the kind of program I wanted to start, and how I would conduct a university taekwondo class, both schools were interested, but in the end I chose TCU. Texas Wesleyan was a very good college, but TCU was a university and had nearly 7,000 students to Wesleyan's 1,000. It was easy to see that teaching there would open many more doors and expose taekwondo to a much bigger student population.

The faculty teaching position TCU offered me, although very low in pay, proved to be a wonderful opportunity to build my reputation in Fort Worth's collegiate community. The best part was that even though I taught at TCU on both Tuesday and Thursday afternoons from one to three, I was still able to run a full schedule of classes at the dojang without adding another instructor.

I began with 40 excited students in the second floor gym of TCU's Rickel Building. Because this room was also home to TCU's ballet classes, it had beautiful wood floors and ballet bars and mirrors along one wall. It was perfect for taekwondo class and, I noted with great satisfaction, the first time I had wood floors for my students since Seoul.

I also soon discovered a wonderful difference in teaching college students. Aged 18 and up, they were in the best mental and physical condition of any students I had taught in a long time. Their focus was sharp and it was easy to demonstrate a technique and then have them follow me exactly and remember every detail. Teaching this class was as easy as my toughest class in Detroit was difficult.

To my delight, many of these college students later came to my school to train to supplement their college class. On the other hand, some of my high school students at the dojang continued their training for college credit once they graduated from high school and enrolled as students at TCU. Some of the faculty and other instructors in the PE department began to show up in my dojang classes, and these overlapping friendships grew right along with my reputation, much as they had during my time on both Korean and American Military bases in Seoul.

When three TCU coeds were murdered, a local outcry arose for a self-defense program for college girls. The next thing I knew, I had been interviewed for the campus newspaper, a story about my class was aired by the TCU TV and radio stations, and my class was featured on Channel 11 News. Standing in the middle of the media response to this tragedy, I was able to explain to a much wider audience that taekwondo training was good for girls — as self-defense and to develop self-confidence that, more often than not, help keep them from being targeted. After seeing how taekwondo built this kind of self-confidence and inner strength in my own daughter, I was able to speak from my heart about how important it was to teach taekwondo to every young woman.

As I worked with these eager and talented college students, an idea began to stir within me. Remembering my days of team tournament competition in Korea, I wanted to share this excitement with my TCU students, to show them what true tournament-style team taekwondo competition was all about. In Korea intercollegiate taekwondo team competition was held just once a year as the culmination of that year's hard training. Only the most highly respected college taekwondo teams were invited, and these spectacular events drew local spectators, inspired other practitioners, and helped build the taekwondo programs of each participating school.

The trouble with trying to duplicate this experience for my American students was that, unlike Korean colleges, few American colleges had taekwondo teams. A traditional Korean taekwondo team required five members and a few alternates. Where could I find other college taekwondo PE programs like mine and inspire them to form a competition team?

After a little bit of research, I discovered that the University of Texas in Arlington (UTA) had a small taekwondo program, as did the University of Texas in Austin (UT), Rice University in Houston, and Sam Houston State University. Excited, I began making plans for a first-ever Texas intercollegiate taekwondo team competition to be hosted by TCU.

I sent invitations to the four other schools I found in Texas, and all but one came. Since we had only four college teams participating, I decided that to give this tournament the splash and excitement I was looking for I would also offer individual events, making this two tournaments in one. To fill out the draws of the individual events, I invited the masters and their students from the 27 or 28 taekwondo schools in Texas at the time.

Since the teams and individuals participating in this tournament were coming at my invitation, I decided to call this tournament the Fort Worth Invitational Taekwondo Tournament. It was 1981, and already taekwondo's rise in popularity across the country and around the world had started the quiet murmur that this new competitive sport may one day become an Olympic event. In keeping with that idea, I decided to use the point system for the team competition — five points for gold, three for silver, and one for bronze — and award medals in all categories in my tournament. Although there were plenty of Karate tournaments and Open tournaments for taekwondo practitioners to enter, the Fort Worth Invitational would be the first dedicated and traditional taekwondo tournament — and definitely the first intercollegiate taekwondo team tournament in Texas.

The excitement of bringing Texas taekwondo students together at the grassroots of what all the masters sensed would one day be something big was fuel for my 41-year-old imagination. The TCU PE department got behind my tournament with a budget and manpower to help support the success of this event. They told me often that they never imagined when we started the taekwondo PE class that TCU would become host to the first-ever intercollegiate taekwondo team tournament in Texas.

The tournament came together exactly as planned. About 20 of my students from TCU entered, the most of any school. In both divisions, intercollegiate and open, combined, we hosted about 218 competitors from all four participating schools — TCU, Rice, UTA and UT. In addition to masters bringing students to compete, many other Korean masters came to the tournament just to watch and be part of this bold new step in taekwondo.

The week following the tournament, my triumphant TCU taekwondo students organized a TCU Taekwondo Club and were already searching for other team competitions to enter. The Department Chair made our tournament budget a special activities budget, so that when we did go to other tournaments, the school would pay for it. By then, everyone involved was catching the excitement of this up-and-coming sport as it began its drive to the Olympics.

◊◊

My excitement over the tournament and the many doors it opened for the future of taekwondo bubbled over in enthusiasm that amused Julie. Always supportive, she worked tirelessly alongside me to help take care of the many critical details of the tournament.

"Slow down! Take a breath!" she had said more than once on tournament day as I rushed from place to place to make sure everything was as it should be.

Julie handled all the registration, and right beside her, even as young as they were, Johnny and Susie did their assigned tasks — Susie made sure that the competitors' paperwork stacks stayed straight and Johnny, sitting next to her, was in charge of handing each person a wristband as soon as they registered, paid, and could be admitted to the tournament floor. A crew of volunteers surrounded them, each with jobs to do, all reporting to Julie. On the rare occasion in which a question arose that Julie couldn't answer, it was Susie's other job to come find me. In addition to TCU students, faculty, staff and friends, the adult students at my dojang provided core support for the details of competition — as referees, judges, scorekeepers and other officials.

Immediately following the tournament, Julie had organized some friends — other masters' wives and friends from the Korean community — to prepare a feast of traditional Korean food for an appreciation dinner to thank the tournament volunteers for their hard work. I watched my students' faces as they took tentative mouthfuls of the sampling on their plates. I smiled at Julie from across the room as I noticed her watching them, too. Soon, caution turned to either delight or disgust as unfamiliar tastes created new friends or foes of Korean food. Some came back for seconds, and it was easy to see which dishes were most popular. *More of this, less of that,* I knew Julie was making a silent notes as she surveyed the leftovers.

I raised my glass to salute this wonderful group of students, saying, "Working together, side by side, we created and ran a successful tournament. Good job and thank you!" Then, as I looked around the room and this special group of people, all brought together by taekwondo, I knew there was something else I wanted to tell them.

"We all have families, we all have friends, but the friendships taekwondo makes are different. Taekwondo "families" have a special bond like no other, and what we are building here, in addition to a successful tournament, is a taekwondo family that will last a lifetime."

Feeling the emotions starting to rise, I sat down quickly. *How can I help them understand how important these relationships could be to them someday?* I wondered. *How can I help them learn to value these friendships as we do in Korean culture so they truly will last for a lifetime?* If I could give this gift to my students, I would consider myself a great success as their master.

◊◊

When I planned the Fort Worth Invitational Tournament, I was thinking of my American students. I wanted to show them all the special traditions of a true Korean taekwondo tournament, just as I and all the masters gathered there remembered from our Seoul competition days. However, when I looked at the crowd of masters, sitting in straight rows of chairs behind the podium where I made my traditional welcome speech as part of a formal opening ceremony, just as we had always done in Seoul, something else occurred to me.

We all knew each other and stayed in touch as well as we could, but we had never, before this tournament, gotten together as a group, here on American soil. Seeing all these masters together was a wonderful sight to me, and at dinner after the tournament we decided that as Texas taekwondo masters, we should start getting together regularly to keep each other informed of what was going on in taekwondo. It was strange to me that while taekwondo associations already existed in many other states besides Michigan, Texas masters, for some reason, had never organized.

We settled on a Korean restaurant we all liked in Dallas, and at our first meeting decided to organize our group as the Texas Taekwondo Association, agreeing this was a move that would be good for Texas taekwondo, good for our students, and good for us.

It was during my time in Detroit that Master Chung and the other Michigan masters formed the Michigan Taekwondo Association. Serving as this group's Secretary General, I had gained valuable experience in state association process. When the Texas masters discovered I had this knowledge and experience, and since I was the only one among us who had ever even been in this kind of association before, their unanimous vote named me president of the new Texas Taekwondo Association.

In 1982, at the age of 42, I set the course for the Texas Taekwondo Association's pursuit of two different kinds of goals. First, to help Texas taekwondo practitioners statewide qualify for the upcoming Olympic trials and pre-Olympic international competitions. Second, we wanted to help these individual practitioners get ready for international competition.

To select our Texas team, we decided to hold a qualifying tournament. Following AAU guidelines, I organized this tournament, to be held in Dallas with the help of two vice presidents, Chang Sik Lee and Sang Jung Kim, a secretary general, Kyu Boong Yim, an organizing committee and a referee committee. Between 200 and 250 competitors came to our first qualifying tournament, traveling to Dallas from taekwondo schools all over the state. Even though none of the competitors on the Texas Team we selected that first year won a medal at Nationals, we were on our way to establishing a system for selection, training and competition in Texas.

◊◊

Consumed by the excitement and challenge of organizing the Texas Taekwondo Association and the first Texas Team qualifying tournament in Dallas, I had been spending far too much time away from home. It was a delicate balance to follow my professional passion as a taekwondo master while taking good care of my personal passion, my family. Julie understood this challenge and often helped me find this balance when it started to slip away.

"I need to talk to you about Sae Jun," she said one night when everyone was asleep.

She said that for the past week our son had seemed upset and angry after school every day, but he wouldn't tell her why.

"Will you see if you can find out the trouble?" she asked. It was rare for her to ask anything like this of me, so I knew it must be serious.

While both of our children did well in school and made very good grades, Susie seemed to have an easier time socially. Johnny's reserved nature seemed to make it hard for him to make friends. Even though he was only in the second grade, everything was very serious to him.

"I don't want to go to school today," he said the next morning at breakfast, opening the door for our discussion.

"Why not?" I asked.

"The kids make fun of me," he said.

"What do they say?" I asked, keeping my tone casual, but feeling anger on the rise.

"They call me Japanese," he blurted out. His face revealed the depth of his pain. "I tell them, ' NO! I'm KOREAN, and they just say 'NO, you're not. You're JAPANESE.'"

"What are you going to do about it?" I asked, curious what his answer would reveal.

"I'm not going to go to school," he said.

"You can't miss school just because of some boys' stupidity," his mother interjected. "You're going to school and you're going to ignore them." That, it appeared, was that.

"But there's another thing that's bothering me," he said, the floodgate was open and tears began to flow. "There's a talent show next week, and we're all supposed to do something." He wailed, "I don't have any talent!"

I thought for a moment. "What about taekwondo?"

"Is that a talent?" he said, as if considering this for the first time.

I laughed. "It can be — if you practice," I teased.

"No," he said, "Taekwondo isn't a real talent — is just something we do. Real talent is singing or dancing or telling funny jokes."

I snorted. "That is talent done by people who don't know taekwondo." I looked at him. "Sae Jun, you know something special that none of those kids know at all." I squeezed his arm. "You are strong, you have power, skill, speed and technique. You have taekwondo because you are Korean. If you want to set them straight on what being Korean means — and to make them remember that you are Korean and not anything else, show them your special Korean talent. Show them your taekwondo."

He was quiet, thinking this over. I noticed he was sitting up a little straighter. "What should I do?" he asked, the decision made.

"Breaking," I said. I looked at Susie. "Will you help him with this demonstration?

"Of course!" She looked at her little brother with a fierce tenderness that I was proud of. It was much the same way I remember Young Soon looking at me when we were trying to solve much more difficult problems together.

Watching the power, beauty and pride of Johnny's taekwondo demonstration in the school talent show brought Julie and me both to tears. It was hard to know whether it was Johnny's newfound courage and power or the support of his sister that touched us more deeply. Regardless, their impressive performance brought down the house. As he smiled and bowed to the crowd, we knew Johnny Park would have no more problems in school — and no one would ever again forget that he was Korean.

Julie and I still spoke Korean to each other and with the children at home, but at school and to each other, my children spoke English. We made friends in Fort Worth's Korean community, including many at a Catholic church with a largely Korean congregation. When the adults got together for frequent social events, our children played together. It was fun to watch all these first generation Korean American children grow up, integrating the two cultures in their language, their tastes, and their perceptions. All day at school and with their American friends, they spoke English, even to each other. At Korean community gatherings and social events, they spoke a combination of Korean and English — darting in and out of both cultures as they interacted with their families and each other.

"You have to be Americanized to live life well as an American," I told them. "But it is also good to observe Korean customs, eat Korean food, and be able to speak and write the Korean language. It is very good to know and practice both."

My family seemed to be doing well in its adaptation to American culture, learning and practicing American ways as needed, yet still keeping our Korean heritage alive and running parallel to our American life. We learned how to do this as we went along, by trial and error, knowing as we did that our only goal was to give our children a sense of comfort and identity within both cultures.

"You are American," I told my children, explaining to them the importance of understanding and embracing their cultural heritage while at the same time being fully and devotedly American. "America is our home. We are American citizens. America has given us a wonderful life and opportunities none of us would have had in Korea."

Then I guided them to stand in front of our large, ornate hallway mirror. "But look in the mirror," I said, looking into the reflections of their beautiful faces. "You are also Korean, because that is your heritage. It is also important to understand the culture of your parents and their native country."

I turned to Johnny. "Johnny you were born here. You have learned American ways and are getting a wonderful American education. But does that change the shape of your face, your hair, eye or skin color?

"No, and I don't want it to," he answered, studying his face as if really seeing it for the first time.

I smiled. "Good answer. You belong to two countries, two cultures. One we have chosen, and one we were born to. We are like adopted children," I said. "America is our adoptive parent, but Korea will always be our birth mother, and it is good to have a special place in your heart for both. No matter how much your life changes, your blood you cannot change."

◊◊

In 1982 we decided it was time to give our children firsthand experience of their cultural roots in a month-long visit to Korea. It was the first time I had been back there since I came to the United States. It was wonderful to show Korea to my children for the first time and watch with delight as they met their Korean relatives for the first time. I welcomed the opportunity to give them a more personal understanding of the deep connection between Korean people that runs in sacred ribbons throughout our ancestral culture.

We stayed with Yunbok's mother so the children could get to know their only grandmother, and a revolving houseful of relatives from both our families excitedly welcomed us all.

Of all the Korean customs they observed firsthand during our trip, the one that left them both mystified was how the oldest son was so blatantly favored — given all the best food, clothes, toys, and opportunities.

"Why is this?" Johnny asked on the long plane ride back to America. For him, our only son, the matter was academic.

Susie, on the other hand was indignant. "It's not fair," she observed. Julie smiled at the American expression.

"Korean custom dictates that in every family, it is the lifelong responsibility of the oldest son to take care of the parents," Julie explained. "Therefore, it is natural that the oldest son is given more benefits — food, clothing and education — both to prepare him well for this important job and to repay him for this sacrifice he is bound to for life. No matter how many children there are, he must be the one to take care of the parents until they die."

They both grew quiet, trying to put this into their own perspectives.

"What do the other children think about that?" Johnny wanted to know.

I laughed. "Over there, there are many things people do not think about or question at all," I said. "They just accept what is." I thought for a moment, remembering how this was in my friends' families. "When they are younger, children may complain inside, 'Why just him? Why does he get everything when we are hungry, too?' and the parents, seeing their younger children hungry, may say inside, 'Because he is going to have to take care of his parents for his entire life.'"

I turned to Susie. "The daughters are free to get married, go and have their own lives; the oldest son can never leave. He has to take care of his parents until they die."

"Wow," they said in unison, each lost in their own reflections on "not fair."

Yunbok (now Julie) and I visited a replica of the traditional Korean village both our families grew up in.

Here we don traditional Korean wedding clothes once again for a photo.

1982 Family trip back to Korea
My children were not sure what to expect, and neither were we. What we all discovered on this trip was that it is possible to nurture your roots in one country and still blossom and grow in another.

In honor of the 25th anniversary of the Fort Worth International Taekwondo Championships, the City of Fort Worth, Texas issued a special proclamation of October 15, 2005 as "Grandmaster Won Chik Park Day"

CHAPTER SEVENTEEN:
Grandmaster Won Chik Park

When I earned my 7th dan promotion at age 36 while I was still in Detroit, I did as my master always instructed — I made a new goal. While I once thought being a Master was as far as I would ever want to go, once my 7th dan certificate was in my hands, I knew that one day I wanted to be called Grandmaster, just as my own master had done.

Kukkiwon sets the minimum age for 8th dan, Grandmaster, promotion at 44. It requires a minimum of eight years of study following a 7th dan promotion, and the criteria is very specific in the kinds of accomplishments and experiences that will make one worthy of this rare and special title. With so much going on in Texas taekwondo and my family life, I had all but forgotten this personal goal. My accomplishments during this time, however, had continued to accumulate.

In 1984, with my 44th birthday circled in red on my wall calendar, I realized I would soon be eligible for my Grandmaster test. After checking into the requirements, I discovered that with all I had done during the past seven years, including university-level teaching, tournament organizing, and leadership of the Texas Taekwondo Association, I more than met these requirements.

Another requirement for 8th dan promotion was to select one technique — I chose speed breaking — and write a paper on how to practice and perfect that technique in order to teach it to others. With my newfound interest in organizing and standardizing taekwondo teaching, this assignment fit very well with everything else I was doing.

To begin the promotion process, I first contacted my master in Pusan for his approval and formal letter of recommendation to Kukkiwon. As always, he was more than happy to do this; in fact, he had said with a chuckle, he had been waiting every day for my call.

Next, I prepared my resume, building upon the accomplishments already listed on my 7th dan resume. With each new entry, I reflected on how it equipped me to be called, "Grandmaster:" teaching experience at an American university; organizing, founding, and serving as president of the first Texas Taekwondo Association; establishing my own annual invitational taekwondo championship; organizing a qualifying tournament for Texas taekwondo competitors who hoped to one day go to the Olympics.

I looked in the mirror at my 44-year-old face. Grandmasters are usually old, having seen, experienced and accomplished much. Looking again at my resume and application before I sealed the envelope, I realized that what was listed there in black and white could well have belonged to a very old man. I patted my young face, sealed the envelope and sent my application to Kukkiwon.

Approval arrived three weeks later. Enclosed with my approved petition to test was the seven-page written exam. First, I was to provide instruction on how to teach a class, and then how to train and develop an instructor to teach a class. Then I was asked to write a summary of the standardized instruction each practitioner should learn at each belt level, including the correct balance of instruction between fighting, poomse, and self-defense.

Then the test asked me to explain the meaning behind each aspect of taekwondo training, why each was important to overall knowledge at each level, and why balance between these elements was so important. My explanation included: why fighters need poomse; how poomse improves self-defense; what purpose practicing specific combinations of techniques serves; how to teach students to combine techniques to achieve this purpose on their own to balance their individual strengths and weaknesses; correct practice of the kihap — and what purpose this serves; how to teach each breaking technique on different materials; the importance of speed; when and how to use jumping techniques as opposed to standing techniques; specific conditioning strategies to improve a student's speed, power, jumping or breaking — the list seemed to go on forever, criss-crossing my entire experience of taekwondo, both as a student and as a master.

I sat back at my desk after I completed the last section of this test, as exhausted as if I had executed all the techniques I explained — in the deep sand and hot sun with no water. I realized that the thick document I mailed back to Kukkiwon contained the sum total of everything I knew about taekwondo. On December 15, 1984, Kukkiwon confirmed that it was enough. For the rest of my life, I would be called Grandmaster Won Chik Park.

◊◊

It seemed like Susie had been on the phone for hours. At age 11, this was starting to be a normal occurrence, but even though I couldn't hear exactly what she was saying, there seemed to be more squealing and giggling than usual coming from behind the closed door of her room. There would be a pause, the sound of dialing and it would all start again with a new person. A couple of times I thought I heard my name, followed by more squealing.

"Who all is she talking to?" I asked Julie as I padded through the kitchen in my socks. "Is there something going on here I should know about?" I had taken a rare day off and was getting ready to go play golf, a delightful and intensely frustrating sport I was just learning to play. It was also, I discovered, addictive. I played every time my schedule and the weather agreed to allow it.

"I believe she is talking to everyone," Julie said, continuing to chop vegetables for that evening's meal. "She's telling all her friends the news."

"What news?" I asked, lacing up my shoes.

Julie stopped and looked at me. Then she laughed. "Your promotion to Grandmaster!"

"Oh," I said. I knew it was big news to me, but I never considered that Susie would be so excited. "Wow. What do her friends say about that?"

"They are very impressed," she said.

"Impressed about what?" Johnny said, appearing at the door of the kitchen. He opened the refrigerator door, looking for a snack.

"Your father's promotion," Julie said, then added, "don't eat anything now, dinner will be ready soon."

"I'm hungry now," he said, not so much in argument, but as a statement of fact.

I poked playfully at his recently expanded little eight-year-old belly. "You don't look very hungry to me," I teased. Julie and the children had just returned from another extended trip to Korea to visit relatives. It had been a month-long party, and from the looks of things, a bountiful Korean expression of love through food.

Even though I almost didn't recognize my son when I picked them up from the airport —they had to buy him new clothes to wear home — it amused me and made me happy to see how much he had enjoyed the abundance of good food in every home they visited, each branch of the family trying to out-do the others.

Remembering how intoxicating the smells of traditional Korean food have always been to me, I smiled. As much as I have always loved to eat, visceral attachment to these special smells were less about the food than the trail of memories they beckoned as only smells can — my mother's cooking in the back of my parents' restaurant, my brother-in-law's house before his wedding, then the food brought to my apartment by my 11 Club friends, prepared by their mothers. The first day I walked into our tiny Detroit apartment to smell Julie's cooking when my family was together at last.

I looked at her now, still cooking, still filling our home with that aroma that always symbolized love in my life. I inhaled these wonderful smells once again and smiled at my son. "When you have the opportunity to eat good Korean food, you should eat a lot of it!"

I knew that with just a few taekwondo classes and a return to his regular eating habits, Johnny's puffy little body would soon return to normal, but the memories associated with those foods would be with him forever.

When Susie joined us in the kitchen, I peered at the side of her head, pretending to be looking for something.

"What?" she asked, patting the spot where I had focused my scrutiny.

"I was looking for the phone," I said. "It's hard to recognize you without it there on the side of your head."

She laughed. "Well I have to tell everyone!" she said

"Tell everyone what?" I teased.

"About my Grandmaster Daddy," she said hugging me. "Everyone thinks it is so cool to know someone whose dad is a real grandmaster! How may people can say that?"

"Cool?" I didn't recall ever being called "cool" before. "So does that make me cool?" I persisted.

"Well, I don't know." Now it was her turn to tease. "You're still a dad."

I pretended to ponder this. "So maybe this makes me a 'cool dad' then?"

"The coolest!"

We settled into our chairs, blessed the food and began dinner. I looked across the table at Julie and smiled. "I'm a cool dad," I said, putting a piece of chicken on my plate.

She returned the smile. "I know," she said.

◊◊

I looked out at a sea of more than 100 faces, turned toward me as one. Almost everyone on the guest list had come. From old friends and masters from Korea to my family — my wife and children and their friends — to some of my newest students, all were here for this huge celebration dinner and ceremony in honor of my promotion to grandmaster.

When my senior students asked if they could organize this party, I hesitated. As much as I didn't like being the center of attention, I did want to share this important moment in my life with the people who were important to me. "OK, but please keep it simple," I told them.

I looked around me. Far from simple, the event that resulted from their weeks of combined efforts, despite their own very busy lives and full schedules, touched my heart. They reserved a big local ballroom, located and invited all the Korean Masters from our tournament list and my private address book, students, families and friends from my Main School and TCU, personal friends from my church and the Korean community, and many others who were in some way connected to my students and wanted to be there and be part of this special celebration.

While my students, enlisting the help of Julie and Susie on a few items, handled all the party preparations, one question troubled me. Who could make this presentation to me? Kukkiwon had already sent my certificate. It came in the mail in a big manila envelope with cardboard to keep it from bending. It seemed wrong to just take it out of the envelope, go have it framed, and hang it on my wall. But I could not present it to myself, and, in what I considered a funny problem to have, every master I could think of was now lower ranking and could not make this presentation.

For my 7th dan promotion, an unrelated visit from Grandmaster Chong Woo Lee to the Detroit area just happened to coincide with receiving my 7th dan certificate in the mail. In a small, informal ceremony at my school, Grandmaster Lee had made a very special presentation to me with my Detroit students and family there as witnesses.

Unfortunately I could think of no one at that level who would be anywhere near Texas any time soon. Then, when I was just about to give up, I learned that Grandmaster Kim Soo, a good friend from Korea who was now an 8th dan grandmaster, was living in Houston. I called him, told him about my promotion, invited him to the party, and asked him if he would be willing to present my certificate to me.

"It would be an honor to make this presentation to you," he said.

Grandmaster Kim Soo repeated this conversation as he addressed the packed ballroom. As both the highest-ranking grandmaster in Texas and my good friend, he told the crowd, how could he not make this presentation?

As he talked, I looked around the ballroom, face to face, soaking in every detail, appreciating each person there. I was humbled not only by the number of people who had come to honor my accomplishment, but also by the many different kinds of people there. All ages, all occupations, all ethnicities, brought together by taekwondo — and their love and respect for me.

One by one, the Korean masters took their turn sharing their own memories and connection to me. Some of my senior students spoke, telling their own special memories of my teaching and how it had affected their lives. There were many gifts, many special presentations, so much kindness, love and respect, I wondered if I had died and was somehow attending my own funeral. I laughed at this image, and if I hadn't been at the center of this stage with so many eyes on me, I might have slapped myself to make sure I was still here.

Then it was my turn to respond to this outpouring. As I stood, I was not at all sure I would be able to speak. The speech I so carefully prepared now seemed so inadequate to express all I was feeling. What words could I say to thank them well enough for all they had given to me? I thought again of the circle my master described, the never-ending exchange created by this relationship forged by taekwondo. Somehow I managed to squeeze out my words of gratitude, and I tried my best to express how important each person there was to me, and what their friendship, love and respect had meant in my life. I never imagined it was possible to feel so proud and so humbled at the same time.

"I am so thankful for my taekwondo life and for all of you," I had told the crowd. "Without you I would not be 8th degree now." I struggled to keep control of my emotions. "I promise you now that I will continue for the rest of my life to promote taekwondo, to do the best I can, to the best of my ability, for you — to honor and celebrate all you have done for me."

Becoming grandmaster was, far beyond a dream come true, an accomplishment I never would have dared to dream. Somehow I was here, at the pinnacle of a climb that began without knowing where it would lead. Always following my master's edict to "choose a new goal" to celebrate each accomplishment, step by step my goals had strung themselves together to bring me here, to the place of Grandmaster.

In the days an weeks that followed my grandmaster promotion, a new awareness dawned of the responsibility of this title. How will I live up to this honor? I asked myself, again and again. For many, the title of "Grandmaster" is honorary — the end of their journey. A time to sit back and reflect on a life filled with proud accomplishment. For me, however, it was time to set a new goal. Considering this promotion to be more of a call to action than ex-officio recognition, I wondered, What contribution can I now make as a grandmaster?

I thought about my Uncle Ki Hoon's description so long ago of the Korean term, *aeyoo naekang,* and how the kind of humble strength he described embodies what I at last determined to be the correct spirit of a grandmaster. Not to be a big shot, but to humbly yet forcefully carry out this role of power and authority to make a contribution that otherwise would have been impossible, to use this power for maximum effect. From the time my uncle first explained *aeyoo naekang* to me, it was an attribute I always hoped I would have if I ever found myself in a position of power. Now my new goal was clear — and the details, I knew, would unfold in their own time as a continuing test of my commitment.

Surrounded by students, friends, family and colleagues, my Grandmaster celebrations were special opportunities to say "thank you," to the people in my life that made all my accomplishments worthwhile.

As I took my place among the worlds Grandmasters, I began to consider for the first time how I would make this role an active expression of gratitude for all taekwondo had brought into my life. Here, celebrating this accomplishment with family, students and friends was an humbling and emotional experience that cemented my determination to live up to the title of Grandmaster.

1985 The Fort Worth Chamber of Commerce ribbon cutting and the Grand Opening of my own building and dojang in Fort Worth marked a big moment of personal accomplishment. Later that same year, when Julie and I also built a new home, our American dream became reality.

1986 at my desk in my new school
Becoming a taekwondo grandmaster carried with it a new sense of responsibility to my students and peers I had not even considered. What would my legacy be?

As I started to understand the master-student circle, I realized that each of my master instructors would now carry a piece of my legacy, just as I and my taekwondo classmates carried my own master's legacy. In the center of their pictures, always hanging in a prominent place in my dojang, is my master's old black belt to remind us all of this sacred connection.

In a touching moment of tribute during the opening ceremony of the 1990 United States National Junior Olympics, I gave a traditional Korean salute of respect and honor to my own master, Great Grandmaster Hyon Chong Park.

The emotion overflowed following my salute to Great Grandmaster Park, for the two of us and for everyone present, Koreans and Americans alike.

CHAPTER EIGHTEEN:
Celebrating the Master-Student Circle

From the first week I was in Texas, Roy Kurban and I tried to meet each week for coffee or lunch. One week he would come to Fort Worth and the next I would go to Arlington. We enjoyed this time to laugh, talk, retell old stories and enjoy being together. We also used this time to talk about our dreams and plans for the future.

Chief among these dreams for each of us was the idea of owning the building that housed our school. As if affirming the power of dreaming out loud, Roy's new school building opened in 1985, and just a few months later, just after my 45th birthday, I broke ground on my own.

Wearing a yellow hardhat just like the ones worn by the construction workers I once mistook for MPs, I stuck the tip of the shiny new shovel in the ground where my new building would stand. I smiled for the cameras. I wanted this moment to last forever.

Even though my new location was just a block from the dojang I opened in 1979, it seemed a world away from that abandoned Kempo school surrounded by cow pastures. As Roy predicted, Fort Worth's growth had wrapped this area in bustling commerce and residential development that brought the city to my door. As the plans came together for this brick-and-mortar expression of one of my grandest dreams, again I felt my life taking an exciting new direction.

Every day during construction, I walked through the tangible expressions of the many decisions my new dojang required. Creating a dojang from my imagination was very different from remaking what was already there, and the excitement of this rare opportunity surpassed even the creation of my first Seoul dojang in the space above Sang Kim's *da bang*.

At last, in December of 1985 I stood in the doorway of, in my estimation, the most beautiful building in the world. From the front reception area with its gleaming glass-front counter, to my private office, to the functional, well-equipped locker rooms with showers, to a special seating area for spectators and a smaller practice room off to one side, to the spacious main training room, mirrored on two sides, every feature was exactly what I wanted my dojang to be. Above the door leading to the training area, in a glass shadowbox frame, was my master's old black belt. With my same American and Korean flags hanging side by side in their place of honor and a picture of my master watching over the room, my dream dojang was mine at last.

For weeks my entire family thought about, talked about, and worked on little else but our Grand Opening. The official Chamber of Commerce ribbon cutting ceremony was at noon, but the celebration would last all day. Four separate demonstrations involving Susie and Johnny and as many students as possible were planned and rehearsed in careful detail, two in the morning and two in the afternoon. Just before the day's festivities began I took a moment to stand back and look around me, taking it all in. In one corner, Susie, now 15 and a second dan black belt, was warming up for her demonstration, surrounded by a group of her friends who had come to watch. Across the room, Johnny, now a sturdy 9-year-old and already a junior black belt, was talking with a group of his friends who also had come to watch. Julie was tending to the last details of the celebration, and students were starting to arrive.

In the evening, after the clockwork success of a day well-planned, we ordered pizza for a private party of 50 or so close friends and family who, sitting in a large circle of folding chairs in the center of the training room, ate, drank, laughed, told stories and sang well into the night. It was a perfect Korean-style welcome to my American dojang.

◊◊

As a steadying rudder in the constant turbulence of my professional life, it was Julie Park whose single-minded focus kept our home and family life on course with the kind of smooth precision that made four very busy lives work together with ease. I didn't know how she did this, always there, always supportive, always a calm, sweet presence that kept our family happily on track.

"Would you like to get out, to go somewhere?" I'd always ask her. As busy and preoccupied as I often was, I wondered if sometimes she got lonely or bored.

"No," she'd say. "I like to be home. I enjoy my life, taking care of our home and family." And then she'd smile. "You go do important things in the world. My job is to do the important things here, making our home a nice place for our family to come home to."

Julie's role in my success could not be underestimated. Every step, good or bad, from the day my heart first fell captive to her smile, hers was the face in the crowd I always looked for first, the first one I looked for when I came home each night. I had to look no further than our two children to see that her successes were far greater than mine.

Still, I worried about her from time to time. "I think you need to be around people more," I'd tell her.

"Don't worry," she'd say, "I'm not just sitting around here. I'm always working on projects. It's what I love."

Looking around our home, I could see that was true — even our trash cans bore her decorative touch. Julie loved HGTV, and nothing, it appeared, was too big for her to tackle. Including wallpaper.

"I need your help," she said one day. She was standing with a roll of wallpaper in her hand, and several more were stacked on the table behind her.

"I don't know how to wallpaper," I told her. Nor did I want to learn.

"You don't have to know how," she said. "I just need your labor — I will show you what to do."

So together, little by little, we wallpapered the whole house. Next she made draperies for every room in the house with a little sewing machine we bought. It was anyone's guess what project would capture her imagination next, but one thing was certain. From painting to upholstery to landscaping and beyond, if Julie Park did it, she kept working at it until she did it well. When friends asked who decorated our house and discovered it was Julie and HGTV, she often helped others with their projects as well.

With my school thriving and my tournament setting new records every year, less than a year after construction was complete on my dojang, I decided it was time to give my beautiful, hard-working wife the home of her dreams.

"Let's build a house!" I said, surprised by the confidence in my voice. Was I crazy for taking on such a thing so soon after building my school? I knew it would be a stretch, financially, but so far, the American Dream had never let me down.

After a few weak initial protests, I could see the light in Julie's eyes as she imagined our new home being built to match her dreams. Even though it was difficult and time consuming, it was a wonderful thing to build a home together to reflect our needs, tastes and priorities. With the kids getting bigger and relatives from Korea coming more frequently for extended visits, we needed more room to accommodate these changes in our lives. In beautiful expression of the American Dream coming true for us yet again, we moved into our new home in 1987.

We soon discovered that with a new building, a new home, and two school-aged children to support, the financial strain was a constant but gentle reminder to work together to keep our expenses low and keep our focus on our priorities.

◊◊

I had been president of the Texas Taekwondo Association for six years when a worldwide challenge was issued to taekwondo masters, grandmasters, and officials. Taekwondo was to be a demonstration sport in the 1988 Olympics, and our job was to make sure that as a sport, it was ready.

Behind the scenes of preparing our competitors, many political wheels began to turn when state taekwondo associations realized that to be eligible for international competition, a team must be governed by the United States Olympic Committee (USOC). Therefore, in 1985 the state taekwondo associations all voted to split from the AAU, which only governs American sports, and form the United States Taekwondo Union, or USTU, which would then be governed by the USOC. This decision would not only put United States taekwondo on the Olympic competition track, but it would also allow the US National Taekwondo Team to compete in the upcoming Pan Am Games for which it just qualified. With this important piece in place, the United States team was able to be part of taekwondo's official international debut at the 1985 Pan Am games.

◊◊

When the Texas Taekwondo Association began, Texas taekwondo had a lot of catching up to do to reach a level playing field with other more established state associations. By the time USTU began in 1985, Texas was leading the nation in terms of competitors, tournaments and organized participation. The tireless work of the dedicated group of masters I had been chosen to lead achieved this primary goal in less than three years, making the Texas Team a force to be recognized.

Due in part to this accomplishment under my leadership — and due in part to the dramatic success of my annual Fort Worth Invitational Tournament, now held in the Fort Worth Convention Center after it outgrew its TCU venue, the USTU appointed me chairman of the 1986 United States National Taekwondo Championship tournament. To be held in Anaheim, California, in less than a year, the purpose of this tournament was significant. It was our final demonstration to the USOC that taekwondo was indeed ready to be included in the 1988 Olympics as a demonstration sport. This, we knew, was the prelude to becoming an official Olympic sport.

Accepting this appointment was agreeing to a tremendous responsibility. Remembering the goal I set with my promotion to Grandmaster, the only answer I could give was yes. Heading up this committee placed me in charge of a board of 21 directors from across the nation. This would be a massive undertaking that would depend upon the help and cooperation of taekwondo organizations nationwide. This, we understood, was part of the USOC test. Ung Young Kim, President of the World Taekwondo Federation and arguably the top taekwondo authority in the world, would be attending; we knew there would be no room for mistakes.

"This is a very big job," Julie observed when I told her the news of my appointment. "Are you sure you want to take this on? What if everyone doesn't work?" She had seen the vast differences in how some committees worked well together and others merely allowed its leaders to do all the work. "Why do you have to be the one to do this?" She wasn't questioning my ability, I knew. She was just worried about how much work it would add to my already full schedule.

"I must do this," I said gently. "It is a great honor to be chosen — and my responsibility as a grandmaster. Because of all I have already done with the Texas Association and my tournament, I have the most experience in both areas." Then, smiling playfully I said, "They called me a 'pioneer' — how could I say no?"

"Yes, you *are* a pioneer," she said. "And of course they were right to choose you. I just hope you won't be a *dead* pioneer because you work yourself to death."

"Please don't worry," I said. "I have a lot of good people to help. Everyone understands how important this is for taekwondo's future. It will be OK, I promise."

"I hope you're right," she said, clearly unconvinced.

"If you want to, you and Susie and Johnny can come too," I said, trying to shift the discussion to something pleasant. "While I'm busy with the tournament you can all go to Disneyland."

Julie smiled. "I always wanted to see Disneyland," she said, fully aware I was trying to sidetrack her worry. "The children may think they're too old for Mickey Mouse, but I'm not!"

After months of planning, countless meetings, tedious checking and double-checking, tournament day for the 1986 United States National Taekwondo Championship arrived. It wasn't until I arrived in Anaheim several days before the tournament to make sure everything was in order that I knew we were ready.

Down to the last detail of the opening and closing ceremonies, the tournament had unfolded exactly as planned; we had taken care of our honored guests with appropriate receptions, presentations and recognitions. The competitors had done well and presented to questioning international eyes an outstanding reflection of American taekwondo excellence that held true to its Korean roots. When President Kim took the podium to make the final remarks of the closing ceremony, for the first time since the day I was appointed, I let myself relax. We did it.

I was very proud of how the committee responded to my leadership, and proud that I was able to lead them. I let my eyes travel around the packed Anaheim Convention Center, from the diverse sea of faces in the audience to the eight now-empty rings stretching across the egg-shaped floor. Watching the audience's reverent attention to President Kim, I was amazed and humbled all over again to have been part of helping to bring this moment about.

◊◊

One sunny Texas afternoon in 1989, one year after taekwondo's successful debut in the 1988 Olympics as a demonstration sport, I found myself in a City of Fort Worth conference room with Fort Worth Mayor Bob Bolen, several key city officials and members of the local media. We were there to make an announcement even I couldn't yet fully believe.

Mayor Bolen had called this press conference to announce a first for Fort Worth —and yet another big moment in taekwondo history I was privileged to be part of. After several months of coordinated effort between the Texas Taekwondo Association, the Fort Worth Convention and Visitor's Bureau, and The City of Fort Worth, we had just won the bid to host the 1990 Junior Olympic Taekwondo Championships.

When the Texas Taekwondo Association voted to pursue this opportunity, I first contacted the Fort Worth Mayor's office and Convention and Visitors Bureau to ask for their support and help. Economically, this tournament would mean at least $2 million over a 4-5-day period coming into the city. After reviewing these economic projections, as well as my track record from running the Fort Worth Invitational, they promised City support of the event if I took the lead in hosting it.

Then, working together with the convention and visitor's bureau staff, we prepared our presentation and, at the invitation of the USTU, traveled together to Colorado Springs to make our pitch. When the vote revealed that Fort Worth had won the opportunity to host the event that would be key to selecting the next United States Olympic Taekwondo Team, it meant that I would be this event's director.

The excitement in the room was high as Mayor Bolen first made the announcement, and then introduced me. I stood and bowed, smiling at the clapping, cheering roomful of people. As questions and answers flew back and forth, Mayor Bolen and the others fielded their questions, but occasionally deferred to me.

I looked around the room, noticing that many of the people there were studying me. Far from the "what is he doing in here" stares in that Birmingham diner, these were more expressions of interest and curiosity. *Who is this little guy?* I could almost hear them wondering. *He seems so friendly and polite, is he really one of the world's highest-ranking taekwondo grandmasters? He looks young. Aren't grandmasters supposed to be old?*

My resume was in their press packet to answer their questions. If they did the math, they could also see that even though I was just 49 years old, I had made each one of those years count. In those 49 years lay several different lifetimes. I smiled as I imagined them looking

Celebrating the Master-Student Cycle

back and forth between that piece of paper and my face, thinking, *Can he really handle this?*

I met their questioning eyes with a smile. Once again, as I felt the weight of responsibility settling onto my shoulders, I remembered what I set out to do as grandmaster. Each time the opportunity presented itself, I was determined to step proudly into the circle of commitment and dedication that gives and receives in equal measure, I would draw on the knowledge that grows with each accomplishment. Step by step, I would lead the 1990 Junior Olympic Taekwondo Championships in the same way I have always led my life, from the core values of my taekwondo training.

◊◊

After the initial fanfare subsided, the real work of the 1990 Junior Olympics began. With the tournament less than a year away, I designated the small training room of my dojang as tournament headquarters, brought in a computer and added a dedicated toll-free phone line. We hired a coordinator, a taekwondo student with event planning experience whose first order of business was gathering information, preparing and mailing pre-publicity materials and detailed competitor information packets to every taekwondo school in the nation — several thousand in all. To compete in the Junior Olympic tournament, each participant had to first qualify in his or her state by finishing first, second, or third in a sanctioned tournament.

Once the packets went out, we turned our attention turned to the event itself, including the program book, souvenir merchandise, pennants, medals, and tournament t-shirts. As each detail unfolded, the magnitude of what we were doing grew. Soon we had, in addition to the coordinator, two additional employees and two full-time volunteers to help make each deadline. Part of the coordinator's job was to make sure that at least two volunteers were there to help her at all times.

Susie, now 19 and home for the summer from her freshman year at the University of Texas, stepped eagerly into a role that expanded every day. Julie and I observed her new strength and leadership with awe as she matched me step for step, clipboard in hand, following up on every detail and keeping communication flowing between various committee heads.

We were expecting more than 2000 people, and when the entries began coming in two months before the tournament, most of them during the last month, the final pressure was on. We doubled our army of volunteers. Michelle Nursalla, the wife of one of my black belts, offered to create a program to computerize the entries, and she worked day and night to first create the right program, and then to enter all the participants and double check accuracy before making a printout of matches for each division. Because of the importance of this tournament to each competitor in it, everything had to be right — one wrong match up could skew the results of an entire division. Michelle's program worked. In fact, it was so flawless the USTU later contacted her for permission to use it.

◊◊

In the stack of acceptances to the invitations we sent to special guests and dignitaries was one that I had to re-read several times to believe. Recognizing very familiar handwriting from the many letters we exchanged through the years, I saw that that Grandmaster Hyun Chong Park, my master, was coming to Fort Worth, Texas, all the way from Korea, to see this tournament.

I met him at the airport with a limousine. It was my first time to ride in a limo, too, but I wanted his arrival to be met with royal treatment. The Hyatt Regency Hotel, the official tournament hotel, just across the street from the convention center, provided us with the entire 12th floor, 10 suites in all, complimentary. I chose the largest and most elaborate, the Presidential Suite, for Great Grandmaster Park.

As we walked in, I smiled as I watched his eyes trying to take it all in, traveling to every inch of the room, absorbing its size and elaborate beauty. He had never been to a big hotel, and I wondered if he had ever been out of Korea.

"Is it OK?" I asked, setting down his single bag.

"Oh yes, yes, it is very nice," he said, his eyes still surveying the room.

I showed him the bathroom with its huge Jacuzzi tub and shower. I showed him how to first fill the tub above the jets, and then turn the jets on. He looked on with interest, but gave no indication that this was something he would likely do. His suite had several rooms, and he went into each one of them and walked all around it, taking it all in.

"Are all the rooms like this?" he asked.

"No, I said, laughing. "This room is the best in the hotel. It is where very important people stay." I turned on a lamp. "It was designed for American President Lyndon B. Johnson when he came to Fort Worth for a visit. Since then, it has always been the hotel's very best room."

"Thank you," he said, "but I did not need all this."

"I just wanted you to know how happy I am that you're here," I told him.

He looked up at the ornate gold filigree that edged the main room's high vaulted ceiling. "Wow," he said.

This was the room where 20-30 masters and grandmasters congregated each night after the tournament day was over. They talked, laughed, drank, sang and shared their stories. In that room was a lot of wisdom. As I sat watching them, I wanted to somehow hang onto every minute of this special time, to somehow preserve these stories I was hearing of the struggles and the triumphs of these masters and grandmasters, each with his own story.

◊◊

I planned the opening ceremony myself. The announcer I hired was a newscaster on a local network. As he welcomed the audience, a horse-drawn carriage entered the convention center floor from a large entry ramp at one end.

"Arriving in our special Texas limousine, the announcer said, "We have a few distinguished guests we'd like to recognize."

I rode "shotgun," sitting up front with the driver, and inside the carriage were several city officials and our visiting taekwondo dignitaries. As the announcer introduced each guest, the carriage continued its slow lap around the arena and stopped just in front of the stage, where we all got out of the carriage and took our places onstage.

In my welcome speech, I extended my personal welcome to everyone in the carriage, then the distinguished guests on stage, and then the competitors, coaches, volunteers and spectators. I was looking out at 2200 competitors and for a moment, I almost got lost in the sensation. We had done it. All of the preparations for the tournament had come together like clockwork. The rest, the actual playing out of the tournament's events and divisions, was the easy part.

As I introduced those sitting with me on the stage, I came last to my master. I handed the microphone to the announcer and gestured for Great Grandmaster Park to follow me. As we made our way to the center ring in the middle of the arena floor, the announcer read a script I had given him. My intention was to demonstrate for the audience the special Korean custom of saluting one's master to show appreciation.

"In Korea, the relationship between master and student is a sacred circle of dedication and commitment, master to student and student to master," the announcer said. "To honor that special relationship, Grandmaster Park's own master, Great Grandmaster Hyon Chong Park, has come here all the way from Pusan, Korea."

He waited until we had taken our places in the center of the arena, facing each other. "In Korea, there is a special salute given only to the most respected and revered people in one's life. Grandmaster Won Chik Park will now make this salute to Great Grandmaster Hyon Chong Park to acknowledge his respect, gratitude and appreciation for all this relationship has brought into his life."

Then, Master Kim from New York asked the announcer for the microphone and what happened next created a memory that no one present that day will ever forget.

"The master student relationship is much the same as the relationship between father and son," Master Kim began. *Who is talking?* I wondered. This was not in my script. But he did a very good job of explaining the traditional Korean salute I was demonstrating.

I knelt down and bowed forward until my head touched the floor in front of me. My master knelt down opposite me and accepted my salute by looking forward, bowing his head slightly. When I came up from the bow, the first thing I saw was his face, smiling at me, wet with tears. Tears were streaming down my face, too, as were, someone later told me, most of the faces in the immense audience that surrounded us. The thing I remember most about that moment was the deafening quiet — a quiet I had never heard. All those people, contained in one gigantic space, and not a sound could be heard as they bore witness to this sacred moment. The masters on stage were all crying, too, each thinking about his own master and his own experience of that special bond.

We hugged, still crying, as the crowd applauded, everyone in that huge convention center standing and clapping and wiping away tears. I climbed the steps back to the stage area where all the masters and grandmasters were seated. I looked into the faces of each of my dear friends seated there Kyu Boong Yim, Jin Song Chung, Hee Sup Lee, and Kyu Il Cho — always eager to help, to offer support, and to tackle any challenge. I looked up at the giant banner welcoming guests to this event, and then out to the sea of expectant faces turned our way.

I scanned the crowd until I found a group of very familiar faces in the audience, sitting together near the front and center section. After traveling all the way from Korea to spend the past few months with my family, Young Soon had at last agreed to come to the tournament as long as I promised not to introduce her. "You'll embarrass me," she had said.

"What do you mean? Do you think the tournament will not be good?" I was puzzled and hurt by her reluctance. This was not like Young Soon.

She smiled. "No, I don't think that at all. I think the tournament will be a big success because you have worked so hard to make it so. But I see that speech you are writing and the grand opening you are planning and you are going to want to introduce me and talk about me and I will be embarrassed to have all those eyes on me."

Sitting with Young Soon were Julie, Susie and Johnny, as well as Kwang Jo Chang and a few other friends who had also come to share this day with me. I thought about my conversation with my sister just the night before.

She was watching me work, papers spread out all over our dining the table, tending to a whirlwind of last minute details. "I'm so proud of you," she said.

I looked up from my work. "Thank you," I said, then confused, added, "What did I do?"

"For all you have done," she said. "For all you have become. Who would have thought that that scared, crying little boy running for his life, living on the streets, nearly dying, sleeping with his feet in a sack of beans, would have done all this?" She gestured toward the table, then, widening it, our beautiful home. "Our parents would be so proud of what you've made of your life after what happened to them," she said.

We were both crying now.

"So many times I have wondered why you came here — why you had to leave Korea," she said through her tears. "When you left I missed you so much it nearly broke my heart. But now I understand. You had a big job to do, and you have done it very well. You have done something very special and honorable here."

"Thank you," was all I could manage to say. I had never heard my sister speak so many words at one time before.

◊◊

Just a few weeks before the tournament, I purchased 600 cowboy hats on a whim. I gave one to each master attending the tournament — and, of course, a special one for Great Grandmaster Park. When it was time to take him to the airport, he answered his door wearing his hat, smiling from ear to ear. "I will wear this back to Pusan," he said, to show everyone there my gift from Grandmaster Won Chik Park from Fort Worth, Texas."

I laughed as I imagined him getting off the plane wearing that hat. How people would stare. How he would enjoy it. How I wished I could be there to see it. Bowing to him, I presented a photo album I made for him of his visit. It held pictures of some of the people he had enjoyed talking to, pictures of Fort Worth and of the tournament, and pictures of us together. He returned my bow, accepting this gift as if it were solid gold.

After the tournament Great Grandmaster Park planned to go to LA to visit some masters and Grandmasters he knew in the LA area. I was to fly out and join them for a few days before Great Grandmaster Park returned to Korea.

Two days before I was scheduled to arrive, he called me. "Can you come to LA now?" he asked.

One master from Seattle who had met them in LA invited Great Grandmaster Park to Seattle to stay overnight in the mountains — in a tent. "He is a young man, but I am not," Great Grandmaster Park said, choosing his words carefully. "It was very cold, and when I wanted to come down from the mountain in the middle of the night, he said it would be good for me to stay overnight in that nice mountain air." He paused. "It wasn't good for me. It was cold. He didn't care about my feelings. So the next day I came back down the mountain by myself and took a bus back to LA. Can you come right away?" He repeated his request, this time with an urgency in his voice I couldn't refuse.

"I'll be there right away," I said.

We toured LA for the next few days in my rental car, talking as we had not talked since I left Pusan to join the Korean military. Like Young Soon, he had some things to say. "I always hoped that one day my school would be yours," he said. "That was why I gave you my belt when you became 2nd dan. Every day since you left for the military I have wished for you to return to Pusan." He paused, letting his words hang heavy in air between us. I felt his eyes turn toward me. "But every opportunity kept leading you further away."

I kept driving, focusing my eyes on the road ahead, not sure where this was going. It was hard to feel like I let him down by not going back. After all he did for me, I regretted not making true that one specific dream he had for me. Now, hearing his disappointment in his own words, my sadness deepened.

We sat silent for a long time.

"You did the right thing," he said, breaking the uneasy quiet. "I came here because I wanted to see for myself — and to try to talk you into coming back. But now that I see you here and see what you have done, I understand why you had to leave Pusan." He turned to face me. "It was a good decision, Won Chik. You were right not to return to Pusan. I am very proud of you for what you have done here. If you stayed in Pusan, you never would have known all you were capable of." He sat back in his seat, marveling. "Just look at all the lives you have touched with taekwondo."

At those unexpected words from my own master, a great weight lifted from my heart. In all my life, my only serious regret was disappointing him by not returning to Pusan. His tattered black belt, now proudly displayed in a shadow box over the doorway of my training room, was a daily reminder of this regret that lived deep in my heart. Now, thanks to the cold mountain air, the insensitive young master, and my quick response to my master's call for help, this thing between us was gone forever. From now on that old black belt would once again represent the love and pride he had for me — both on the day he gave it to me and today.

1990 The Texas Masters who became pillars of the Texas Taekwondo Association with my friend and taekwondo classmate Man Sup Lee (center) Left To Right: Grandmasters Kyu Boon Yim, Dae Sup An., Man Sup Lee, Won Chik Park, and Hee Sup Lee.

Won Park Institute Instructors, circa 1994.

1989 with my old friends and classmates from Korea. Next to me in the center is Kwang Jo Chung, and right, Kyon Yeon Won, a middle school classmate.

Working with Fort Worth City officials to win this hosting opportunity for Fort Worth was an accomplishment that earned me the "Keys to the City," and a Proclamation of "Taekwondo Week" presented by Fort Worth Mayor Bob Bolen.

US taekwondo masters and grandmasters gathered from across the nation to attend the 1990 United States Junior Olympic Championship, Pictured here with our special guest, Great Grandmaster Hyon Chong Park, standing next to me in the center.

Of all my favorite moments of the 1990 tournament, seeing my master wearing his special cowboy hat with pride was one of the best. Here Kwang Jo and I prepare to go to dinner with Great Grandmaster Hyon Chong Park, still wearing his hat.

Tournament Director, 1990 US Junior Olympic Championships, Fort Worth, Texas Entering the tournament in our Texas Limousine, I rode "shotgun" in my ten gallon hat.

Opening ceremony of the 1990 United States Junior Olympic Championships.

On the tournament floor of the Fort Worth Convention Center venue, competitors in required divisions squared off simultaneously in 15 rings.

As taekwondo gained national exposure in many different arenas, I was glad to support and take part in high-profile events such as Grandmaster Chuck Norris's Kick Start Foundation, designed to help at-risk youth stay away from drugs and violence and embrace the healthier lifestyle offered by taekwondo. Left to Right: Grandmaster Won Chik Park, Grandmaster Chuck Norris, Master Roy Kurban, and my wife, Julie Park.

CHAPTER NINETEEN:
Taekwondo's Changing Image in the World

It was 1993, nine years since my 8th dan promotion. The calendar told me that at the age of 53 I was eligible to apply for my 9th dan promotion, but I was uncertain. In my mind I needed to be much older to be a true 9th dan. But when I looked around me at others being promoted, I realized I had done as much or more than they had. It was with these thoughts in the back of my mind that I boarded the plane for a trip to the Netherlands.

Earlier in the year I was selected by the United States Taekwondo Union (USTU) to accompany the US Taekwondo team to the 3rd Annual World Games in The Hague, Netherlands. While this competition had no official connection with the Olympics, the World Federation of Taekwondo (WTF) leaders believed that if taekwondo was well-represented in this international competition, it would help raise its Olympic status from demonstration event to medal sport. During the World Games, World Federation President Un Young Kim was scheduled to deliver a speech and to meet with the heads of each participating country's taekwondo teams. As the head of the United States team, I would represent the US team in these meeting with WTF President Un Young Kim. Traveling with me to this one-week competition were one coach, one referee and six competitors .

I settled into my seat, surprised to feel a flutter of nerves. Not only was it my first time to travel to a foreign country since I came to the US, but also I felt the weight of this responsibility. The USTU had placed its faith in me and I didn't want to let them down.

A van met us at the airport and took us to the hotel where we would stay for the next five days. Soon after I checked in, I discovered that Un Young Kim had been unable to come, but in his place was the World Federation Vice President Chong Woo Lee, my master's old friend and the Jidokwan President who presided over my very first Grand Opening in Seoul. I was excited by this unexpected opportunity to spend time him. An important part of taekwondo organization since 1960, Grandmaster Lee was very well respected in the taekwondo world. I looked forward to hearing his insights and thoughts about the future of Taekwondo.

As everyone else arrived and checked in, I recognized several other masters and grandmasters, as well as about a dozen coaches and referees from all over the world. On the first morning after we arrived, we began our talks about taekwondo and its future. When the talks turned to our ranking system, Grandmaster Lee asked each of us to introduce ourselves and tell our ranking. When it came my turn, I said I was 8th dan.

Grandmaster Lee looked puzzled. "When was your promotion?" he asked me. My master always asked him for his recommendation for promotions.

"1984."

"1984," he repeated, then said, "I remember your 8th dan recommendation." He paused. "1984? That's almost ten years ago! That means you are qualified for 9th dan."

With my 53rd birthday just past, I knew it was getting close to time to apply, but for him to remember my recommendation and to tell me it was time for another was another matter entirely. "Do you think it is possible for me to apply this year?" I asked.

"Yes," he said. "When you get back to the United States, call me or send me a letter."

"Yes, Sir," I said. "Thank you!"

Promotion at any level is something you cannot ask for, and, since I was now in the United States, I had wondered whether I would ever get the opportunity to apply for my 9th dan promotion. With no master here to say, "Won Chik, you are ready now," this recommendation would have been difficult, if not impossible, to earn. My trip to the Netherlands had proved to be a good opportunity for me, a good opportunity for the United States Taekwondo Team, and a good opportunity for taekwondo.

As the WTF predicted, the 1993 World Games proved to be a pivotal point in Taekwondo history. With 63 countries in the world now training taekwondo teams, this solid international performance in the World Games laid the next step toward achieving official medal sport status for the 2000 Olympics in Sydney, Australia.

After its 1988 Olympic debut as a demonstration sport, followed with a second good showing in 1992, also as a demo sport. taekwondo organizers and officials only had to prove to the United States Olympic Committee (USOC) that its organization, rules and regulation management, referee education, and structure were consistent from country to country. As the USOC scrutinized each national team to see how well it handled both the competition and organization aspects of our sport, we all held our breath that they would deem taekwondo ready to be an Olympic medal sport.

In the United States, each state taekwondo organization's growth and competence was reflected in the US team's selection of competitors for the national championship sanctioned by the USTU. All this hard work paid off in the US Team's 1993 World Games showing — the United States women's team won second place and the men's team took third.

◊◊

The day after I returned from the Netherlands, I called Great Grandmaster Lee. I didn't want to take any chances that he might forget his advice to apply for my 9th dan promotion. I wasn't sure exactly what the requirements were for 9th Dan or how they differed from 8th Dan.

"Have you chosen a subject to write about?" he asked.

I had. "I want to write about sport taekwondo and traditional taekwondo and how to find good balance between these two aspects."

He said nothing.

"Both are important and must be supported," I continued, voicing a concern that had been growing in me for some time. "Without tradition, taekwondo loses its heart," I said. "Without a heart its future will be limited."

"That's good," he said." Send it to me whenever you get it ready. I will read it first, and if there are areas that need improvement, I'll tell you what needs to improve."

Great Grandmaster Chong Woo Lee had been one of those shadowy figures of importance throughout my entire taekwondo career. He was one of the officials presiding over my first black belt test, he spoke at the Grand Opening of my first school in Seoul, and through every promotion, every Korea Taekwondo Association tournament, and every major taekwondo event—he was always there. By offering to read my paper first, Great Grandmaster Lee would then make sure that everyone of any importance at Kukkiwon would see it. His approval of my topic — and his name on my recommendation — would carry a lot of weight with Kukkiwon. At that time there weren't very many 9th dan grandmasters, and few, if any, who were as young as me. Great Grandmaster Lee's support would improve my chance of success. I worked on my paper until I was satisfied it was the very best I could do, and then I sent it to him.

"Won Chik?" His voice at the other end of the telephone line surprised me. It had not been very long since I mailed my paper to him. This was either very good news or very bad.

"Yes?" I said, holding my breath.

"Your paper is good, but it needs more explanation in a few areas."

I listened as he described the areas he felt needed more detailed explanation. His comments made it clear he had read and absorbed every word of my paper.

"The reason I am asking this," he said, "is that what you have here is good enough for promotion purposes, but not good enough to become part of Kukkiwon policy. With a little more information and the details I have mentioned, I think it can be."

Kukkiwon policy? I was confused.

"Kukkiwon has a research group that selects all the best papers and uses them to create its policies," he explained. "I want to make sure your writing is good enough for them to consider using it for this purpose."

Wow, I thought. I didn't know what to say. This was a surprise that both flattered and terrified me. It was one thing to be writing a paper for my own promotion, but the thought of creating a document for Kukkiwon to consider as policy was very intimidating. "Thank you, sir," I said. "I will make these changes right away."

I got right to work, making the changes and adding the details Great Grandmaster Lee requested. My topic voiced a concern we were all feeling. With so much emphasis on the sport side in our excitement over Olympic taekwondo competition, there was a danger, especially in other cultures, of the less exciting things like tradition and philosophy slipping away. This, we feared, could reduce taekwondo to little more than a hollow shell of its former beauty and purpose. We all wondered how we could ensure that tradition stays forever connected to taekwondo training. In this paper I sought to present some solid answers.

My first recommendation was that Kukkiwon create a separate traditional taekwondo research institute, led by a bright, high-ranking person on a level with Kukkiwon leadership. This institute would capture and record all the taekwondo traditions, philosophy and practices and document the connection between the physical, mental and spiritual aspects of each technique. This institute should not be just in Korea, I wrote, but should include five major branches worldwide to make sure other countries and cultures understand and incorporate this information into its taekwondo training. I proposed that each branch be required to travel to Kukkiwon each year to attend a seminar in which Kukkiwon would keep them updated on the specific research topic completed that year. The five branches would then be responsible for distributing this information worldwide. This, I wrote, would bring the whole scattered world of taekwondo together and make sure that tradition is preserved and integrated into training. Most important, its time-honored roots would not be sacrificed in Olympic fervor.

Part of the detail Great Grandmaster Lee requested was how to select, organize and structure this Kukkiwon Research Institute and its' international branch committees, as well as its' areas of research. After giving it a lot of thought, I outlined the details of creating the Kukkiwon Research Institute and identified seven specific areas of research. When I was satisfied I had covered every single question well, I sent the new document to Grandmaster Lee. A week later, he called me to say that this time my written paper was acceptable and ready to send to Kukkiwon. All I needed now, he told me, was to send a copy of my application to my master and to request a formal letter of recommendation from him.

I called Great Grandmaster Park that same day to let him know this package was on its way.

Happy to hear this news, he said, "Of course I will give my recommendation!" He laughed. "Won Chik, you are more than qualified. I will send my letter right away." I could tell by his tone that Great Grandmaster Park was pleased that it had been Great Grandmaster Lee's idea for me to begin the 9th dan application process. "You have continued with taekwondo while many others have stopped," Great Grandmaster Park said, his pride radiating through the phone line. "This promotion is important to the continuation of your activities."

◊◊

Even with so many exciting things happening in my professional world, it did not escape my notice that important milestones were also arising at home.

"Dad, tomorrow is my 16th birthday," Johnny said after waiting a respectful seven minutes after I walked in the door one evening. His face was trying to cover boyish eagerness with teenage nonchalance — and failing. This was a birthday of unusual interest, and for one reason only.

"Yes, Sae Joon it is," I said, pretending not to grasp the significance of this birthday. "You are growing up fast." I looked at my son, up and down. How could he already be 16 years old?

"Can we go to the driver's license place?" he asked, ignoring my comment. He was in no mood to reflect on the passage of time.

"Why do you want to go there?" I couldn't resist the opportunity to tease him a little bit.

"To get my license," he said, trying very hard not to sound exasperated. "I can get my real license when I turn sixteen." He paused. "And that's tomorrow."

In his focus he didn't even notice that I was teasing him.

I sighed. "I suppose we can go some time tomorrow," I said.

"I want to go at 8:00," he persisted.

"Oh, that's too early," I said. "Why would you want to go so early?"

"I want to be first in line."

I laughed then, and ruffled his hair, just the way I did when he was a little boy. "Yes, Sae Joon, we can go tomorrow," I said. "Early, to be first in line."

When we arrived at the Department of Motor Vehicles at 8:00 am the next morning, no one was there. Johnny smiled. "See?" he said, "Now we are first in line. I can get my license without having to wait in line."

I looked around us at the empty parking lot and laughed. "You're right Sae Joon," I said. "There's no line. But still we are standing here, waiting. What's the difference?"

Now it was his turn to sigh. I just smiled and patted my now-16-year-old son on the back. He was a good boy, and well on his way to becoming a good man. I was thankful that, unlike my own father, I was able to watch this amazing transformation in my son. I tried to imagine myself at 16 and wondered, as I always did in moments of parental reflection, what my father would have thought of me at that age.

It's no secret that fathers and sons have a very different relationship from fathers and daughters. For example, I had managed to somehow teach both Julie and Susie to drive well enough to pass the driving test, but we all agreed that if I tried to teach Johnny it would be nothing but trouble. That Johnny would go to driving school was a decision without question. Although Johnny's demeanor held the quiet sweetness of his mother, his other qualities were enough of mine that clashes were frequent and inevitable.

"Now what?" I asked Johnny as we got in the car so that he could drive us home with his new license.

"What do you mean?' he asked, concentrating as he turned the key in the ignition for the very first time.

"When you reach every goal, you must set a new one right away." He had heard that from me many times before, and like all my master's favorite sayings, it grew more worthy of repeating.

He looked over at me. I could see he was way ahead of me — a new goal already in his sights. "Now I need a car."

I looked at my son sideways, but the earnestness in his face stopped me from teasing. "That is a good goal," I said.

◊◊

Now in her third year of college, Susie, too, set a new goal. Changing her direction from political science and international law to student ministry was a surprise to us, but we were proud that she wanted to mentor others, and we respected this decision to follow her own dream and calling.

She graduated from the University of Texas in 1983 and joined a faith-based non-profit organization in California that would allow her to fulfill yet another dream — living in California. Her new job would allow her to work at three different campuses: UC Berkeley, UC San Diego, and UCLA.

"What do you do there?" we'd ask her in our weekly telephone calls. We missed her terribly, but knew it was important to her to experience living in California. Every night we prayed that one day she'd come back to Texas.

"I am director of the ethnic student initiatives." She loved her job, and her enthusiasm bubbled across the miles and told us she was happy. We just wished she could be happy closer to us.

"What does that mean?" I'd say to her various job descriptions.

"Oh it's basically a fancy way of saying that I help implement leadership initiatives with Asian American students."

"Oh," Julie and I said in unison. "Good for you!" We still didn't know what she did, but were glad to hear her sounding so happy doing it.

◊◊

On December 15, 1993, I received an official-looking package from Kukkiwon that confirmed my promotion to 9th dan, making me one of just a handful of 9th degree Grandmasters in the United States at that time. I gathered my senior students together to make this announcement and to ask their help in planning a celebration.

Years before, in planning my 8th dan celebration of becoming a grandmaster, I was concerned that throwing a party for myself would seem self-laudatory. What I discovered instead was how meaningful it was to bring together the important people in your life to say, "Thank you," to mark a accomplishment and acknowledge the role they played in your success.

One afternoon shortly after the planning began for my 9th dan celebration, I got an unexpected phone call.

"Is this Won Chik Park?" Despite the passage of time, it was easy to recognize the voice of the Kyu Ryun Park, my old school principal.

"Yes, Mr. Park!" I said. "Where are you?"

"I'm here in the United States visiting my son in Florida!"

"How long will you be here? I asked, plans already forming in my mind. We had not yet set a date for my 9th dan celebration, but if it were possible, it would be wonderful for Mr. Park could come. It was to him I owed special thanks, and now I might have the chance to deliver my gratitude in person.

"I'll be here for a few more weeks," he said.

"I am having a big celebration here, and I would love for you to come," I said. "If I send you a plane ticket, can you and your wife come to Fort Worth Texas to my party?"

"When is the party?" he asked.

"When you get here!" I said. I laughed and told him we were just starting to plan the event and would be happy to set the date around his attendance.

He laughed. "That would be wonderful, Won Chik. I would love to see you. What is this party about? Christmas? New Years?"

"No," I said. "I just received word from Kukkiwon that I have been promoted to 9th dan grandmaster."

"Wow," he said. "Congratulations! Of course I would be very happy to be there! What good timing that I called today!" He paused. "I always knew you would be successful," he said, "but even I never could have imagined all that you've done."

He told me he had heard from others from time to time about my accomplishments and had always hoped that he would be able to see me again. "You were always a leader to everyone around you, even at a young age," he added. "Even the teachers looked up to you. We all knew that despite your background, your success in academics and in your taekwondo training were only hints of what was to come."

Mr. Park arrived three days before the celebration, and Kyung Yeon Won, my best friend from Korea who by then lived in Irving, invited us to his home for dinner. The next day, remembering what fun the other Korean masters had with their cowboy hats, the three of us went to Fort Worth's annual rodeo.

This was an afternoon of many firsts for Mr. Park. For the rest of my life I will remember his smiling face beneath the brim of his new cowboy hat. We ate popcorn, took many pictures, and laughed and told old stories. After the rodeo, we all went to dinner and continued to laugh, talk about old times, our families, and all that had happened in each of our lives. In the true Korean tradition of any joyful reunion, we sang all the old songs from home. People at the restaurant stared, and perhaps thought we had had too much to drink, but we didn't care. We were so happy to be together again.

Korean people often say that if you have one really good friend for your entire life, you are lucky. I had such a friend in Kyung Yeon Won. From middle school until now, for more than 50 years, Kyung Yeon Won has been part of my life. One of the 11 Club, he is the one friend who knows my whole story — most of it firstand because he was there.

When he came to the United States, Kyung Yeon Won and his family settled in Irving, partly, I think, because my family was here. Starting with that first year, and because Julie was the only one who knew how to cook a Thanksgiving turkey, Kyung Yeon and his family came to our house to celebrate every Thanksgiving; in turn, we went to his house every Christmas.

We grew up together, our children grew up together, and now that all of our children are grown and pursuing their own lives, we are all growing old together. Korean culture also compares personal friendship to building a house. You start with two people, the raw land. Common interests and shared experiences are the foundation, and times spent together form the walls, the roof and, with enough time, the fine details that give it character, strength and uniqueness. My lifelong friendship with Kyung Yeon Won has layers of understanding and experience like no other.

◊◊

To make the actual presentation of my 9th dan certificate to me, I invited Grandmaster Hwa Chong, another old friend who was at that time the president of USTU, to my 9th dan celebration. He lived in Detroit, Michigan and said he would be honored and happy to make the presentation. I invited many other friends, masters, students and their families, and other people for whom this event would hold meaning.

The dinner, presentation and party was in the same ballroom as my 8th dan grandmaster party. Remaining holiday lights and greenery added to the festive, lively atmosphere, as did the many flowers sent by friends and well-wishers. As the huge crowd began to assemble, music played and the air was alive with happiness. I was humbled by the turnout, and so happy to see each familiar face.

A massive crew of volunteers from my main school and its branches took care of all the preparations. Looking around the room as people began to take their seats, I was pleased to see that almost all of my black belts and senior instructors were there, seated at the special table near the front reserved for them. I looked at each one of them, remembering the first time I saw him or her, how they went through their training, and the qualities I appreciated most in each one.

These instructors were the support system of my school. Without good instructors, one master cannot serve very many students well. For as long as I can remember, Dan and Betty James, Terry Avery, Winifred Harvey, Greg Gafford, Ryad Nusrallah, and Sid Nelson were always there to help me and help train my school's students. While many other instructors had come and gone through the years, these were the ones I relied on, the ones I will always remember in the way every master remembers his best and brightest instructors. I knew that each of these instructors would themselves become masters with their own unique taekwondo legacy.

Dan James spoke first. Expressing his deep respect for my teaching and my school, Dan told the crowd how important being part of the Won Park Institute family was to him. He spoke of my reputation and how this respect and recognition automatically carried over to my students. He told a few of his favorite stories about the difference his taekwondo training made in his life, his family, and his long career as a private investigator. "The family that kicks together sticks together!" he said, drawing laughter from the crowd.

Roy Kurban spoke next about our times on the US military base in Korea, his memories of training and tournaments with me there, being in my wedding and at the Grand Opening of both my first school in Seoul and my school here. He talked of our long, close friendship and all the memories we shared from experiences to dreams to celebrating each other's accomplishments. Roy's natural gift as a speaker held the room's attention, and his words showed my students and friends a new reflection of me and my life that few of them had ever seen.

Next, Master Kyu Buong Yim, my good friend from Dallas, spoke of our work together for the development of taekwondo in Texas. He spoke of our leadership of the first Texas Taekwondo Association, I as president and he as Secretary General, our tireless work together on so many projects, overcoming challenges and our great friendship and respect for one another. He spoke highly of my leadership at a pivotal time in taekwondo history, and how with our help, Texas had emerged as a leader in US taekwondo.

Next, a succession of children came forward to speak, representing the coming generation of taekwondo. Each was asked to say a few words about what taekwondo meant to them in their life. They were sweet in their expression of respect and appreciation to me, talking from their hearts in the simple and direct way only children can.

Grandmaster Hwa Chong was the last to speak. "I am very proud and honored to present this 9th dan certificate on behalf of Kukkiwon to my good friend, Grandmaster Won Chik Park," he began. He went on to talk about my taekwondo activities and contributions, as well as how my leadership and accomplishments had helped to organize taekwondo in the United States. He talked about how people followed and liked me, and how, because of this I had been able to help people with differing opinions to find common ground for the good of taekwondo.

"Texas is number one in its taekwondo membership and its organization," he told the crowd. "This is because the Texas Taekwondo Association, under Grandmaster Park's leadership, learned to work well together, handled its resources wisely, and accomplished its goals. Because the Texas Taekwondo Association created its own system for funding its activities, meetings and championships, it is now an example for other states." He looked at me and smiled. "When you began, Texas did not even have a taekwondo organization. Because of your leadership, Texas now makes the other states jealous."

Each speaker, from the highest ranking to the oldest friends to the youngest child, brought up a different kind of emotion in me. These words, coming from so many different people and so many different perspectives, created an overwhelming mixture of pride, joy, and humility that tumbled over one another in my head. Every time in my life that circumstances caused me to stop and consider all of its blessings, accomplishments, and achievements laid out end to end, my heart has been touched in a special new way.

During the planning of this event, I thought it would be easier emotionally than the first one, because I knew what to expect. Hadn't they said it all at my 8th dan celebration? Wouldn't these presentations be very much the same? I'm still the same man, with the same life and the same accomplishments, I reasoned. With just this one new thing to add, I thought I was prepared. But just as my 8th dan Grandmaster celebration was a milestone event like no other, the celebration of my 9th dan promotion reached deeply into my heart in a whole new way.

Fighting my emotions, I stood up and said, gesturing with my arms to encircle the whole room and everyone on stage as well, "All of this is because of taekwondo. Without taekwondo I would not have had any of this — these students, these friends, these accomplishments, this life. So I say thank you to each of you for all you have done to support me, thank you to taekwondo for the many opportunities it brought into my life, and especially, thank you to God for taekwondo."

With the US Team at the 1992 Friendship Games with Kyong Hee University, Korea. Standing to my left and right are Texas Taekwondo Association leaders Grandmaster Kyu Boong Yim, and Hee Sup Lee.

1992 at Susie's graduation from The University of Texas. Johnny, standing next to her, is a junior in high school and already making college plans. Both of my children are well on their way to the educations and futures Julie and I dreamed of for them in Korea.

1993 World Games in The Hague, Netherlands. As Head of the US Team I was responsible for representing the US Team in meetings with Great Grandmaster Chong Woo Lee, Vice President of the World Taekwondo Federation, seated next to me in the center.

1993 World Taekwondo Championship in Madison Square Garden, New York.

1994 Special Achievement Award for efforts in the Taekwondo and Korean communities, presented by Minister Kong Ro Myong, The Foreign Ministry, Republic of Korea, at the Korean Consulate General's office in Houston.

1995 When I hosted a Fort Worth Convention Center demonstration by the Korean National Taekwondo Demonstration Team, I was surprised at the turnout — and the increased public awareness of taekwondo. Here I award a young student first place in the kicking competition for children that opened the event.

1997 Observing the 13th World Taekwondo Championships in Hong Kong with a group of Jidokwan leaders attending the event.

Standing on my right is my master's old friend, Great Grandmaster Chong Woo Lee, Vice President of the World Federation of Taekwondo. On my left is Grandmaster Jin Song Chung, my former assistant instructor in Seoul.

2003 Fort Worth International Championship referees, officials and instructors.

CHAPTER TWENTY:
A New Dream

"Dad, I want to go to a big college," Johnny said. It was early in his senior year of high school, and his college decision had moved from vague speculation to pressing concern.

"Why do you want to go a big college?" I asked. I thought with his shyness he might prefer a smaller school, much closer in size to his private high school experience.

"I'm tired of feeling so different," he said. "I want to go somewhere I can just sort of blend in."

I stiffened. Was he struggling with the same feelings that bothered Susie, but never mentioned it? Remembering how Susie blossomed after her trip to Korea, I asked carefully, "Would you like to find a college where there are more Korean Americans — and study abroad programs?" I asked.

"No," he said slowly, looking at me as if I had lost my mind. "Why would I want to do that?"

"Well," I said, your sister found it difficult to be one of the few Korean Americans in her school. She wanted to be in a place where there were more Asian people." I searched my mind for her exact words, then found them. "For cultural identity."

Johnny laughed. "No dad, it's nothing like that for me. That stuff never really bothered me as much as it did Susie. I guess I got it all straight in my head in the second grade."

I smiled, remembering his second grade taekwondo demonstration and how respectfully the other kids treated him after that.

"What made me feel different in my school was that even though we were very comfortable and I always had everything I needed, we were one of the only middle class families in a very high socioeco-

A New Dream

nomic group of families."

Where did my children get these complicated words?

Seeing my puzzled expression, he laughed. "Dad I'm just tired of only being around rich kids."

Then it was my turn to laugh. And laugh. And laugh.

Johnny started laughing too, but it was clear he had no idea why this was funny. This made me laugh even harder, until tears rolled down my cheeks. "I was so worried that something was wrong," I said, still chuckling as I wiped my cheeks. "I'm glad you're just looking for something different."

"I just want a little bit of freedom," he said. He paused. "Dad, I know you and mom love me and want the best for me, and I do appreciate all that, but sometimes I think you may have sheltered me too much."

Again the irony was amusing, but this time I managed to keep a straight face. "What is it you think you've missed?"

"I don't know," he said. "I just don't feel like I know much about the real world."

"And where is this real world you are looking for?" I asked, hoping he wouldn't say, "California."

"University of Chicago," he said. "I've already applied."

"Oh," I said, trying not to let my disappointment show. Chicago wasn't California, but it might as well be. "We should go visit there and make sure you like it before you go."

Although Johnny selected the University of Chicago with careful consideration of all its merits and what he thought he wanted, seeing it in person it was a different picture from the image in his head. It was impressive, but simply too big, too much.

"Daddy, I don't want to go to school here," he said on the second day of our visit.

"Why not?"

"I just don't like it. It doesn't feel right to me."

"OK," I said, trying to conceal my relief. "I respect your choice."

I also admired Johnny's courage to speak up and say what he felt;

A New Dream

other young men his age might not be so trusting of their intuition — and so willing to admit a mistake. After speaking of nothing but the University of Chicago for months, for Johnny to recognize that it wasn't right for him and to change directions even when that was a more difficult path, told me that my son was becoming his own man. This, I realized, is one of the proudest moments a father can have.

A few weeks later Johnny came to me with information about his next choice — Boston University. Even farther away. Truly on the opposite coast from Susie, splitting our children by an entire continent. I tried to listen without questioning his choice.

"Can we go visit there?" he asked.

My schedule was packed. There was simply no way I could go in a timeframe that would allow him enough time to apply if he decided to go. Just as well, I thought. It's time to let go. He needs to make this decision by himself. I bought him an airline ticket and made reservations for a three-day visit.

He came back elated. "I want to go there," he told us. "It feels just right."

Boston University would be expensive, but Johnny had a scholarship and grant that covered about half his tuition, so we agreed to pay the rest of his tuition and he would have to work for the rest. He got a job as a valet and security guard for a large Boston hotel and in 1998, graduated with a degree in business.

Years later I learned of a presentation he made to his Leadership class during his junior year at the Boston University School of Business. The assignment was to write a paper and give a 10-minute presentation about a leader. While most of his classmates chose famous business leaders like Jack Welch, or famous coaches like Rick Pitino as their topics, my son chose me. The boy who was so shy he wouldn't order his own food at McDonalds when he was a little boy, who barely spoke up in groups and avoided most social situations at all costs, stood before a class of his peers and called me his hero.

I cried like a baby when I imagined him standing up before his business class, telling them about my life, my early struggles, my taekwondo and how I became an American grandmaster and influenced so many lives through my teaching of Taekwondo. He got an A on that project, but I give him an A+ as my son, because I'm the only one who knows how much courage it took for him to do that.

With Susie and Johnny finishing college and finding their own paths in the world, Julie and I celebrated the fulfillment of our dream that began long ago in Korea with the difficult decision to leave our homeland to give our children a better life. When we looked at these two well-educated, kind-hearted, family-centered and grounded young adults we knew our decision was worth every moment of difficulty.

◊◊

In 1998, the Korea Taekwondo Association and the Korean government invited 100 masters and grandmasters who had been in the United States for at least 10 years for an official visit. The letter of invitation explained that the purpose of this visit was to show us the "new Korea." With special tours of business, industry and development, they arranged to show us how much things had changed in the ten years since we left. As ambassadors of taekwondo, they considered us to be representatives of Korea, and they wanted our information and perceptions to be current.

We would tour not just Seoul, but other areas in the country as well. The official visit would last for five days, and then each individual was invited and encouraged to extend his trip for more personal visiting, touring, and exploring. They would provide everything, the letter promised. Hotel, food and tour buses were reserved for us to ensure that our stay was comfortable and enjoyable, and several smaller organizations would also host us for meals and activities. The trip would also feature an official visit to Kukkiwon so we could first learn about taekwondo activities worldwide.

When we arrived in Seoul, everything was as promised. We were greeted like royalty at the airport, then ushered to our hotel where many welcome gifts awaited us in our well-appointed rooms. The only trouble was my luggage was lost somewhere along the way. The

A New Dream

hotel representative told me they would locate it and deliver it to my room. The next morning, the day of our scheduled visit to Kukkiwon, my luggage still had not arrived. I was up early, calling the front desk, then pacing back and forth in my room, growing more agitated and despondent with each passing moment.

The Kukkiwon visit was the thing I looked most forward to on this trip, but without a suit and tie to wear, I could not go. We would be visiting Kukkiwon President Un Young Kim, and to go there in casual clothes would be the height of disrespect. My disappointment was overwhelming, but what could I do? The bus would be leaving before any stores opened, and time was running out for getting my suitcase in time.

A knock sounded at the door. *Maybe they found my suitcase,* I thought as I hurried to open the door. Instead, it was one of the other masters, Master Jeon, an Olympic team coach. I tried not to look disappointed, but seeing the expression on my face, he said, "What's the matter, Grandmaster Park? Are you not feeling well?"

I told him about the lost luggage and how I would not be able to go to Kukkiwon.

He thought for a moment, and then said, "Grandmaster Park, I'm about your size, and I have an extra suit. Please wear my extra suit so you can join us at Kukkiwon."

I was so surprised and grateful I hugged him. "Thank you!" I said, over and over, "Thank you so very much!" Because of Master Jeon's generosity, I got to go and take part in the meeting with Un Young Kim at Kukkiwon. I smile and remember Master Jeon and his kindness every time I look at our group picture in front of Kukkiwon, with me, smiling, and wearing Master Jeon's suit.

◊◊

After the official part of the visit was over, I traveled to Inchon to see my family. Ung Chik still lived in Inchon, as did Julie's family, and a crowd that represented both families was waiting for me when I arrived.

A New Dream

Surrounding me with love, laughter and food — and a huge celebration that lasted for days — we ate, drank, sang and told family stories. In between our trips into the past, the memories we all shared, and memories I had missed being part of because I had been away for so long, they took turns pelting me with questions about our life in America. They also took turns speculating whether I had become "Americanized."

"Have you turned into an American?" someone would ask, moving closer and scrutinizing my face as if just living in America could somehow visibly change it.

"No, still Korean," I said, laughing, playfully pushing that person away. "But I do live a very nice American life," I would say, smoothing my clothes. It was hard for them to grasp that although I had become an American citizen and loved American ways, I was still the same person they had always known, still very proud of my Korean heritage.

"But you talk like an American," they would argue. "You act like an American."

I laughed, thinking how funny it would be for my American friends to hear this. "No," I argued, "I'm very traditional in my taekwondo teaching. Even though I do speak English to my students and American friends, I'm still very much Korean." And then I'd laugh. "I'm very much a Korean who loves America and my American life."

"But what about your children?" they would challenge. "Do they even know who they are?"

"They understand this all better than anyone," I assured them. "They know the importance — and the way — of loving both cultures. Yunbok and I have taught them, with words and by our example. They have also explored their identity on their own," I said, thinking of Susie. "Both my children know exactly who they are: proud American citizens with deep love and respect for their Korean roots."

◊◊

A New Dream

One last important stop before I returned to America on my 1998 visit to Korea was a trip to Pusan to spend some time with Great Grandmaster Park. When I told him I was coming, he gathered together about 10 of my former classmates and we all went to dinner together.

We laughed, sang, and relived old taekwondo memories — and we marveled at all that had happened in our lifetime to this ancient art that had gone centuries at a time with nothing changing, now taking huge leaps of change in the span of a single lifetime. As the evening drew to a close, Great Grandmaster Park pulled me aside to ask if I could meet him the next morning for breakfast. There was something he wanted to show me, he said, and something important to discuss.

What could this be about? I wondered, looking around at the others still laughing and talking. *What is it that can't be discussed here tonight?*

We met at a *da bang* near the harbor he told me about. After coffee and small talk reliving favorite moments of the gathering the night before, he said, "Let's walk."

So we walked, in the direction of the harbor. "Won Chik, I need to tell you about something that is happening, " he said.

I held my breath, praying he wasn't about to say he was sick or dying.

"I'm about to become a very rich man," he said.

I sighed my great relief. "Rich? What do you mean?" I asked. "How?"

"Pusan is now the second largest city harbor in Korea," he said. "Did you know that?"

I did. The tour of "new Korea" had made sure of it. But what did that have to do with Great Grandmaster Park?

"You see, Won Chik, a long time ago I bought some land here, some almost worthless beachfront property right on the harbor. When the city changed its plans for developing this area, it made my little piece of land worth about $2 million American dollars."

I stopped walking. "Two *million* dollars?" I echoed, incredulous.

He laughed. "Yes, Won Chik. Two *million* dollars."

"Wow," I whispered. Even with my very comfortable American lifestyle, I couldn't even imagine that much money. "Kwan Jang

A New Dream

Neem, what will you do with all that money? You'll be rich for the rest of your life!"

He laughed. "With that much money I could be rich for several lives!" He paused. "I don't know what I'll do with all of it, Won Chik," he said. "But I do have a plan for part of it."

"What is it?"

"I want to make an investment in taekwondo," he said, looking out across the water. "I want to create a taekwondo foundation in my name that will take good care of future students. I want to build a school that I can be sure will continue on, teaching just as I have taught, for future generations. I want to make sure people who study taekwondo always remember the roots of taekwondo and continue to practice it as our ancestors taught."

He turned to look at me. "A lot is changing in taekwondo, Won Chik, and a lot of it is good. Good for practitioners, good for taekwondo and good for Korea." He paused. "But what concerns me is that in all this excitement over "Olympic-style" taekwondo, if we don't work very hard now to preserve and protect the ancient teachings, they may someday be forgotten. As the world clamors for more and better and higher levels of competition, the ancient art of taekwondo as we know it, what our ancestors have protected for centuries, sometimes at the risk of their lives, could be lost forever."

His words rattled me. Even though this was the subject of my 9th dan dissertation, and the topic of debate at nearly every meeting I attended these days, especially those with older masters and grandmasters present, to hear him express his concerns with such passion awoke in me a fierce new protectiveness of our traditions.

"How can I help you make this foundation?" I asked. "Tell me what you need and I will find a way to help you make it happen."

He explained that he would like to make an initial investment of maybe $100,000 to establish the foundation. In Korea, foundations are named after their primary benefactor, followed by a short foundation name.

"By your name, this foundation will build up a permanent school," I

A New Dream

said, "and forever your teachings will be here. It will continue your legacy as it preserves and protects the roots and traditions of taekwondo."

He nodded, clearly pleased at how I was taking hold of this mission.

We continued to walk and talk all morning. By noon when we stopped for lunch, many specific ideas for creating his foundation were taking shape. With my experience in forming organizations, I promised my help with that part, and I proposed that he appoint five directors and a president of his foundation board.

He agreed that this was a good idea. "I will do that right away," he assured me. He looked at me and smiled. "And of course, the first person I appoint to this board will be you."

I bowed, just as I had in the old days. "Thank you, sir," I said, feeling the familiar rise of humble tears. "It would be a great honor to serve on your foundation's board."

Before I left, we bowed, hugged, shook hands, and hugged again. I was excited to be part of my master's new mission and honored to be part of this wonderful tribute to Great Grandmaster Park's teaching and to the ancient roots of taekwondo.

We agreed that the following year we would hold the foundation's first official meeting in Pusan, inviting all of my classmates from the dinner the night before to its formal launch. The time frame for everything else would depend on the actual sale of his land, determined by the city of Pusan. Based on what city officials told him, Great Grandmaster Park believed that the sale would be final within the next year.

◊◊

The phone rang just before 6:00 am on a cold December morning as 1998 drew to a close. "Won Chik?" The voice on the other end of the line was Man Sup Lee, one my taekwondo classmates, calling from Korea. His voice sounded strange, but I recognized it right away. Man Sup, who had been at the dinner with Great Grandmaster Park during my trip to Korea earlier that year, was another constant in my life since we tested

A New Dream

for 2nd dan together in that long ago trip to Seoul. When I left Pusan, Man Sup had more or less taken my place in the dojang, and throughout our lives, we had stayed in touch. He was a great friend who loved telling people about my success in America.

"Yes?" I said, struggling to see the clock.

"I'm sorry to say that I am calling with some very bad news. Great Grandmaster Park has passed away."

I sat straight up in the bed, hoping this was a bad dream. Man Sup kept talking but I couldn't make my brain process his words. The details really didn't matter. My heart felt as if it had been wrenched from my chest.

"When?" was all I could manage to say, once I was able to speak.

"Three days ago," he said.

In Korea, the funeral was always held within three days of someone's death, so he was obviously calling after the funeral.

"Why didn't you call me sooner?"

"If I had called you sooner, you would have come," he said.

My fury flamed. How dare he make that decision for me? "Yes. I would have," I snapped. "That was not your decision to make."

"I'm sorry, Won Chik," he said. "I was just trying to help. It is so expensive to come here and I was trying to do you a favor. If you had known, you would have come, and even if you had come, there was nothing you could do here that you can't do there." He started to sob. "All any of us can do is cry and say goodbye to him in our own hearts in our own way."

Man Sup's reasoning dissolved my anger into deep uncontrollable sobs. No use being angry with Man Sup. He did make a mistake. I would have been there for the funeral and to be with my classmates in this time of great sadness. I took slight comfort that we were all together with our master the last time I was in Korea. It was good that Great Grandmaster Park had that chance to enjoy all the old stories one more time and to see us all together, laughing and singing. It had been our happy farewell — and probably for the best that none of us knew we were also saying goodbye to Great Grandmaster Park.

1998 The Korea Taekwondo Association and the Korean government sponsored an official visit for 100 United States taekwondo masters and grandmasters to reveal "the new South Korea."

The visionary leadership of the Texas Taekwondo Association put a system into place that helped produce an outstanding Texas Team that included the very first Olympic Taekwondo Gold Medalist. Among these leaders, pictured here left to right, are Grandmasters Hee Sup Lee, Dae Sup An, Man Sup Lee, Won Chik Park, first TTA president, John Kim, second TTA president, and Kyu Boong Yim, 3rd TTA president.

2010 Seeking to bring together the past, present, and future of taekwondo in America with the United States Taekwondo Grandmasters Society and the United States Taekwondo Grandmasters Society Museum and Hall of Fame.

> *"Human life has limits, but the spirit of taekwondo is forever."*
>
> — *9th Dan Grandmaster Won Chik Park*

CHAPTER TWENTY-ONE:
Rally Cry for the Future

Throughout 1999, excitement pulsed through the air at every taekwondo gathering, event and tournament. Even when masters and grandmasters met socially, their talk was of little else but the upcoming Olympics in Sydney, Australia, when taekwondo would at last make its debut as an official medal sport.

Although I was chosen as a delegate to attend the 2000 Olympic Games in Sydney, Australia, in the end I decided to allow someone else to go in my place. It was too far, too many days away from home, and because Julie and I had already planned a very special trip to Korea later that same year, it made more sense to surrender my delegate seat to a young master just beginning his career.

As the Games drew nearer, excitement rippled throughout the taekwondo community. We read every word of the newspaper coverage, got the TV schedule ahead of time and tried to find out when taekwondo was scheduled. As a new event, it landed in odd time slots, making it necessary to record it and, often, watch matches after we already knew the result. Nevertheless, we followed every second of our first Olympic taekwondo media coverage before, during and after the 2000 Games.

The most exciting moment came when a member of the Texas team, Steve Lopez from Sugarland, Texas, won the first Olympic gold medal in taekwondo history. It also turned out to be the only U.S. medal won in taekwondo in the Sydney Olympic games.

"He did it!" the group of Texas Taekwondo Association members gathered to celebrate kept shouting, slapping each other on the backs. "Our Texas boy won the first gold medal in the world!" Not only was this good for the future of taekwondo in America, it was especially good for taekwondo in Texas.

I smiled to myself, amazed at this incredible outcome. Who would have thought when we decided to organize a Texas Taekwondo Association to create and support a Texas Team that we were laying the pathway for one of our state's young men to win Taekwondo's first Olympic gold medal? It was humbling to look back and see how the pieces had fallen into place as we worked, aware of the importance of what we were doing, but unaware of where it would lead. Life is that way, I thought. Sometimes you really don't know what you're building, but when you work hard and follow your heart, your efforts can add up to impact you've never even imagined.

◊◊

As much as 2000 was a banner year for taekwondo, the year of my 60th birthday and our 30th wedding anniversary held special personal meaning for me. Giddy with excitement, Julie and I boarded an airplane for the long flight to Seoul in early November — back to the eager awaiting homes of our extended families and days of nonstop parties and celebrations the likes of which we had not seen since our own wedding 30 years before.

We walked into Ung Chik's home first, shocked by the huge crowd of people gathered there. Korean people tend to cry easily, especially when overcome by emotion, so this joyful reunion was a hysterical scene of talking, hugging, and crying all at once. It was a sweet, beautiful time with our families that made us very glad we came.

Food and gifts were everywhere we looked. It was also a Korean custom to give money to family visiting from far away to help pay for their travel expenses and their stay. Ung Chik and my side of the family had gathered a generous donation in US dollars for this gift. Later, when we went to a very similar celebration in my mother-in-law's home, Julie's side of the family presented us with a hotel reservation for five days on Jeju Island in its brand new 5-star hotel.

After spending a few days with each side of the family, Julie and I departed for Jeju to rest, relax, and celebrate our anniversary together.

"Thirty good years," I said to her as we walked together, taking in the beauty of the volcanic island's beautiful Olle trails.

She smiled, and in that smile I still saw the beautiful young woman, now even more beautiful with time, that I had first met in that coffee shop in Inchon. "Thirty wonderful, interesting years," she said, squeezing my hand.

"Are you ever sorry you left here?" I asked her, not at all sure what she would answer. Watching her with her family these past few days reminded me of all Julie gave up to come with me to America.

"I've missed my family very much," she said. "And at times that was very hard." She paused, then turned to look at me with the directness I have always loved so much. "But if I had the chance to make the decision again, I'd still do the same thing. It has been an adventure and a life I never could have dreamed of." She waved her arm, her gesture at once taking in the island around us — and all of Korea. "I know all of this," she said. "I know the life I probably would have had, and as long as you were here with me, it still would have been a good life." She looked deep in my eyes. "But I never would have seen all the things you have shown me, all the experiences we have shared, the life we have been able to give our children."

My eyes welled up with tears, and she squeezed my hand. No one on this earth loved or understood me as completely as she did.

Julie frowned, an unexpected shadow crossing her face as she remembered something disturbing. "You know," she said, as if fully realizing this for the very first time, "with the trouble I had when Johnny was born, if I had been here I might not have survived."

We continued walking for a time, quiet and thoughtful. And thankful.

"So yes, *Yeo Bo*," she said using that sweet Korean term of endearment I loved to hear her say, "I'm glad. I'm glad for everything."

◊◊

Something had been troubling me since we landed in Korea, something I would not allow myself to think about. Something I was glad to sweep away in all the celebrations and our delightful five days on Jeju. But as we left Jeju Island, I felt its full weight crashing in on me.

Great Grandmaster Park was gone from this earth, and I felt his absence everywhere I looked. In the States, it was easy to put his passing out of my mind after the initial grief subsided. In the States, there were only a handful of things that reminded me of him. But everywhere here held a memory of him, every memory like a knife in my heart. Here it was as if I had just heard the news of his death, as if my true mourning for him was put on hold until I got here .

After three days of struggling with this oppressive grief, I went to the cemetery to visit his grave. Even though we were half a world apart for most of my adult life, my master was always there for me. If I needed him, I could always call. If I wanted to hear his voice or know his thoughts on a particular subject, all I had to do was write or call. For all my life, Great Grandmaster Park was the voice of balance in my life. "Breathe, Won Chik," I could almost hear him say to me when I found myself in difficult or challenging situations.

I knelt beside his grave, just as I had in the opening ceremony of the Junior Olympics tournament, and, again, did a ceremonial salute. I was crying so hard by then I could barely breathe, but it felt good to finally be able to let all these emotions out, here where it was just the two of us again.

After a time, I sat near the head of his grave, cross-legged in meditation. My mind was finally clearing itself of this huge sorrow I had kept packed down inside me since Man Sup's devastating call. At last, I began to feel peace. I opened my eyes, and allowed myself to remember.

I recalled the memories one by one just as we would do if we were sitting together over a few drinks, laughing and telling the old stories, singing and remembering. I laughed out loud as I imagined someone walking by just now, thinking I was crazy or had been drinking, just sitting there talking to myself, laughing, crying and singing. These were special memories, treasures in my heart, and I unpacked and examined each, one by one, thanking him as I did for his guidance, understanding, advice, friendship, love and respect.

I thought about the day he came to watch me teach at the US military headquarters, how he stood silently and watched my class full of high-ranking American officers, all bowing to me, eager to absorb my instruction. I remember the look of pride and amazement on his face that day and didn't understand. I understood now.

I remembered his trip to America, seeing him again in my mind's eye as he got on the plane to go back to Korea, wearing that cowboy hat I gave him, clutching the photo album I made to commemorate his visit. People told me later that he took that album everywhere he went, telling anyone who would listen about his trip to America to visit Grandmaster Won Chik Park and to his big Olympic-style taekwondo tournament — and how he was honored as a special guest. Of all the things I am glad about in my life, near the top of the list is that I made his visit so special to him and that he knew without any doubt how much I appreciated him and all he did for me.

More than just my taekwondo master, Great Grandmaster Hyun Chong Park was the parent I didn't have, the guiding influence who molded my character, held me accountable, delighted in my success and encouraged me through failure. "If you fall down seven times, you must get up eight," was another of his favorite sayings. In a life filled with challenges, I always knew that whenever I fell down Great Grandmaster Park was there to make sure I always got up and tried again.

I thought of my own children, and how differently they had grown up. Even though they had parents and every advantage, the one thing they would never know is the bond of the master student relationship. Growing up without parents, I always felt like I had less than other people. Now I realized that in some ways I had more. In that moment I saw the fortune in my misfortune, and that almost every good thing in my life somehow grew out of adversity. I thanked my master for this understanding, and then I thanked God for my master.

◊◊

In 2002, when USTU President Sang Lee invited the grandmasters and masters involved with the USTU to what he called a celebration of United States Masters and Grandmasters, I realized we were nearing a generational "changing of the guard," the time for our younger generation of masters to begin its era of leadership. This put my generation of masters and grandmasters in a place of unique opportunity.

"This is a time," Sang Lee told us in his speech on the first night of this three-day meeting, "to celebrate what we have done. We are the generation of masters who brought taekwondo to this country; we are the reason for America's new place of honor in taekwondo history."

There were about 55-60 present at this meeting, about half masters and half grandmasters. More than just a meeting, it was a three-day, two-night gathering that included a nice dinner with entertainment, golf, social outings and special events. In this grand celebration, we laughed, sang, told stories, and had a wonderful time seeing one another again.

Then, sometime after dinner on the second night, our talk turned to our individual feelings about taekwondo's past, present, and future. One by one, everyone present expressed heartfelt opinions and feelings. Then, a gentleman I didn't know stood up and said to the entire group, "This is a very valuable meeting. I would like to say thank you to Sang Lee for inviting us all here to share our friendship and memories."

The room murmured its agreement. Then someone else said, "Why does it have to end here? Why don't we start having a friendship meeting regularly for United States taekwondo grandmasters and masters?"

Someone in the back of the room began to applaud, and others joined in. Within seconds we were all on our feet, giving a standing ovation to this grand idea.

Everyone began talking at once; the room buzzed with observations and ideas — why we needed this kind of thing, what our role will be in the coming years, how important it is to build good, relationships with one another.

When we were young, we were competitors. Now that we're older, we realized it was time to become friends. At once we realized the true value of celebrating the experiences we shared, the spirit of taekwondo, and the friendships forged of common dreams.

With great enthusiasm, everyone agreed that we would form a group whose sole purpose was to celebrate the unique bond of being America's first generation of taekwondo masters — the builders of this special bridge of friendship between Korea and America. But who would lead this group? Who would organize these events? Who would manage the details of such a gathering?

Dr. Ken Min, the first president and a founding member of the USTU, stood up. "I'd like to make a recommendation," he said. "For the past 20 years, Grandmaster Won Chik Park has been an outstanding leader in helping take taekwondo in the right direction."

Everyone stood up and applauded.

"Grandmaster Park is a powerful organizer," he continued, "and someone who is respected by many different groups of people."

Again everyone, still standing, applauded.

This was completely unexpected. I sat there in complete shock, with no idea of what to say or do. There had been talk for the past three or four years about appointing me to this or that position of leadership, but I always declined, saying, "No, thank you," "Not now," or "I'm sorry, but this is not a good time. Thank you anyway."

But this was different. Without question, I knew I must accept. I stood up. "Thank you very much for this honor," I said, "I am happy to accept." I looked around me at all the faces now turned my way. "I will be calling many of you to help me get things organized."

Once back home I composed a letter to everyone who attended the meeting. "We have a very serious responsibility to taekwondo," I wrote, remembering my master's last words to me. "Because we are the first generation of masters — and now grandmasters — in the United States, we hold within us an important part of taekwondo history. We cannot let these 40 years of taekwondo history fade away when we are gone. If I lead this group, its purpose will be to strengthen and preserve taekwondo history and traditions for future generations of US taekwondo practitioners, masters and grandmasters."

Our group didn't yet didn't have a name, but I thought it should be called a grandmaster's meeting, even though it would always include masters as well. Another concern I had was the invitation list. Those who attended that first year came to support Sang Lee, and recent politics and unrest between the USTU and the USOC made everyone a little uneasy.

I believed that our group should be above these issues, and open itself to all masters and grandmasters in the United States, regardless of personal politics. "I will not leave anyone out," I told the leaders of the group who had been appointed to help me. I personally called all the masters and grandmasters in the United States to tell them about the group and to invite them to attend our next annual meeting. Most of this diverse group of people did support me in doing this; even those who questioned what I was trying to do encouraged me to do what I thought was right.

Some warned, "There will be too many members. You are going to have a lot of trouble. Some of these people don't get along."

"It's once a year," I told them. "Even those who don't get along can be nice to each other for a few days for the good and future of taekwondo in the United States. Once a year we can all meet and have fun together despite our differences. We are not young men any more, and we need to include everyone."

Next, I turned my attention to our legal structure. To begin this process, I knew from previous experience that we needed to file the correct documents to establish ourselves as a not-for-profit — organization. This required an official name, rules, mission statement and objectives. I studied the structure and organization of other groups with characteristics similar to ours and fit this to the information I gathered during our many discussions to arrive at a pretty good idea of what this group wanted to be.

I did my best to put our collective ideas into writing, and then I sent them out with a letter asking each person to vote "yes" or "no" on each of several items. With about a 50 percent return on these letters and the predominance of "yes" votes, I moved forward.

With the paperwork filed, and while we waited on 501c3 approval, I set to work designing an emblem for our group, which I had begun to call "The Grandmasters Society." I smiled as I sketched out several different ideas for this logo, remembering the day of the 11 Club initiation.

I chose the *moogunhwa,* the Korean national flower and symbol of peace as my base, to represent the peace now between us, formerly competitors, now working peacefully together for taekwondo's future. In my design the eight petals of the moogunhwa flower symbolize the eight-fold path, and a bold, black G in the center of the flower stood for Grandmasters. The Korean term, *"Godanja,"* means high-ranking, or grandmaster, and the black color of the letter stood for black belt. All other lettering was in gold to signify the value of what we all accomplished individually and what we would accomplish as a group. A circle to signify the never-ending spirit of taekwondo surrounded the entire design.

I sent this design out to the group with another letter asking for a vote. "This is just an idea," I wrote in my letter. "Please tell me what you think." I also made a list of each element and what it symbolized, adding, "If you want to change anything or make a suggestion, please do. If you agree, write 'OK' beside this design and send it back as your vote." The votes came in and every letter I received had "OK" written beside my design.

"I can't believe you did all this!" was a common response among the handwritten notes scrawled across the bottom of the ballot pages. "So much work!" "Did you do this by yourself?" "Good job, Won Chik!" I felt gratified by all this support and began preparations for our first official meeting to be held in Dallas, Texas in March of 2003.

◊◊

It was Friday evening, nearly a year after that initial meeting hosted by Sang Lee, when they began arriving in Dallas for the first official meeting of the United States Taekwondo Grandmasters Society. I had thought of little else during the past year, spurred by a new dream and renewed sense of purpose. At last I had found a way to repay taekwondo for all it had done for me — and to honor my master's own dream.

They arrived from all over the United States — New York, Los Angeles, Chicago and many points in between. Several local grandmasters and I chose 20 of our local black belt instructors to serve as greeters to those flying into DFW airport. Each had studied the person he or she was assigned to pick up in order to recognize his face. Each had been instructed to greet the grandmaster or master by name, bow, introduce themselves, and present the grandmaster or master with a flower to wear, extending a formal welcome to the Dallas meeting of the United States Grandmasters Society.

At the hotel, a special banner greeted them, and in each room a welcome basket was waiting, filled with gifts our volunteers had gathered for the event. Attached to each basket was a nametag. We knew that while we were certain to recognize each other's names, recognizing each other's faces after so many years apart could be more difficult.

I arrived at the airport to pick up Grandmaster Henry Cho, whom I had not seen since 1991, and Grandmaster Tae Hi Nam, whom I had not seen since 1976. I passed an Asian man who looked vaguely familiar, but I was certain he was neither of the men I was there to pick up.

After we passed each other the fourth time, I stopped. "Excuse me," I said. "Are you looking for someone?"

"Yes," he said, peering at me as if trying to solve a puzzle. "I'm looking for Won Chik Park."

Now it was my turn to solve the puzzle. "I'm Won Chik Park," I said, bowing. "What is your name?"

"I'm Henry Cho."

I laughed. "Welcome!" I said, shaking his hand and then hugging him. "I'm sorry I did not recognize you!"

"I'm sorry I did not recognize you!" he said. He looked at the top of my head. "What happened to all your hair?"

I laughed. "I don't know," I said, rubbing my head and pretending to be baffled. "What happened to your face? Where did you get all these wrinkles?"

He raised a hand to his cheek. "I don't know," he said, echoing my bewildered tone.

Then we laughed and hugged each other again. "It is good to see you, old friend," he said, "now that I know who you are!"

This scene repeated itself somewhat less than an hour later with Grandmaster Tae Hi Nam. Henry Cho and I waited until the baggage claim and surrounding areas were empty. Just about to give up, we spotted a gray-haired Asian man walking back and forth in front of the terminal, peering through the glass at us. He couldn't hear us, so I waved, smiled and pointed to my nametag.

He read the tag, laughed, and then picked up his bags and came out to meet us.

"It's good that we're doing this now," Henry Cho said, laughing. "In a few more years we might not even remember the names!"

After our first meeting, some of the more skeptical masters, the ones who didn't think it possible to organize this group, were standing back, watching to see what would happen. This time, however, once we were all together again, every single master agreed, "This is a good thing. We must continue."

All jokes about our advancing ages aside, we realized the urgency. We did not want our stories to die with us, so for the sake of future generations of taekwondo in America, we felt a pressing obligation to preserve our legacy before it was lost forever.

◊◊

It was important to me that the welcome dinner for the first official meeting of the United States Taekwondo Grandmasters Society be memorable, so I chose Southfork Ranch, a meeting venue that was once the filming location for "Dallas," the popular 1980s TV show that revolved around the fictitious Ewing family, a wealthy Texas oil and cattle-ranching family. Among Korean people, this TV show was an American pop culture icon. When I discovered that Southfork Ranch's beautiful white mansion, pool and grounds was now an international tourist destination and conference center, I met with Southfork representatives. After discussing this idea with our planning committee, the decision was unanimous to hold our first official meeting there.

The last rays of the Friday afternoon sun still tempered the slight March chill as more than 100 people — grandmasters, masters, and a few special guests — boarded the busses at the hotel to take everyone to Southfork together, "like a high school trip!" I told them. Excitement crackled in the air as they settled into their seats, eager to see the famous "ranch," reliving favorite moments of the "Dallas" TV show.

About 15 minutes into the trip, as the bus eased into the Dallas rush hour traffic, I looked around me and laughed softly to myself. Almost everyone was asleep. *Good,* I thought. *At least everyone will be well-rested for the evening!* A nap sounded good to me, too, but my excitement would not let me sleep. I used the quiet time instead to go over my notes for the evening and think about my speech. I sensed the importance of this meeting, and I couldn't wait to see what new ideas would come out of it. Whatever we decided our next step would be, I had a very good feeling it would be good for taekwondo.

The bus whined to a stop before negotiating the turn into the large double entry gates of Southfork Ranch. Everyone awoke at once — and immediately started clapping. Excited conversation began again as everyone looked around and pointed out to each other the things they recognized from the TV show. In a true display of quirky Texas weather, a sudden downpour of unexpected rain began with the sun still shining, but by the time we stopped at the unloading place just minutes later, the rain had stopped, leaving everything fresh, sparkling and beautiful.

We took a group picture in front of the bus before touring the mansion, and then we gathered around the pool for drinks and a welcome reception. Looking at these happy faces all around me, I thought how funny it was that we were all here together in this place so far from all we had been through to get here. Former rivals and competitors, all grudges now set aside for at least the evening, were laughing and talking around J.R. Ewing's pool.

Just as the servers came out to tell us it was time to go inside for dinner, a commotion on the front lawn caught our attention. Someone out there was yelling, and then we heard shooting. Everyone stopped talking and looked frightened.

"Hey, what's going on out there?" I asked, strutting like a tough guy in the direction of the noise. I knew very well what it was — cowboy actors staged a shootout every evening on the front lawn — but I hadn't mentioned this show to anyone else. It was a surprise.

"Won Chik, don't go over there!" someone yelled at me. "They're shooting!"

"I know," I said, "but I want to know why!"

"Are you crazy?" said another. "Come back here!"

When I saw the true fear on these former happy faces, I realized their worry for my safety was genuine, so I put an end to my charade. Laughing, I said, "No, it's a show! Come see! They're just pretending to have a cowboy shoot-out on the front lawn! Maybe it's the same person who shot J.R.!"

Everyone laughed then and we all hurried over to watch the show.

I asked several different people to speak after dinner, people whom I considered to be true pioneers of taekwondo in the United States. Grandmaster Henry Cho spoke first, telling the group his own story about opening the first taekwondo school in the United States — in New York in 1961. He told of his first tournaments here, and how in 1965 he began hosting a tournament in New York's Madison Square Garden. After 40 years of hosting this tournament, he reflected on the pride he felt in being part of bringing taekwondo to the United States.

Next came Grandmaster Tae Hi Nam, who had been the right-hand colonel of General Hong Hi Choi, the South Korean army general and martial artist who issued the order that all ROK troops be trained in taekwondo. Although General Choi later became a somewhat controversial figure in taekwondo history, with that landmark decision he single-handedly elevated taekwondo from relative obscurity to national priority. Grandmaster Nam talked about his military experiences and of bringing taekwondo to the Korean military, particularly during the Viet Nam War.

Two other speakers followed, including Grandmaster Yoo Jin Kim, who related his own personal experiences, how much this meeting meant to him, and how he hoped we would continue. Grandmaster Myung Kyu Kang spoke of his decision to come to the United States, his experiences here, and his hopes for taekwondo's future in America. He also emphasized the importance of what we were doing to preserve all these memories and stories and why we needed to continue this meeting.

At the end of the speeches, everyone stood and applauded them all. Each speaker emphasized the importance of our group and this gathering, and all of them thanked me for opening this meeting to all the taekwondo grandmasters and masters in America. Even though many still chose not to attend, they all knew they were welcome. Everyone agreed that it could take a while, but as we continued they would see the value in what we were doing. Someday, maybe they would all join us.

The next morning was our first official United States Taekwondo Grandmasters Society (USTGS) meeting, followed by a choice of golf or tour of Dallas. Our talks centered on our purpose as a group, what we would like to accomplish, and what was most important to us as leaders of taekwondo in the United States. It was March 27, 2003, less than two months before my 63rd birthday when their unanimous vote gave formal approval to me as the first president of the USTGS.

With everyone now very relaxed and comfortable with one another, we laughed together over our competition days. In this historic moment, all old grudges were laid aside for good. "Let's let the younger generation have that part," we decided.

Then the discussions grew more thoughtful. As this country's first generation of taekwondo grandmasters, we considered our responsibilities as role models for future generations. How will we share this information and knowledge? We realized that each of us held a unique piece of United States taekwondo history, and if any of us dies before sharing what we know, that piece of taekwondo will die with us. As we grew more somber with the comprehension of both the urgency and importance of our actions, I felt a shift in the group that set the stage perfectly for my speech later that evening.

When I first prepared this address, I considered the two kinds of steel. One kind is very inflexible, and although it is strong, it cannot bend. When enough force is applied, it breaks — snapping in two with no possibility of mending. I compare this kind of steel to people who are too rigid in their beliefs and opinions. When enough pressure is applied to a relationship, it is broken forever. The other kind of steel is flexible steel. It bends, but it is very difficult to break. When enough force is applied, it can move and even change shapes, but it can always be re-straightened. In providing example to the younger generation of taekwondo practitioners and masters, we must be like flexible steel — strong in our beliefs, yet humble enough to bend so the traditions and roots we sought to preserve could never be broken.

I thought of my Uncle Ki Hoon's words to me long ago on Yeon Pyong Island, when he first described *Aeyoo Naekang*. Of all the leadership qualities of a Grandmaster, this is the one I now understood to be most important. *Aeyoo Naekang* is what I must inspire and support in the others, I thought as I entered the elevator to go to dinner.

After dinner I addressed the group, first summarizing the day's discussions, decisions, and insights. Then I moved on to sharing my thoughts, hopes and ideas about how we could act on our decisions. I pledged my support and sincere effort to help accomplish the goals we set for the coming year. The applause and positive comments afterwards affirmed the success of our first annual meeting. This diverse group had come together in a decisive and exciting way, and now we were ready to move forward on the specific goals we set for the coming year. Can we really accomplish all we hope to achieve? I wondered the next morning as I watched them disappear one by one into the taxicabs that would take them back to their daily lives. I vowed to do everything I could to make sure of it.

Rally Cry for the Future

◊◊

While everyone was busy with their own lives, health issues, and retirement planning in the year between our meetings, I could think of nothing else. I realized that to reach the goals we set as a group would require a tremendous amount of legwork, thought and effort. I also understood that while this group sincerely wanted to make these things happen, to really get these things done while most of us were still alive required making Grandmaster Society work a priority. Thinking of my own master's dream that died with him, I redoubled my determination to make sure our dream became a reality we could all celebrate together.

At the third official meeting of the United States Grandmasters Society, held in Las Vegas, our direction changed from talk and dreams to action. Following the Dallas meeting the year before, after careful consideration of everything we talked about, I wrestled our ideas into three main vehicles for action. I proposed this plan of action at the Las Vegas meeting.

First, I proposed that we put our knowledge and experiences into the tangible form of a United States Grandmasters Society Museum. Second, to honor the accomplishments that would shine the light of example for future generations of taekwondo, I proposed a specific recognition system in the form of a Grandmasters Society Hall of Fame. Third, to ensure that the knowledge of taekwondo's roots and traditions from its mother country are preserved and taught to future generations, I proposed a unified system of testing, promotion and instructor training in the United States to mirror Kukkiwon in Korea. After my formal presentation of these ideas, and several discussion sessions that followed, the United States Grandmasters Society voted to approve this direction.

I discovered that within this diverse group of grandmasters lay all the keys to the success we dreamed of; all we needed to succeed was someone willing to turn the key. That someone was me. I also discovered that once I organized and laid out our ideas, they rallied behind me. When I gave them jobs to do, they did them. With every new step, I saw our dreams beginning to take shape. We had a long way to go with time in limited supply, but at last our journey was underway.

◊◊

We petitioned Kukkiwon for support in creating a special testing system for the United States, asking for input and permission to govern United States taekwondo testing. We reasoned that Kukkiwon itself most likely began as a way to meet a similar need for consistent leadership in Korea. In the United States there was no central place for people to go, no organization with one true set of answers, no consistent guidelines, requirements, or sources of information about taekwondo in America. As taekwondo continues to spread throughout the world, we reasoned that each country needs its own mirror image of Kukkiwon to lead its practitioners while staying true to the roots of Kukkiwon.

This was not an attempt to replace Kukkiwon, our petition emphasized, but on the contrary to permanently align taekwondo in America with Kukkiwon so that future generations would have consistent information, guidelines, and standards. We felt that setting it up this way now would earn the respect of America's young masters and give them a consistent model to follow once we were gone.

Kukkiwon said no.

I think Kukkiwon misunderstood our request as a challenge of its power, but nothing was further from the truth. The idea we were proposing would, in fact, guarantee Kukkiwon's permanent control of taekwondo standards, practices, and requirements in the United States, and we would administer this control like a branch school, setting an example the rest of the world could follow. Our goal was to work with Kukkiwon, not against it.

"Kukkiwon cannot take care of the whole world without help," I told the group at our Las Vegas meeting. "One day Kukkiwon will see that, but until then we must move forward."

Although we would remain open to working this out with Kukkiwon in the future, the vote at the Las Vegas meeting of the USTGS was to move forward with our testing system without Kukkiwon. We would still request testing certificates from Kukkiwon for those students who wanted them, but we would also design and began issuing our own certificates.

At the Las Vegas meeting we also decided on the eight categories for our Hall of Fame awards and established the criteria for each award, as well as the selection process. At our next meeting, which was set for New York City the following year, we would be ready to induct the very first honorees in the United States Taekwondo Grandmasters Society Hall of Fame.

◊◊

When I returned home from the Las Vegas meeting with a much more concrete vision of a Grandmaster's Society Museum and Hall of Fame taking root in my imagination, my first phone call was to my old friend, Roy Kurban.

Roy, now a grandmaster himself, had also been very busy in his life and career, which included not only a thriving dojang and continued involvement in tournament fighting as a referee, but also active community involvement that most recently resulted in his election as Justice of the Peace.

The idea of rambunctious Roy Kurban as Justice of the Peace struck me as funny at first, but the more I thought about Roy's good natured influence on everyone he knew, the more right it seemed. It warmed my heart to remember how his students campaigned for him, going door to door wearing their doboks to tell every single household in his precinct about master, Roy Kurban, and why he deserved their vote for Justice of the Peace. For the past 15 years my friend Roy had become a powerful influence in the lives of others, and now as a new member of the Grandmaster Society, his talent and connections would be very valuable.

Roy had not been able to attend the Las Vegas meeting, but when I outlined for him the decisions made there, his only response was, "What can I do to help?"

As I predicted, Roy's connections with several outstanding attorneys and business leaders proved crucial to taking wise first steps toward making the USTGS Museum and Hall of Fame a reality. After many months of meetings and paperwork, The United States Grandmasters Society Museum and Hall of Fame was an official entity ready to move forward into its future. Roy explained that all this took so long because the American Government was so closely scrutinizing all non-profit organizations with overseas connections. Roy recruited not one but three attorneys who were among his black belts, and they donated their time to create what Roy described to me as a "bulletproof, fireproof organization," doing something he called "due diligence" and "creating successful monitoring mechanisms." These terms were all unknown to me, but I was grateful that Roy knew how to speak them with people he trusted to make sure we did everything the right way.

As the boards we appointed to lead the development and fundraising for the Grandmasters Museum and Hall of Fame, more ideas emerged. These ideas included a black belt testing and training center modeled after Kukkiwon and a Korean Culture Center featuring food, music, and other highlights of Korean culture. The museum would provide its host city with an international drawing card for meetings, tournaments, testing, instructor certification and special demonstrations and cultural exchange programs.

As our vision crystallized, we realized we were creating a place that would bring together all the elements of the friendship forged between the United States and Korea by taekwondo. So much like my own master's dream, but also very different in its cross-cultural focus, the United States Taekwondo Grandmasters Society Museum and Hall of Fame had a very good chance to become reality in my lifetime. Less than five years remained before my own *koh cui,* or 70th birthday celebration, and I hoped with all my heart that unlike my master, I would live to see my legacy become reality. Still, I willed myself to be patient.

As our fundraising plans began to take shape, Roy explained that the way the Foundation was set up was to first create an endowment fund for the museum's construction, exhibits, and operation, then a second endowment fund would be started to provide scholarships for black belts, training scholarships for Olympic hopefuls, and education scholarships for taekwondo instructors and tournament officials. As someone whose life was changed by two scholarships, one for school and one for taekwondo training, this was an idea very close to my heart.

My excitement surged as the museum's specific features fell into place: interactive displays, videos of the championship fights taekwondo's greatest competitors, and best of all, an exact replica of a traditional dojang training area in tribute to Great Grandmaster Park's dojang in Pusan.

"I can see the uniforms, hanging on hooks all around the room, just the way we did back then," I told Roy in the planning meeting that gave birth to this idea. I gestured with my hands, pointing to each feature as if it were already in place. We'll put a window in the back with the broken glass that let the cold air in, the old wooden bucket in the corner that held water to clean the floors after practice."

Moving on to more practical issues, we tried to imagine what the outside of this place might look like, the brick and mortar reality? As if in answer to this lingering question, and article in the newspaper about an architecture exhibit at the University of Texas at Arlington, just a short distance from my school, featured the work of Nak Chun Kim, a Korean architecture professor from Chung Buk University, a smaller state university not far from Seoul. Professor Kim was visiting UTA as part of a six-month exchange program. He had been here three months, and this exhibit displayed his many different sketches.

I called the phone number listed for the exhibit and a student answered. "Would it be possible to speak to Professor Kim?" I asked.

"Yes," the student replied, "but he is not here right now. I will have to take your number and ask him to call you back."

Rally Cry for the Future

Days went by, then a week. No word from Professor Kim. Then one day, when I had just about given up on his call, the phone rang.

"Is this Won Chik Park?" the voice on the other end of the line asked.

"Yes," I said.

"This is Nak Chun Kim. I'm very sorry, but I just found the note on my desk to call you . How can I help you?"

We met for lunch the next day and I told him about the museum. As I told him about the Grandmasters Society, who we were, what we represented, and how this museum and hall of fame was the culmination of all our collective dreams of leaving a legacy for future generations of American taekwondo practitioners, he grew more and more excited.

He leaned forward, on the edge of his seat as I told him about our most recent meeting and our vote to move forward to create this place.

"I'll be glad to help you, Grandmaster Park," he said. "It would be a great honor and privilege to be part of something so wonderful and important," he said. He began to ask me questions about my vision for this place, drawing excitedly on one napkin after another as we talked. As my answers to his questions tumbled out, ideas began to take shape.

Three hours later, he gathered up the napkins now covering the top of our lunch table and put them carefully in his coat pocket. "Grandmaster Park, you have given me some great thoughts and ideas," he said, patting his pocket. "Let me give it more thought and put some sketches together for you. If you like what I do, I will talk with the architects at HKS, the Dallas architecture firm where I am working while I am in the States, to see what we need to do to move forward. This is very, very exciting and I am so glad you called me!"

"I am so glad you called me back!" I said. "You understand how important this is to America's grandmasters and to the future of taekwondo. I truly appreciate your time and help in getting this idea started."

"It's already started!" he said, excitement glowing in his eyes. "This will be a place where everyone who visits will see the beauty, grace and strength of taekwondo and Korean culture. In this museum, the Grandmasters will live on forever!"

Professor Kim's enthusiasm was infectious, a boost to my own spirit and determination. By talking through his questions, the museum and hall of fame was coming to life, becoming a place I could see with my eyes as well as my heart. That night, I was so excited I could not sleep, replaying our conversation over and over, trying to imagine how his wonderful napkin sketches would manifest into a design that reflected all our dreams.

Three days later, Professor Kim called again. "Grandmaster Park, I've got something to show you."

His sketches were magnificent, beyond anything I had imagined. He had developed several different ideas, one contemporary, one very Asian in its architecture, and another, which was my favorite, combining clean flowing lines with a hint of the Asian influence. "This is it," I said, tapping one page with my finger. I pointed to the tall, rounded atrium, visualizing what it would be like to walk inside. "American people will be able to feel the spirit of taekwondo alive in here. They will look all around this big circular room, and then look up and see the beautiful stained glass yin and yang, and say, 'Wow.'" I tapped his drawing again. "This is a wonderful design."

"Good!" he said, delighted with my response. "I will take this one to HKS and present this idea to them. If they like it, they will send it through engineering to work out the specifics of structure, and then we can go from there!"

One week later, Professor Kim was back with floor plans, elevations and a color rendering that took away my breath. I called a meeting of the grandmasters who lived around Dallas and showed it to them.

"We have to make an announcement to the Korean media," they agreed. The next day I contacted a reporter for the Korean newspaper, the Dallas Newspapers, and several others and invited these reporters to a Dallas restaurant to make this announcement and to introduce Professor Kim and his design.

Eight reporters came, and the room was filled with questioning faces. Representing the grandmasters, I, as USTGS President, Grandmaster Kyu Boong Yim, Secretary General, and Grandmaster Hee Sup Lee, Event Director, told the reporters about the United States Taekwondo Grandmasters Society and its dream of building a museum — and how Professor Kim had now come forward with this design. Cameras snapped pictures, microphones were everywhere, and I felt the momentum building behind this wonderful dream that was now on a fast track to reality.

Roy was working hard with the attorneys and materials were being prepared for presentation of this design to potential sponsors and contributors. The next obstacle would be raising the funds to buy land and build the museum and hall of fame, but Roy said with the legal paperwork in place, the ideas solidified and presented in such a beautiful way, a major fundraising event couldn't be far behind. "It's going to happen, Grandmaster Park," he'd say, every time we met. "And it's going to be a beautiful tribute to the legacy of the grandmasters."

"You're crazy," Julie said to me one day as I went on and on about the museum. "I've never seen you so obsessed with anything. Are you *sure* about this?"

I laughed and hugged her, "I've never been more sure of anything in my life," I told her. Then I smiled at my pretty wife who supported me even when she thought I might be crazy. "Except you."

She laughed. "*I've* never been this much work!"

◊◊

"Grandmaster Park, I need to talk to you." The troubled voice on the other end of the phone line belonged to Sid Nelson, one of my students who had begun training with me long ago as a white belt. A naturally gifted teacher, Sid started leading class very early and then teaching as a first dan. Today he was a 4th dan who taught at one of my branch schools; he had trained many of his own black belts including a 3rd dan instructor now teaching under him. I didn't like the tone in his voice.

"Come today. We'll have lunch," I said, hoping that whatever it was could be resolved over a good meal together.

He sat across from me a few hours later, looking tired, dejected, more discouraged than I had ever seen him.

"Grandmaster Park, I think it's time for me to retire," he said.

"Retire?" I said. "You're kidding! You're younger than me!"

"I know, sir," he said, not meeting my eyes. "But I just need to quit."

"Why?" I asked. I looked him over carefully. "What happened?"

"I'm tired, Kwan Jang Neem," he said. "I've been involved in taekwondo long enough. My knees hurt, I'm tired of teaching, and my heart's just not in it anymore."

I let him talk for a long time without interrupting. When he was finished, I said, "If you want to quit, it is up to you." I paused, then continued, "but when you began, you had a good reason to start. To finish, you need a good reason to end."

"What do you mean?"

"You are not just talking about being finished with taekwondo," I said, leaning forward with my hands outstretched on the table in front of me. "Your classes, your students, your instructors are your responsibility. If you quit taekwondo, you are also quitting them."

He sat, quiet, taking this in.

"My opinion is that anybody can quit," I said. I looked at him for a moment. "But not everybody can keep going when it gets difficult. Sid, you're not just anybody."

Sid looked at me, meeting my eyes for the first time.

"Think about the past 20 years," I said. "Think about the experience you have gained by being a taekwondo instructor — and how valuable your knowledge and experience is to your students. Think about what they have learned from you, how they have grown up with your help, and how they will forever respect you and respect themselves because of you. Aren't you proud of that? Aren't you proud of them?"

"Oh, yes, I'm very proud," he said.

"Then as long as you can, you have to take care of them."

"So I can't ever quit?"

"Not this way," I said. "The correct way to do that is to keep building your taekwondo community so that in the future when you retire you can choose one of your black belts to take over for you."

"Why can't I just do that now?"

"Too soon for that now," I said. "You have to choose your successor and train him until his entire life is taekwondo, just as yours has been. I highly respect the community of taekwondo you are building in your school. Your students have great respect for you anywhere you go. I've been with you in restaurants when they come in and recognize you. I see it in their faces, hear it in their voices. Doesn't that feel good?"

"Yes, sir."

"That doesn't happen in one day."

He nodded.

"As long as you can stay with it, taekwondo is good for your life," I said. "If you don't believe that, you have to quit."

He looked up, confused.

"You're too young to quit," I said. "It's too soon for you. If you quit now, you will be giving up too much." I made a fist, then opened my hand, palm up. "Empty hand," I said. I looked at his knees. "You have to take better care of your conditioning. If you quit now, you will just get bigger and your knees will get worse."

He laughed. "OK, Kwan Jang Neem, I will stay with it," he said. "Thank you for your advice."

We shook hands and he left, resolved to continue. The following April, Sid tested for his 5th dan, earning him the title of Master. Although his knees still hurt, I could see that his mental focus was better than ever. I felt a pride in Sid that day that must have rivaled what my own master felt when I rose above my own discouragement to pass my own next test.

Afterward, Sid came to me and bowed. "Thank you, sir, for talking me out of quitting," he said.

"You made a good decision," I said. "And now, because you didn't quit, you are forever Master Sid Nelson." I bowed to him. "Good Job, Master Nelson."

◊◊

After months of what seemed to be endless preparation, checking and rechecking every detail, the time came at last for the first United States Taekwondo Grandmasters Society Hall of Fame induction ceremony. We chose all of our first honorees very carefully; we were very aware that these were the charter members, the gold standard for future inductions.

Of all 10 honorees chosen, only two couldn't be there to accept the award in person. Grandmaster Chung Eun Kim, chosen for the Literary Achievement Award, was having surgery and a friend would accept the award on his behalf; Grandmaster Chuck Norris, chosen as our first Ambassador of Taekwondo Award, had a previous commitment but sent a heartfelt acceptance letter to be read by his friend, now Grandmaster, Roy Kurban.

Bringing along Julie and Susie to witness this momentous occasion, we arrived in New York a few days early. As I met with hotel staff and organizing committee members, Julie and Susie were a blur of activity whose paths I crossed several times each day on their way to sightseeing, shopping and exploring New York City. It was good to see them having so much fun together, mother and adult daughter. I watched them get into a taxi cab the morning of the awards, trying to believe that Susie was now 33 years old. Johnny, now 30, was unable to join us, but had called several times to stay connected with all that was going on.

Later that afternoon, I walked back into the room to find packages strewn everywhere and the two women in my life talking and laughing together like old friends. I closed the door and they looked up, startled.

"What's going on here?" I asked, teasing them with a stern tone.

Susie, not fooled at all, laughed and came over and hugged me.

"Daddy you won't believe where all we went!"

"Where all?" I was a little confused by this term.

"Everywhere," Julie said. She looked tired, but very happy. "We rode the subway."

"You rode the *subway?*" I asked, incredulous. I looked at Julie, then at Susie, then back at Julie. "How did you get your mother to ride the subway?" I couldn't imagine my wife doing such a thing.

"Our daughter also knows how to bargain," Julie said, smiling at Susie, and then gesturing at the pile of purses on the end of the bed.

I raised my eyebrows.

Susie laughed at my expression. "I bought them on the street — and got a very good price."

"A very good price," echoed her mother.

"Why so many?"

"Gifts!"

"Oh." I looked again. "Where did you learn to bargain like that?" I asked.

"At the market in Seoul!" she said. "When I went to Korea that summer, I got to spend a lot of time on my own and with different family members. Everyone went to the market, so I learned how to bargain like a native! And guess what? It works even better here in New York!"

"Wow," I said. I looked at Julie. "Did you buy things on the street, too?"

Julie laughed. "No, I left that up to Suyun. It was all I could do just to keep up with her!"

"She's a trooper!" Susie said, now hugging her mother. "I dragged her everywhere and we saw everything!"

"I'm a trooper," Julie echoed, smiling. Everything about the City made her nervous, and I couldn't imagine how hard it must have been for her to get on that crowded, fast moving, underground subway. But she did. And of course, I already knew she was a trooper. Our life together had proven her quiet courage, her own *Aeyoo Naekang*, many times.

◊◊

I tightened my bow tie and asked Julie for the third time if it was straight. She smiled. "You look good," she said. "Very handsome in your tuxedo."

I bowed. "Thank you, beautiful lady." I offered her my arm the way I had seen the American movie stars do on the Academy Awards. Then I offered my other arm to Susie. "Shall we go?"

They both giggled at my formality and took my arm.

To me, this night was bigger than the Academy Awards. It was the culmination of everything I had worked for in my life, the moment of triumph over every struggle, the ultimate reflection of who I had become. I have always known that when your mind is right, your heart is right, and your effort is sincere, the right people will appear to help. My life itself is proof of this truth. It was April of 2006 and the very first induction ceremony for the United States Taekwondo Grandmasters Society Hall of Fame. Tonight we would celebrate the accomplishments of ten outstanding taekwondo practitioners and give them a permanent place in United States Taekwondo History. I was so proud to be part of that, and I imagined the face of my master, smiling down on this occasion from heaven.

As I entered the lavishly decorated hotel ballroom, I was taken aback at the beauty of how this first-ever Taekwondo Hall of Fame induction came together. *This is the first one ever,* I thought, looking around the room. *Even in Korea they have never done this.* I thought about all the people involved in making this happen, both in the ceremony and in my life.

The organizing committee met in the ballroom the night before to check the set-up, do a sound check, and to double check the readiness of the beautiful PowerPoint presentation we had prepared to present Professor Kim's museum design and the mission and objectives of the Grandmaster Society. Laughing and joking with these old and dear friends, it seemed as if we were back in Seoul, working together on any other important taekwondo event.

I climbed the steps to the stage area where all the grandmasters were now seated. I looked into the faces of each of my dear friends,

Kyu Boong Yim, Jin Song Chung, Hee Sup Lee, and Kyu Il Cho — each of whom had been there every step of the way, always eager to help, there to offer support, and ready to tackle any task that needed to be done. I looked up at the giant banner welcoming guests to the First Annual United States Grandmaster Society Hall of Fame Awards Ceremony, and I let those words sink in, one by one.

I sat down, taking my place on the brightly lit stage, and I looked out at the room as it filled with all the different kinds of people who had traveled here for this historic event. The United States Grandmasters Society had come together as one guiding spirit to make this happen. I watched people's faces as they sat down, enjoying the expressions of surprise and delight when they picked up the program and saw the photograph of Professor Kim's rendering on its cover.

Roy looked over at me and winked. "Are you ready, Grandmaster Park?" he asked in that tone that always meant a new adventure was about to begin.

I looked back at him and smiled. "I'm ready," I said.

The End . . .
And Always, Another Beginning

2000   I made a visit to the fence that still separates North and South Korea, leaving a message there with so many others for my relatives still in the North.

2000 Together again at last, our trip to Korea to celebrate our 30th wedding anniversary and my 60th birthday was a chance to spend time once again with, left to right: my brother, Ung Chik, my sister in law, Soon Jun, and my sister, Young Soon.

Celebrating my Jang Mo Neem (mother-in-law)'s 80th birthday during our 2000 trip, I thought of my own parents and wondered what they might think about the life I have lived.

2003 The first official meeting of the United States Taekwondo Grandmasters Society in Dallas, Texas, at the "Dallas" TV show's Southfork Ranch. It was funny to watch everyone put his differences aside and join together at this icon of American pop culture.

2005 Local dignitaries attending the 25th Fort Worth International Championships, Pictured left to right: Tarrant County Commissioner Marti VanRavenswaay, Great Grandmaster Yoo Jin Kim, Texas State Representative Bill Zedler, and Fort Worth Mayor Pro Tem Chuck Silcox. During the opening ceremony, the mayor's office presented a proclamation declaring it "Won Chik Park Day" in Fort Worth, and I received a Presidential Sports Award from President George Bush, and a letter of commendation from the State of Texas for my work with children and youth in taekwondo.

2005 With Mayor Pro Tem Chuck Silcox and my dear friend, Taekwondo Master and and now Judge Roy Kurban at my 25th annual Fort Worth International Taekwondo Championships.

Joining me at the 2006 Hall of Fame ceremony gave my daughter, Susie, left, and my wife, Julie, right, an opportunity for New York City shopping before accompanying me to the formal evening event.

2006 The first United States Taekwondo Grandmasters Hall of Fame honorees. This historic event marked both the culmination of an old, cherished vision and the beginning of a new dream. Pictured left to right: Woo Jin Kim representing Jung Eun Kim, Great Grandmaster Yoo Jin Kim, Grandmaster Roy Kurban representing Grandmaster Chuck Norris, Grandmasters Dr. Ken Min, S. Henry Cho, Jae Joon Kim, Won Chik Park, president, USTGS, Dong Keun Park, Great Grandmaster Myong Kyu Kang, and Grandmasters Michael Warren and Lynette Love.

2006 Presenting a Lifetime Achievement Award to Great Grandmaster Yoo Jin Kim

2006 The 60th Jidokwan anniversary celebration in Seoul was opportunity for renewing old friendships and celebrating the many connections of taekwondo. Left to right: Professor and Grandmaster Woo Kyu Kim, Dong-A University, Pusan, Korea, me, Grandmaster Jin Song Chung, Olympic Gold Medalist Dae Sun Moon, Greece, now also a professor at Don-A University, and Grandmaster Hee Sup Lee. As taekwondo classmates, Woo Kyu Kim was once my junior, and he later trained Dae Sun Moon for his Olympic Gold.

2006 Fort Worth International Taekwondo Championships welcomed special guests from HKS Inc., Dallas, the architectural firm that designed the concept for the USTGS Museum and Hall of Fame. Pictured far left is HKS Vice president Taama M. Forasiepi and far right is HKS Creative Director David Brehm.

2005 Renderings of the proposed United States Taekwondo Grandmasters Society Museum and Hall of Fame. This inspired design by Nak Chun Kim, a Korean architecture professor from Choongbuk National University, put all our thoughts and wishes for this place into a tangible vision. Professor Kim was visiting UTA as part of a six-month exchange program and was also working for the Dallas Architectural Design firm, HKS, during his time in the United States.

Acknowledgements

I would like to thank and acknowledge everyone in my life who has supported me with love and direction — my taekwondo seniors, my juniors, my students, and most of all, my family and friends. To my taekwondo students, the extended Won Park Institute Family, I want to say here how much I appreciate your hard work, your dedication, and your support, especially from masters Dan and Betty James, Greg Gafford, Winfred Harvey, Riad Nusrallah, Terry Avery, Richard Sacks, Sid Nelson, and author and instructor Melinda Kaitcer.

Helping to establish the United States Taekwondo Grandmasters Society has caused me to consider how my accomplishments, abilities and leadership experiences can improve and support this organization. My generation of grandmasters has seen many changes in taekwondo, and through our friendship and mutual support, we have accomplished many meaningful things together.

Special acknowledgement goes to my seniors, Grandmasters Yoo Jin Kim, Dr. Ken Min, Henry Cho, and Myong Kyu Kang. To my good friends and peers who have worked so hard and so well together for the benefit of the Unites States Taekwondo Grandmasters Society, I thank you for your friendship and the opportunity to share the spirit of taekwondo: Grandmasters Kyu Byong Yim, Kyu Il Cho, Roy Kurban, Jin Song Chung, and Hee Sup Lee. I would also like to thank Grandmasters Ho Young Chung, Dae Sup An, John Kim, Seung Ryul Yang, Woo Jin Jung, Professor Woo Kyu Kim, Sam Jang Kim, and Yeon Hee Park for your friendship and support.

I also extend my special appreciation to Great Grandmaster Chong Woo Lee, whose leadership, guidance, and support throughout my taekwondo career has earned my deepest respect, and to the late Great Grandmaster Hyon Chong Park, whose support and guidance made all my accomplishments possible.

United States Taekwondo Grandmasters Society Outstanding Leadership Award
2010 Hall of Fame Induction Ceremony

Appendix

Accomplishments of Grandmaster Won Chik Park

- Born in May 15, 1940
- Achieved the Rank of Taekwondo 9th Dan by Kukkiwon in 1993
- Began Taekwondo Training under Great Grandmaster Hyon Cho Park 1954, Pusan Taekwondo (Kong Soo Do) Jidokwan
- Has been teaching Taekwondo since 1960 in Korea and 1972 in the U.S.
- Graduate of the Pusan Deok Won High School

Taekwondo Achievements

- Inducted into the United States Taekwondo Grandmasters Society Hall of Fame in 2010 and honored with its "Outstanding Leadership" award
- Honorary President United States Taekwondo Grandmasters Society
- Chairman, Taekwondo Museum and Hall of Fame Building Committee 2006- present
- Founder, U.S. Taekwondo Hall of Fame Award System
- First President, United States Taekwondo Grandmasters Society 2003 - March, 2008
- Founder and Chairman, Pan Am Foundation Masters of Taekwondo 1999-2005
- Chairman, The National Board of Martial Arts, United States Taekwondo Union
- Head of Team, United States Taekwondo Team for World Game in the Netherlands 1993
- Chairman, United States Taekwondo Union Tournament Committee 1986-1988
- Tournament Director and Chairman of Organizing Committee for 10th U.S. National Junior Olympic Taekwondo Championships 1990
- Founder and First President, Texas State Taekwondo Association 1981-1987
- Founder and Tournament Director, Fort Worth International Championship 1981

Honors and Awards

- Proclamation, "Grandmaster Won Chik Park Day" by the State of Texas, May 15, 2010
- Proclamation, "Grandmaster Won Chik Park Day" by City of Fort Worth, 2005
- Achievement Award of World Taekwondo Jidokwan 60th Anniversary in Korea 2006
- Resolution Award by The State of Texas 2005
- Presidential Sports Award by President George Bush 2005
- Resolution Award by Texas Tarrant County Judge Tom Vandergriff 2005
- Excellent Citizen " Key Award" by City of Fort Worth
- Appreciation Award by Minister, The Culture and Sports Ministry, Rep.of Korea 2003
- Inducted the Texas Martial Arts Hall of Fame for Outstanding Leadership 2001
- Achievement Award by Minister, The Foreign Ministry Republic of Korea 1999
- Proclamation Taekwondo Week by City of Fort Worth, Certificate Award 1995
- Coach of the Year by United States Taekwondo Union 1995
- Special Award Excellent Leadership by United States Taekwondo Union 1993
- Achievement Award by World Taekwondo Federation President Dr. Un Yong Kim 1990 for Tournament
- Director, 10th U.S. National Junior Olympic Taekwondo Championship
- Special Appreciation Award by U.S. Taekwondo Union 1990 for Chairman of Organizing Committee and Director, 10th U.S. Jr. Olympic Taekwondo Championship
- Achievement Award for as presidency 1981-1987 by Texas State Taekwondo Assoc.

- Letter of Commendation by Kukkiwon, Seoul Korea 1983
- Sam Wee Great Award by World Taekwondo Jidokwan, Seoul Korea 1977

Teaching Achievements

- Faculty member, Physical Education Department of Texas Christian University Fort Worth, Texas 1979-1986
- Won Park Institute of Taekwondo - Fort Worth, Texas Since 1978 - Present
- Chief Instructor, F.B.I. Detroit Branch in Michigan 1973-1974
- Won Park Institute, 1st open in the Detroit, Michigan 1972-1978
- Founded Won Park Institute in Seoul, Korea 1968 Move to U.S.1972
- Chief Instructor, Headquarter U.S. 8th Army and U.S. Military Force in Yong San, Seoul, Korea 1965-1972
- Instructor, Headquarters Korean Army Non San Basic Training School 1962-1964

Community Service

- President of Korean Association of Fort Worth, Texas 1982-1984
- Member of the Advisory on Peaceful and Unification of Korea 1983-1987
- Chairman of Board of Directors, Korean School of Fort Worth, Texas 1992-1994
- Committee Member of Youth Discipline Committee, City of Fort Worth 1996-1998

2010 Hall of Fame Recipients
Left to right: Grandmasters Moon Sung Lee, Kim Soo. Y.H. Park, Roy Kurban,
Won Chik Park, Jung Um Hwang, Ho Young Chung, Sun Hwan Chung, and Seoung Eui Shin

United States Taekwondo Grandmasters Society Advisors
Front Row, left to right: Grandmasters Hee Young Kim, Dr. Ken Min, Myung Kyu Kang,
Shi Hak Cho, Young Ho Jun, and Young Rae Cho

Left to right: Grandmaster Jin Song Chung, Mrs. Chung, Grandmaster Woo Jin Jung, Grandmaster Won Chik Park, Texas State Representative Bill Zedler, Mrs. Zedler, Grandmasters Dae Sup An and Dr. Hee Young Kim

Left to right: Texas TKD Association President In Seon Kim, Grandmaster Kyu Il Cho, Hall of Fame Selection Committee Chairman Dr. Chong Woong Kim, Grandmaster Won Chik Park, Longtime friend, Grandmaster Ho Young Chung, and Grandmaster Young Rae Cho

Left to right: Grandmasters Sam Jang Kim, Dae Sup An, Dr. Chong W. Kim, Jae Kyu Lee, Moon Sung Lee, Yeon Hwan Park, USTGS President Kyu Boon Yim, Won Chik Park, Nam Kwon Hyong, Kim Soo, and John Kim

Left to Right: Grandmasters Dae Sup An, Won Chik Park, Ho Young Chung, Jin Song Chung, and John H. Choi

The State of Texas Proclamation
"Grandmaster Won Chik Park Day"
Presented by Mr. Bill Zedler, Representative of the State of Texas
With Retired Judge and Grandmaster Roy Kurban

2010 United States Taekwondo Grandmasters Society Annual Meeting
Dallas, Texas

www.ingramcontent.com/pod-product-compliance
Lightning Source LLC
Chambersburg PA
CBHW071959150426
43194CB00008B/928